Dangdut Stories

DANGDUT STORIES

A Social and Musical History of Indonesia's Most Popular Music

ANDREW N. WEINTRAUB

OXFORD
UNIVERSITY PRESS

2010

OXFORD
UNIVERSITY PRESS

Oxford University Press, Inc., publishes works that further
Oxford University's objective of excellence
in research, scholarship, and education.

Oxford   New York
Auckland   Cape Town   Dar es Salaam   Hong Kong   Karachi
Kuala Lumpur   Madrid   Melbourne   Mexico City   Nairobi
New Delhi   Shanghai   Taipei   Toronto

With offices in
Argentina   Austria   Brazil   Chile   Czech Republic   France   Greece
Guatemala   Hungary   Italy   Japan   Poland   Portugal   Singapore
South Korea   Switzerland   Thailand   Turkey   Ukraine   Vietnam

Copyright © 2010 by Oxford University Press, Inc.

Published by Oxford University Press, Inc.
198 Madison Avenue, New York, New York 10016

www.oup.com

Oxford is a registered trademark of Oxford University Press.

Recorded audio and video (marked in text with 🔊)
www.oup.com/us/dangdutstories.
Access with username Music3 and password Book3234
For more information on Oxfordwebmusic.com, visit www.oxfordwebmusic.com

Library of Congress Cataloging-in-Publication Data

Weintraub, Andrew N. (Andrew Noah)
Dangdut stories : a social and musical history of Indonesia's most popular
music / Andrew N. Weintraub.
p. cm.
Includes bibliographical references and index.
ISBN 978-0-19-539566-2; 978-0-19-539567-9 (pbk.)   1. Dangdut—Indonesia—History and
criticism.   2. Popular music—Social aspects—Indonesia.   I. Title.
ML3502.I5W45   2010
781.6309598—dc22   2009027535

9 8 7 6 5 4 3 2 1

Printed in the United States of America
on acid-free paper

Acknowledgments

I would like to express my gratitude to all the dangdut singers, musicians, composers, and fans who provided the stories that constitute this book. I am particularly grateful to Rhoma Irama, Elvy Sukaesih, Mansyur S., Munif Bahasuan, Zakaria, Fazal Dath, and Dadang S. for their kindness and generosity.

I would like to thank my friends and colleagues for their sound advice and strong criticism. Philip Yampolsky pointed me in all the right directions and gave me access to rare materials in his vast collection of music recordings. Henry Spiller was a constant source of friendship and moral support. I am grateful to Shamsul A. B., Sandra Bader, Sharon Berk, Siddharth Chandra, Tony Day, Laurie Eisler, William Frederick, Jocelyne Guilbault, Toriq Haddad, David Harnish, Marty Hatch, Ariel Heryanto, Ritaony Hutajulu, Lambertus Hurek, Kaoru Iijima, Irwansyah Harahap, Peter Manuel, Scott Marcus, Goenawan Mohamad, Nelly Paliama, Dana Rappoport, Anne Rasmussen, Ismet Ruchimat, Jerome Samuel, Rizaldi Siagian, Ishadi S. K., Ati Sumiati, R. Anderson Sutton, Katsunori Tanaka, Ricardo D. Trimillos, Jeremy Wallach, Sarah Weiss, Sean Williams, Tinuk Yampolsky, Bell Yung, and Ben Zimmer.

The Dangdut Cowboys band helped me playfully work through many of the musical ideas in this book. I thank Mathew Rosenblum, Mike Witmore, Ben Pachter, Kavin Paulraj, Margot Goldberg, and Ben Rainey for their camaraderie and willingness to try new things.

For assistance gathering permissions I am indebted to PAMMI (Persatuan Artis Musik Melayu Indonesia). I am thankful for having three excellent research assistants: the late Yoseph Iskandar, Tiur Manalu, and Indra Ridwan. Kerrith Livengood helped me reformat the music transcriptions in the book.

Ening Rumbini was an insightful and provocative interlocutor since the beginning of this project. I offer her my deep and heartfelt affection. And to my son Noah, who traveled to Indonesia with me for five months and put up with loud rehearsals in the basement of our Pittsburgh home, I dedicate this book to you.

A Fulbright Senior Scholar Award and travel grants from the Asian Studies Center and the University Center for International Studies at the University of Pittsburgh supported this project.

Contents

Note on the Web Site

The companion Web site, found at www.oup.com/us/dangdutstories, contains streaming audio and video of many of the songs analyzed in this book. The Web site is designed as an educational resource that allows readers to fully appreciate key points presented in the book. Each audio and video example is cued in the text, and readers are encouraged to refer to the recordings while contemplating the points addressed in the text.

Each audio and video example has its own caption that includes (a) title; (b) year of recording (issued); (c) record number or name of album; (d) singer(s); (e) accompanying band and director; and (f) composer.

An effort has been made to limit the access time of videos by reformatting them into .wmv files. However, the reformatting of videos has resulted in a slight loss of quality. Despite this reduction in quality, the points made in the analysis can be clearly seen from these examples.

Accurate information about the dates of dangdut recordings are often difficult to obtain because data are either not available or not accessible. In some cases, the recording artists, composers, and producers could only estimate the year of production. Based on estimated dates of recording, as well as the sound and style represented on the recording, I have provided the most accurate information possible. A complete discography of dangdut recordings awaits further treatment.

Many other audio and video examples of dangdut, including examples of songs discussed in this book, are available on commercial recordings as well as the Internet.

Dangdut Stories

Chapter 1

Introduction

A dentist, a police officer, and a soup peddler were competing against each other in Dangdut Mania, an "American Idol" version of dangdut, Indonesia's most popular music.[1] Men and teenage boys crowded the dance floor in front of the stage, and in typical dangdut fashion, they danced with each other as they sang along with songs about heartache, suffering, and loss. Women and children sat on risers in the back of the studio, cheering on the singers and gossiping with friends about the singers' outfits, dance movements, and stage demeanor. A parade of promising singers strutted across the stage (see figure 1.1).

The television show was being recorded for Indonesian Educational Television (Televisi Pendidikan Indonesia, TPI), a station known for its heavy rotation of dangdut programs.[2] Originally the music of disenfranchised urban youth in the 1970s, dangdut had become part of a hugely profitable commercial industry of musical recordings, films, videos, TV shows, tabloids, and ring tones. But it retained its earlier symbolic associations as the music of the underclass. Middle- and upper-class commentators had given TPI the demeaning moniker "Televisi Pembantu Indonesia" ("Indonesian Domestic Workers' Television") for its large fan base of female domestic workers who watched dangdut contests at home and sent in their votes for their favorite singers via cell phone text messages. The television station capitalized on the popularity of dangdut by inserting an extraordinary number of commercials for laundry detergent, cold medicine, and packaged noodles. These commercials enticed consumers by including dangdut sounds and images in the commercials themselves to make a seamless connection between the entertainment contest and the commercial product.

FIGURE 1.1 Dangdut on television in Jakarta, 30 June 2005 [courtesy of *Tempo*].

One of TPI's stated mandates was to glamorize dangdut so that it would have commercial appeal not only for its core working-class audience, but also for "the middle classes and up" (the so-called "A-B" audience).[3] For example, female national dangdut recording stars made guest appearances on the show wearing glamorous evening attire to give the show some "class." And the band that accompanied the contestants was directed by pop/jazz musician/arranger Purwacaraka, who did not even consider himself a dangdut musician. TPI and several other national television stations had increased the exposure of dangdut by bringing dangdut images and sounds into middle- and upper-class living rooms. Upgraded to produce higher ratings and at the same time denigrated for its underclass roots, dangdut was a symbolic marker for reflecting and shaping cultural values and aesthetic standards based on social class.

Hundreds of miles away in Madiun (East/Central Java), dangdut superstar Rhoma Irama and his veteran band Soneta performed at a campaign rally for the election of governor of East Java (see figure 1.2). Since the 1970s, politicians had used dangdut, a form of "people's music" (*musik rakyat*), to gather crowds at rallies. Rhoma Irama enjoyed a privileged position in political campaigns

FIGURE 1.2 Dangdut superstar Rhoma Irama performing at a campaign rally in Madiun, East/Central Java, 7 July 2008 [photo: Andrew Weintraub].

because of his long-standing identification with "the people." His songs about male-female relationships, moral behavior, and sociopolitical issues spoke directly to the everyday lives of ordinary Indonesians. His large underclass male audience identified with Rhoma Irama's biography, which has been publicly narrated in popular print media interviews, over 20 feature films, and even some of his own songs. He had long been involved in national politics, first as a member of the United Development Party (Partai Persatuan Pembangunan, PPP), and then, switching allegiance, as a member of the Functional Work Group (Golongan Karya, or Golkar). He had also developed a successful second career as a religious preacher (*juru dakwah; mubalig*). Invited by the Nahdlatul Ulama (NU), the country's largest Muslim political organization, Rhoma Irama was sure to draw thousands of potential voters to the event.

Reports of violence, drunkenness, and debauchery followed large dangdut concerts like this one, and police were brought in to guard the front and sides of the huge stage. But the atmosphere was more like a carnival or an outdoor rock concert. Food sellers pushed hot soup and cold drinks, along with noise-makers and toys. Some in the audience were waving banners advertising the political candidate, while others were wearing the political party shirts that had been handed out earlier that day. As Rhoma Irama's band began to play, people packed into the town square, and those standing near the front of the stage began to dance and lift their friends up on each others' shoulders. The sun was painfully hot, and the sound system was piercingly loud and distorted, but no one seemed to mind. People cheered as Rhoma Irama beckoned them to "vote for candidate number 1," the number of the party's candidate. The candidate came on stage and sang one of Rhoma Irama's songs, showing that she too was a fan of the people's music. In large public gatherings sponsored by political parties and religious organizations, dangdut helped to organize and define "the people."

The dangdut scene that I viewed in 2006 in North Sumatra was just as lively, although not nearly as regulated and official. A small stage was constructed on the side of a busy truck route connecting the large city of Medan with the town of Perbaungan to the south. The sounds of the latest super-charged dangdut band could be heard from far away, calling people to the site. Keyboard groups like this, called "keyboard *bongkar*" ("transportable keyboard") have standard offerings: (1) eroticized dangdut; (2) dramatic scenes featuring local characters (for example, the female ghost character named *sundel bolong* and the witch *mak lampir*); and (3) male transvestites (*waria*) who dance with pythons (*tari ular sawar*) (see figures 1.3 and 1.4). The atmosphere was busy and excited: a throng of people crowded the front and sides of the stage, which was no more than ten by ten square feet. The audience nearest the stage included

FIGURE I.3 Dangdut performer Irma (Camelia group) and child performing at a wedding reception party in Perbaungan, North Sumatra, 18 November 2006 [photo: Andrew Weintraub].

middle-aged and young men, teenage boys, as well as a group of older women, school-age boys and girls, and young mothers with babies and small children in tow. Further back, teenage boys and girls flirted with each other, and people in cars slowed down to see what all the excitement was about.

FIGURE I.4 *Waria* dangdut performer onstage in Perbaungan, North Sumatra, 19 November 2006 [photo: Andrew Weintraub].

Onstage, the electronic keyboard player accompanied a female teenage singer/dancer (*biduan*) dressed in a bra, panties, high knee-length boots, and a mini-skirt. As she sang, she crouched, thrust her hips, and swayed back and forth. She rubbed her body up against a corner pole holding up the tent and performed a "pole dance," imitating movements usually reserved for strip clubs. Lying face up with her feet and hands supporting her arched body, she performed bouncing movements that simulated sexual intercourse. Four *biduan*—three females and one *waria*—sat idly by with bored facial expressions awaiting their turns to entertain while male band managers, sound technicians, and bouncers looked on.

The young mothers in the audience seemed to particularly enjoy the show, and one mother even placed her one-year-old baby right in front of the dancer as she performed hip-thrusting movements against a pole. In other such events, women have reportedly thrown stones at these same performers. In 2005, due to pressure from Islamic religious groups, local government offices prohibited this group and others from obtaining permits to perform in public because of the erotic nature of the staged dances. At this event, dangdut became a space for representing widely divergent positions about the meaning of women's bodies. For some, eroticized female dance signified commodification and religious blasphemy, while for others it represented economic opportunities and freedom of expression. These positions were dramatized within the increasingly Islamic public sphere of post-Suharto Indonesia.

Compared to the erotic spectacle in Perbaungan, the dangdut party that I attended in 2008 in Banjarmasin (Kalimantan) was quite ordinary. I accompanied a dangdut band hired to play at a ritual event (*selamatan*) to celebrate the marriage of the host's daughter. When we finally reached the neighborhood on the outskirts of town, we were escorted through a few narrow alleyways to the home of the bride's family. The bride and groom were dressed in elaborate traditional clothing and were seated on a couch framed by decorations on the front porch of the house. The parents of the bride ushered us to a table of food and we filled our plates with *soto Banjar* (chicken noodle soup spiced with lemongrass) and *saté* (skewered meat basted with sweet soy sauce). A makeshift wooden stage was set up in an open clearing between houses in the community, filling in the space usually used for soccer or badminton or just hanging out watching passersby (*nongkrong*). We made our way to folding chairs set up on the dirt floor in front of the stage. Bamboo poles constituted a floor directly in front and to the sides of the stage, and a ramp allowed people in the audience to flow freely on and off the stage.

The host had chosen dangdut for the evening's entertainment because it was certain to create a lively and fun mood and the band was relatively inexpensive to hire. Dangdut performance practice and the themes of dangdut songs are thought to fit well with marriage celebrations. Dangdut performances open up a space for telling jokes full of sexual innuendo and dancing in erotic and comedic forms. The songs often narrate nostalgic yearnings for lost love and anxieties about present and future relationships.

Everyone can dance to the basic rhythmic pattern of dangdut, a four-beat groove with an accent on beats 4 and 1, and most people have memorized a song or two. It was expected that guests would jump onstage at some point during the evening. To encourage them, the emcee skillfully wove stage patter and bandstand chatter with comments directed at particular audience members. Around 10 PM the emcee began calling people onstage to sing and dance: an older man wearing long shorts, cowboy boots, and a leather jacket; a middle-aged mother in Muslim attire; a 20-something girl in tight pants and high heels; and a gay man dressed for the office (see figure 1.5).

A teenage girl, a local community religious leader, a single mother, a group of five-year-old girls, and the American ethnographer joined them. I jumped on stage to sing a few songs, and, despite slips in intonation and some awkward hip movements, the crowd cheered me on enthusiastically for participating in the celebration. My performance became even more of a spectacle when I was joined by a boisterous and large woman whose erotic movements, heavy makeup, and facial expressions reached comical proportions (see figure 1.6). Everything about the event was as it should have been. A steady stream of

FIGURE 1.5 Dangdut at a party in Banjarmasin, South Kalimantan, 13 July 2008 [photo: Andrew Weintraub].

FIGURE I.6 The author singing dangdut at a party in Banjarmasin, South Kalimantan, 13 July 2008 [courtesy of Muhammed Uhaib Asad].

visitors dropped by to extend congratulations, to offer small gifts to the family, and to receive nourishment and entertainment. Hundreds of people came, and everyone left fulfilled. Nothing unusual happened. The event ended just around midnight and was considered a great success.

Consumerist media display, political campaign rally, eroticized dance spectacle, and everyday communal party—these are sites where dangdut frames meanings about class relations, national belonging, and gendered power and difference in Indonesia. As I will show in the following chapters, dangdut sets the stage for organizing and dramatizing social unity out of difference for large and diverse audiences.

Named onomatopoeically for its characteristic drum sounds "dang" and "dut," the music is heard in streets and homes, public parks and narrow alleyways, stores and restaurants, and all forms of public transportation. *Dangdut Stories* is a social and musical history of dangdut within a range of broader narratives about class, gender, ethnicity, and nation in post-independence Indonesia (1945–present). Denigrated as a debased form of popular culture in the early 1970s, dangdut was commercialized in the 1980s, resignified as a form of national and global pop in the 1990s, and localized within ethnic communities in the 2000s. With roots in popular music of urban post-colonial Indonesia, dangdut is a privileged site for narrating stories about the modern nation-state of Indonesia.[4]

Dangdut and Genre

Since the 1980s, the number of books, journal articles, conferences, university courses, and scholarly organizations dedicated to popular music has increased dramatically. Popular music is now, finally, a staple in introductory world music courses, upper-division area studies courses, and graduate seminars. Yet, despite the attention to issues of identity and culture in popular music studies over the last few decades, richly contextualized ethnographic studies of particular genres are lacking.[5]

Despite the recognition of popular music studies as an object of analysis, the processes of genre formation and the practices that constitute specific genres remain undertheorized and underresearched (Holt 2007). The stylistic qualities and characteristics that constitute specific genres are important to analyze because they reveal a unified set of texts, a vocabulary, and specific ways of speaking. Music genres represent historical continuity and stability, and mark common training, aesthetics, techniques, skills, and performance practices. Genres play a major role in authorizing canons, cultural hierarchies, and decisions about censorship and government support.

My interest lies in genre both as a fixed set of elements marked by sameness, as well as a discursive practice that represents difference and social struggles over meaning. Discourse has a material dimension involving economic, political, educational, and religious institutions that establish social relations of power and authority. The construction of meaning depends on such relations of power that either sanction and institutionalize or prohibit and marginalize symbolic production. The stories people tell about how dangdut came to be, or what it represents, or who belongs to its history and who does not, can be read and interpreted as part of its discursive formation (Foucault 1972). Genre distinctions have social effects, as I will show in my analysis of dangdut as a system of representation, in which sounds, texts, images, and meanings symbolically mark one group socially from another.

Dangdut Stories situates the production and circulation of meanings about a musical genre within particular social (political and economic) and cultural (ideological) conditions. Since the genre's inception in the early 1970s, dangdut's meaning has changed from the voice of the popular masses to a central element of modern consumer culture. In the case of dangdut, these shifts in popular music production, discourse, performance practice, and meaning have profound implications for the study of social relations in Indonesia, namely class, ethnicity, gender, and nation. For example, in the 1970s, dangdut was targeted largely to urbanized male youth, and it became a platform from which to proselytize about Islam. Women's voices took center stage in dangdut performance in the 1980s, introducing both dominant representations of women as well as emergent ways of speaking the unspeakable in the public sphere. In the 1990s, officials within the central government and national media apparatuses defined dangdut as a national genre that had the potential to speak for everyone. In the 2000s, new regionalized forms of production, circulation, and consumption began to challenge the center-periphery model of popular music discourse and practice. This genre-centered approach to dangdut clarifies issues of worldwide significance, including local discourses of Islam, the role of women in modernizing societies, and the role of popular culture in the formation of a developing nation-state.

In a seminal article about dangdut, historian William Frederick states that the genre represents a "sensitive and useful prism through which to view Indonesian society" (1982, 104). I argue that not only is dangdut a vivid reflection of national politics and culture, but that dangdut as an economic, political, and ideological practice has helped to shape people's ideas about class, gender, and ethnicity in the modern nation-state of Indonesia.

Despite dangdut's tremendous popularity in Indonesia and other parts of Asia, it has seldom received the serious critical attention it deserves. Even the number of articles, theses, and working papers about the genre is surprisingly low, scattered among the disciplines of history (Frederick 1982; Lockard 1998), music (Hatch 1985; Yampolsky 1991; Wallach 2008), anthropology (Simatupang 1996; David 2009); and Asian studies (Pioquinto 1995 and 1998; Sen and Hill 2000; Browne 2000). Missing from these earlier studies are focused analyses of music, and attention to the stylistic development of new creative forms. *Dangdut Stories* is the first musicological study to examine the stylistic development of dangdut music itself, using vocal style, melody, rhythm, harmony, form, and song texts to articulate symbolic struggles over meaning in the realm of culture. The book illuminates historical changes in musical style, performance practice, and social meanings from the genre's origins to the present day.

During the field research for this book, I listened carefully to how dangdut structures stories in particular musical forms at particular historical junctures. People often told me that dangdut songs dealt with universal themes, for example, love and relationships. In love, everyone has experienced the same emotions—excitement, passion, and joy, as well as loneliness, anger, and frustration—and these constitute the raw material for dangdut songs. Yet, dangdut songs address social issues that other genres avoid; for example (a) drunkenness and gambling; (b) poverty; (c) prostitution; (d) infertility; (e) infidelity; (f) broken families; and (g) homelessness, among others.[6] Further, songs by dangdut superstar Rhoma Irama have introduced populist messages about (a) human rights; (b) social class inequality; (c) social struggle through religion; and (d) government corruption, among others.[7]

However, this is not simply a study of music and texts. Using a synthesis of ethnographic, historical, and musicological approaches from ethnomusicology, anthropology of media, and cultural studies, *Dangdut Stories* connects the aesthetic properties and the uses and effects of the music to shifting social and material conditions in modern post-independence Indonesia. I approach dangdut as a form of cultural politics in which social actors activate symbolic forms in struggles over what counts as valuable and meaningful in culture.

Seven interrelated chapters, or "stories," about the meanings of dangdut in modern Indonesian society comprise the main text. These stories are arranged chronologically within the larger historical narrative of the Indonesian nation-state.

Why Dangdut?

Indonesians chuckled when I told them that I was writing a book about dangdut. Scholars of Indonesian performing arts, including myself, have typically focused on forms, practices, and discourses of tradition in genres of music (e.g., *gamelan*, the gong-chime ensemble), dance (e.g., classical), and theater (e.g., *wayang*, the puppet theater). Until 1990, musicological research in the English language had largely ignored the study of popular music in Indonesia.[8] Further, the nature of dangdut songs and performance itself tend, on the surface at least, to be cute, playful, funny, and light, rather than serious, contemplative, and heavy.

Academic colleagues had mixed reactions about my project. Some reacted positively, expressing the sentiment that "it's about time!" Negative reactions tended to be based on monolithic views of the genre. One colleague remarked: "Dangdut? It's just a bunch of women in skimpy outfits shaking their hips around! Why would anybody want to study *that*!" Indeed, in chapter 7, I ask: What is the nature and meaning of eroticized dance in the public sphere, especially in the largest majority Islamic country in the world? Some critics argued that dangdut was more accurately a rhythmic treatment rather than a genre, which somehow made it less valuable as an object of study. They noted that *any* song could be made into a dangdut version by treating it with dangdut rhythmic and melodic elements, much like any song can be made into a reggae version, or a bossa nova version. Indeed, there are numerous pop songs that have been made into dangdut versions. But the ability to "cross over" seems to indicate the power and distinctiveness of dangdut, a genre defined by very small and detailed musical gestures.

In this book, I focus on dangdut as a repertoire (of songs, texts, and spin-off styles), a community (of singers, arrangers, musicians, producers, and fans), a performance style (spectacular, excessive, and over-the-top), and a discourse about social relations of power. One of the main goals of this book is to show how dangdut has changed during the last forty years, giving rise to a diversity of styles and contested social uses, functions, and meanings.

Colleagues questioned me about the aesthetic grounds of the music: "Do you really *like* that music? It's so tacky!" ("I do!" I answered). In contrast to tra-ditionalized objects of musicological study, dangdut was perceived as loud, aggressive, crass, derivative, inauthentic, and lacking creativity and imagina-tion. But these claims may be countered by understanding dangdut's performance practice, style, and aesthetics within particular historical contexts, rather than in relation to aesthetic criteria developed for other kinds of music in different historical periods.

Another colleague lambasted dangdut's commercial nature: it existed solely to sell products (primarily beer and cigarettes) and it functioned as a form of escape to distract its largely underclass consumer base from contemplating and acting on real social problems. Dangdut is a commercial mass-mediated music, and the economic stakes of its production and circulation are high. I argue that a study of music, style, and aesthetics in late-twentieth-century Indonesia has to be articulated with the economic base, commercial networks, and the circulation of cultural products that inform so much of contemporary cultural practice. The dangdut music industry exerts tremendous influence and power. But people consume and use dangdut in a variety of ways and they create a variety of mean-ings out of dangdut texts and practices.

In Bandung, West Java, a respected intellectual and colleague at the music conservatory warned me: "If you go to dangdut concerts, you will have to deal with the fact that the music encourages violence, prostitution, and the use of alcohol and drugs." His comments implied a causal relationship between dang-dut and these activities. Later, I learned that dangdut was a discursive space for mediating a variety of social meanings about poverty, unemployment, infi-delity, sex, and drunkenness. Its lyrics reflected a social community based on everyday material conditions, and its music and performance style encouraged pleasure, fantasy, and desire. In some social spaces, dangdut could not be separated from the violence and disorder of modern Indonesian history. It did not take long for me to realize that dangdut was an ideal site from which to understand the symbolic role of music in mediating the tensions and contradictions of contemporary Indonesian culture and society.

"Dangdut is no longer popular with the younger generation," an Indonesian undergraduate student at my university reported in January 2007. Dangdut was never very popular among university students, although universities have hosted conferences and even performing groups since the 1970s. And yet, I had just returned from five months of Fulbright-sponsored fieldwork in Indonesia, where it seemed that dangdut shaped the soundscape of urban life: in buses and taxis, roadside food stalls, nightclubs, karaoke bars, and luxury hotels, and on television and radios at home. In 2006, an informal survey of weekly television programming showed that 29 out of 43 music programs were devoted exclusively to dangdut (67%), while another calculation showed that dangdut could be viewed on television nearly ten hours per day.[9] Clearly dangdut was one of the most—if not the most—popular music on television. Yet, how could dangdut be both rising and falling in popularity?

I include these commentaries and reactions from colleagues and students to exemplify conflicting interpretations about the nature, function, and meaning of dangdut that have led to its relative exclusion from scholarly discourse about Indonesian culture.[10] These comments illustrate a politics of culture surrounding dangdut, a way of strategically invoking ideas, symbols, and practices to make social distinctions among groups (Bourdieu 1984). Dangdut stimulated conversations about the nature and meaning of class, gender, ethnicity, and nation, and these conversations grew into the subject of this book.

Why Stories?

I have chosen to frame this book as a series of stories for several reasons. Dangdut songs themselves constitute stories. In the historical transition from Malay band music (orkes Melayu) to dangdut, composers moved away from texts composed in four-line verses (pantun) based on metaphor, allusion, and language play toward a narrative style more common in Indian film songs (Frederick 1982, 111). Indonesian composers in the 1950s began adopting the cinematic quality of Indian film music to create characters and situations in song. People visualized themselves in these songs, which are mostly about love, and often involve an intersubjective dialogue about "me" (diriku) and "you" (dirimu). Songs cut to the emotional core of these stories through direct language and a melodramatic style of performance (including crying and screaming). A dangdut song frames a theme, establishes a setting (time, place, event), and represents a certain point of view. As a distinct genre of storytelling, we can speak about formal narrative conventions in dangdut. These song-stories, accompanied by elaborate costumes and dance, transferred easily across visual media including films, television programs, and video.

During my fieldwork, I was particularly attentive to the way that people told stories about dangdut. Musicians, critics, fans, scholars, and media personnel emphasized or excluded certain actors, places, themes, and sequences of events in order to construct social meanings and values around a genre of popular music. Not surprisingly, one person's telling would often conflict with others, giving rise to a multiplicity of meanings about the same subject or historical event. I have tried as much as possible to preserve and explicate those contradictions in the text in order to provide as much "backstory" to the material as possible.

Stories are important not only for what they reveal but for what they hide. *Dangdut Stories* are tales about dangdut and its relationship to commercial music and media institutions (music recording, radio, and television), government institutions (regulatory agencies), and critical institutions (news media and education). These institutions do not represent one coherent position, but they have their own hierarchies and internal ideological conflicts. The forms of discourse that emerge from these institutions raise ideological questions about storytelling as a cultural practice. What cultural and material conditions make it possible to tell certain stories and not others? Where do stories originate, and what routes do they travel? Whose stories become valuable economically? What stories are excluded from being told?

My own participation in the work of representation should not be left unexamined. Throughout this book, I will speak on behalf of dangdut's main audience, "the people" (*rakyat*), who constitute the majority of Indonesia's 220 million inhabitants. I have relied on a stereotype of the *rakyat*, "who often suffer from injustice inflicted by the rich and powerful" (Heryanto 1999, 162). I have imagined the *rakyat* as a group excluded from centers of power, a group that requires either protection or intervention from powerful commercial, media, and government institutions. The interpretations presented in this book are necessarily limited by my life experiences and are framed in terms of my own subject position as a white heterosexual male, a citizen of the United States, an employee of a university, a musician, and a fan of the music. The reader will get a selective glimpse of dangdut, and that perspective is shaped by my own ideological and personal interests. In order to be critical of my own authority in the representation of culture, I acknowledge throughout the book that ethnographic writing is partial and at least partially fictionalized. For example, as the first major study to address the stylistic elements and aesthetics of dangdut, *Dangdut Stories* focuses on canonical songs, recordings, and recording artists whose songs have become widely successful in Indonesia. Myriad local artists who never made recordings, as well as new localized forms of dangdut, are only examined briefly in chapter 8.

The story I will tell begins with dangdut at the center of a dialogue about social relations in modern Indonesia. I believe that dangdut opens up texts that can "speak" in very revealing and significant ways about the value and meanings of class, gender, ethnicity, and nation. In this approach, dangdut mediates and organizes social meanings through its articulation with corresponding moments in Indonesian history. A large body of scholarship can be found on political and economic developments in Indonesia, especially for the period leading up to and during the New Order regime of Indonesia's second president, Suharto (1967–1998).[11] I will refer readers to this extensive literature throughout the book. In the following section, I will summarize the relationships between dangdut and the broader narratives addressed in the book.

Ethnicity and Nation

In chapter 2, I discuss the notion that dangdut is based in ethnic Melayu (Malay) music and culture. In the Malay/Indonesian language, "Melayu" is one of the most difficult words to define.[12] In Indonesia, Melayu ethnic identity has been defined in terms of cultural geography (a Melayu "culture area"), religion (Islam), language (Melayu or Malay), and customs and ceremonies (*adat*) (Yampolsky 1991). The Melayu region includes the modern nation-states (with dates of independence) of Indonesia (1945), Malaysia (1957), Singapore (1965), Brunei (1984), and southern Thailand (never colonized politically). Melayu is a culturally hybrid and evolving category that extends across these modern nation-state boundaries. However, in the discourse about the roots of dangdut, Melayu-ness is often invoked to link dangdut with a royal historical lineage (in North Sumatra) and a core ethnic and racialized culture. Rather than privileging a source of origins, I examine the history of dangdut in specific locations involving specific actors within specific historical circumstances. In chapters 2 and 3, I describe Melayu music of the 1950s in Jakarta, Medan, and Surabaya.

Throughout this book, I examine the historical construction of dangdut as a national music that is said to appeal to *all* Indonesians. As arguably the dominant form of popular music in Indonesia, dangdut has an important role to play in defining what it means to be a proper citizen. Music is part of a discursive formation about belonging to a national community. This discursive formation conditions people to imagine themselves as part of a community in terms defined by the institutions or apparatuses of the nation-state. Its important role in shaping what it means to be a citizen has made dangdut a site for government appropriation, regulation, monitoring, and censorship.

How did the state become involved in the production, circulation, and meaning of dangdut as a national music? Since the 1970s, political parties have used dangdut to gather crowds at rallies for the purpose of promoting candidates in local and national elections. But the discourse about dangdut as a form of national music accelerated through public pronouncements about dangdut made by government and military officials in the 1990s. Sung in the national language, and mediated far and wide across the archipelago, dangdut became identified as the music of Indonesia. In chapter 6, I address the following questions: What does it mean to be a national music in Indonesia? What forms of dangdut were used to promote national culture? What can these forms tell us about national belonging and identification?

In the national-popular model of Indonesian music elaborated by Hatch (1985) and Yampolsky (1991), music is analyzed as a signifier of either local (also defined as regional or ethnic) or national identity. Indonesian national-popular music genres are characterized by the following criteria: (1) they are sung in the national language; (2) musical elements (instruments, timbres, melodic, rhythmic, and formal organization) are based on Western models, or at the very least, not associated with one ethnic group or another; and (3) recordings of the music are produced in Jakarta by a centralized group of producers and circulate within a nationalized media network. Genres considered national art forms, ironically, often originate from elsewhere. As dangdut singer and composer A. Rafiq told me: "What is the original Indonesian art form? *Wayang* [puppet theater] is from India! *Kroncong* [string band music] is Portuguese!" (A. Rafiq, pers. comm., 18 July 2005).

On the other hand, local popular musics are characterized by the following criteria: (1) they are sung in local languages; (2) they have indigenous musical elements, and (3) they are produced in local recording studios for a local market. "Local" refers to musical practices of an ethnic or regional group in relation to the national level (for example, Minang, Javanese, Acehnese), representing local interests in the realm of culture. Local popular musics rarely cross ethno-linguistic borders. The basic premise of this model is that local music is defined by local content, whereas national music is constituted by non-local elements. Unlike local forms, dangdut was defined as national because it did not belong to any one group in particular.

National forms not only stand for national affiliations, but they help to produce these affiliations, and these affiliations become symbolic markers of national cultural identity. Yampolsky (1991, 1) writes:

In Indonesia, the distinction between national and regional is extremely important: what is national—Indonesian language, mass media, government, the educational system—unites the country, and what is regional—local loyalties, languages, customs, music—has the potential to fragment it.

The national-popular model describes the way in which the production of Indonesian national culture emanates from the center (Jakarta) and works its way out to the peripheries (everywhere else). For example, in the national-popular model, dangdut was produced in Jakarta and circulated throughout the provinces. Furthermore, due to its hegemonic force in media, dangdut maneuvered in such a way as to threaten and displace local music, exerting a homogenizing force in the realm of culture. Like the national language (*Bahasa Indonesia*), people began speaking the same musical "language."

Sutton expands on this center-periphery theoretical model by placing musical forms within specific media frames. The tripartite framework of local, global, and national is the focus of Sutton's analysis of dangdut on television (2003). He traces the outlines of dangdut by analyzing its musical elements, musical instruments, and media representation as signifiers of locality, globalization, or nationality. A picture of dangdut's meaning emerges through a comparison of dangdut with other forms (mainly *pop Indonesia*). For example, "Dangdut is NOT trendy, does not give its viewers a finger on the pulse of the world, of the global now. It is not 'traditional,' not 'regional'; but neither is it 'modern' in the same way that the more Western forms of pop are" (Sutton 2003, 16; emphasis in original). I will not attempt to define dangdut as local, national, global, or some combination of the above, because dangdut as a signifying system does not correspond to such fixed categories in all times and places. Rather, I will situate dangdut's meaning within specific discursive communities shaped by historical, political, economic, and ideological factors.

At the turn of the twenty-first century, a flurry of new hybrids blended local music and dance genres with dangdut. This is the story of a genre that started out in the centralized media environment of Jakarta. It then gave rise to localized forms, which reestablished the genre as Indonesia's "de facto" national music (Sutton 2003, 13). In chapter 8, I describe the uses, functions, and meanings of national popular forms in local settings. I show that the terms and ideological stakes with which dangdut has been labeled "national" and "ethnic" have changed over the last 40 years, especially in the post–New Order era. These new forms challenge the center-periphery model of national popular music.

Dangdut and "the People"

Dangdut musicians expressed a common trope about dangdut that is true for many kinds of popular music. While its production and circulation are thought to be highly controlled by a powerful and manipulative music industry, dangdut simultaneously represents the aspirations and desires of the *rakyat*, the vast majority of Indonesian citizens. Dangdut illuminates notions of the *rakyat* not only directly from the people's perspective, but through representation: in songs, statements by musicians, and stories about the genre in popular print media. When and how did the notion of the *rakyat* become formulated through both the music itself and discourses about the music?

In the 1970s, dangdut fans, synonymous with the masses, were discursively produced in popular print media according to middle-class and elite notions of the *rakyat* as explosive and uncontrolled. Benedict Anderson writes that the *rakyat* have long been perceived as a central symbol of Indonesian nationalism, but they were "*masih bodoh*" ("still stupid," ignorant, and unformed) (1990, 61). I will describe the contours of this relationship by addressing questions about music and cultural representation in chapter 4. I concentrate on the ways in which stories about the *rakyat* have been narrated and mobilized within a discourse about dangdut in popular print media.[13] What kind of story has been told about the *rakyat* through dangdut in popular print media? How are they called into being by these stories? Where and when are they represented? For what purposes are they invoked?

The association between dangdut and *rakyat*, according to artists as well as critics and scholars, is based on lyrics of the songs themselves, which are allegedly simple, easy to understand, and utilize everyday situations that audiences can relate to. But this association was produced under specific social and historical conditions through a media industry that developed around dangdut superstar Rhoma Irama in the 1970s. His songs became a voice for the underclass as well as a tool to proselytize about Islam. In chapter 4, I discuss these myriad ways of understanding constructions of the *rakyat* in dangdut.

Gender and the Body

But regardless of class, ethnicity, and nation, the mention of dangdut during my fieldwork inevitably elicited conversations and commentaries about dance, gender, and the body. Munif Bahasuan, one of dangdut's senior composers, noted that dangdut has always been synonymous with dance (pers. comm., 16 July 2005). Unlike other kinds of popular music, dangdut "invites" people to dance, as described by singer Camelia Malik (italics mine):

I view dangdut as a unique kind of music. It's a type of
entertainment not only for listening, but it *invites* listeners to
participate, to dance, *automatically*. As soon as they hear it, people
want to dance. With pop, people have to be encouraged. Not so with
dangdut. (Camelia Malik, pers. comm., 18 July 2005)

A newspaper article reflected the common attitude that dangdut's appeal lies in
the fact that one does not need any special training to participate:

This type of music, besides invigorating a scene, makes people feel
confident to dance. There are no prescribed foot movements, hand
gestures, or body postures to dance dangdut. This is quite different
from cha-cha, salsa, samba, or line dancing which have lots of rules.
("Asyiknya Digoyang Dangdut" 2001)

"*Goyang!*" ("Dance!" or "Shake it!") was a common response when I mentioned
to Indonesians that I was studying dangdut. *Goyang* simply means "to move,"
but in dangdut it refers to the swaying movement of the hips, waist, and buttocks. *Goyang* is not only the movement of the body, but it is a "natural" and
"unconscious" reaction to dangdut's distinctive drum rhythms, as indicated by
the quotes above as well as the lyrics to a classic song entitled "Dangdut" (composed by Rhoma Irama): "Because it's so enjoyable, without even realizing it /
my rear end begins to sway, and I feel like singing" (*Karena asyikna aku, hingga
tak kusadari / Pinggul bergoyang-goyang, rasa ingin berdendang*).

By pressing the left hand palm against the top (head) of the dangdut drum
(*gendang*), the drummer tightens the head, compresses the physical space
inside the drum, and produces the ascending glissando of the "du-ut" sound.
Notably, males often use this downward pressing movement of the wrist to signify sexual intercourse. Commentators have written that the sound of the
"du-ut" produces a "psychological effect [of] heightening its erotic spell"
(Setiawan 1989, 226–227). Yet, as I show in chapter 6, *goyang* does not have
one specific meaning. In public settings where males dance as audiences and
patrons, female performers may use their sensual voices, seductive movements, and songs full of sexual innuendos to call men to dance. Yet, males
dancing to dangdut can also create a social space for defining masculinity
(Spiller 2001). Further, women dance for many reasons, as noted by dangdut
singer Cucu Cahayati:

Even goyang has to have some sort of parameters, so that people can
identify one person's distinctive type of goyang. You can't just do it
freely to capture the desires of your audience. ("Terserah Orang"
1996)

Women's dancing bodies are the subjects of many songs.[14] Males generally compose the lyrics and music, play the instruments, and produce the albums. In public performances, males are the main audience. Yet, my research shows that women are a significant focus of dangdut songs. Composers consistently reminded me that they compose with women audiences in mind. Further, female singers currently dominate the genre. At home, where dangdut is broadcast on radio and television, and played on inexpensive video compact discs (VCD), dangdut's audience is primarily women.

How are women represented in dangdut song texts, images, and discourses? Are women as economic actors empowered through dangdut more than other arenas of popular culture? How are they as a class simultaneously degraded in performance? Several different images of women are available in song texts, images, and discourses about dangdut. One dominant representation is the seductive singer/dancer who is sexually available. Dangdut is the music that accompanies the sale of sex in the corridors of prostitution districts in Indonesia. In dark and steamy clubs, or dimly lit karaoke bars, women work as singers, dance partners, and hostesses, as illustrated by the following edited field notes from my fieldwork:

> The "Top 1" Club is located in the Mangga Dua area of Jakarta, a center for nightlife in this city of 9 million. The three-story building houses several clubs, one on each floor. We hear dangdut, and enter one of the clubs. Inside, the large, dark and steamy room smells like alcohol and sweat. Booths surround a dance floor, with tables in back. When we walk in, there are six "couples" on the dance floor, all men, dancing in two rows, stepping to the rhythm of the music.
>
> At one end of the dance floor, two men, about 35–40 years old, are locked in a tight embrace, heads facing upward, cheeks together, eyes closed, with arms outstretched. Hands clasped, they move their arms in and out and around, singing a song about a lost love, while the music swirls around them. The song "Mabuk Janda" (Crazy/ Drunk about a Widow/Divorcee) portrays the voice of a long-suffering wife admonishing her irresponsible husband: "You're already drunk, you've already gambled away your money, Still you're tempted by a young divorced woman, I can't take it!" [udah mabuk minuman, ditambah mabuk judi, Masih saja kakang tergoda janda kembang, tak sudi ku tak sudi].
>
> Women work the club. They are dressed in colorful miniskirts, tight tops, and high heels, and wear thick masks of makeup. Men pay

by the hour to ogle, hold, and touch them. A female dancer who works as a hostess at the club thrusts her hips in short quick movements, accentuated by the short staccato jabs of the drum rhythms. She knows dangdut songs better than anyone. The song "Putri Panggung" (Princess of the Dance Floor) accompanies the persona she performs at the club: "I'm a princess, a princess who sings on stage, I'll come here whenever you want me" [*Saya si putri, si putri sinden panggung, datang kemari menurut panggilan anda*]

Money passes quickly from men to women. Dangdut fans like to sing, and for a small fee they can sing their favorite songs in public. After a song, the female singers hold their hands out to each man until the exchange is complete. The women may or may not engage in sexual acts with men. Their interactions with men within the realm of music and dance events reminds me of the "ronggeng image" (Spiller 2007): a representation of attractive and flirtatious Sundanese female singer/dancers which appears in a variety of performance genres and supports a structure of gendered power and difference in Sundanese society ("gender ideology").

Scenes like the one described above have become dominant in video recordings, circulated on VCDs and via the Internet, in which female performers are filmed dancing in sexually provocative ways. However, dangdut is also a forum for celebrating eroticized female dance and power, which has long been an important part of Indonesia's cultural history, at least on the islands of Java and Sumatra. As we shall see in chapter 7, women do not apologize for expressing their own sexuality in dance. Further, as described in chapter 6, dangdut in the 1990s engaged with the image of the good wife/mother, the head of household who suffered for her husband even as he destroyed the family.

Women present different images in popular print media and discourses of self-representation. Tabloid stories about sex and scandal attach to dangdut singers, especially women, more than any other genre of music in Indonesia. The grouping together of "female," "dangdut," and "singer" conjures images of sexual pleasure and seduction for some, while for others, it can signify sexual freedom, economic possibilities, as well as Muslim identifications (see Figure 1.7 with parts [a], [b], and [c]).

FIGURE I.7 *Continued*

FIGURE I.7 *Continued*

(c)

FIGURE 1.7 Visual representation of women in dangdut performances, 2004–2005:
(a) Nita Thalia portrays an image of female sexuality and power, 4 December 2004
[courtesy of *Tempo*] (b) Cici Paramida represents a modern glamorous woman,
10 March 2005 [courtesy of *Tempo*]; (c) Evie Tamala appears in a Muslim head scarf
(*jilbab*) at a political campaign rally, 28 March 2004 [courtesy of *Tempo*].

Dangdut and Islam

The strong associations between dangdut and Islamic culture, and the fact that
the majority of its practitioners and fans are Muslim, make dangdut a privileged
site for analyzing music and Islam in Indonesia. Scholars of music in Indonesia
have become increasingly aware of the importance of Islam in Indonesia, the
country with the largest majority Muslim population in the world (Capwell
1995; Rasmussen 2001; Berg 2007; Harnish and Rasmussen forthcoming).
Many of dangdut's first generation of star singers, including Ellya Khadam,
A. Rafiq, Mansyur S., and Elvy Sukaesih, cite their training in Islamic recitation
(*tilawah*) as a major aesthetic component of proper dangdut vocal style. Islamic-
related genres, including *orkes Melayu* and *gambus* (Middle Eastern–inspired
lute-based music), are often cited as precursors to dangdut. Although dangdut
is not a form of Islamic music, its main figure Rhoma Irama is also an Islamic
preacher. The relationship between dangdut and contemporary debates about
Islam, women, and censorship is the subject of chapter 7. In 2003 a female

dangdut singer named Inul Daratista became famous on national television for dancing in ways that infuriated conservative Muslims. Her rise to fame coincided with transformative political events, including the fall of ex-president Suharto in 1998, the subsequent calls for political reform in the name of democracy, and the ascension of an Islamicist discourse in the public sphere. The story of Inul Daratista came to symbolize the shifting relationship between politics, religion, and the role of women in post-Suharto Indonesia, involving a certain segment of Muslim leadership, moderate political leaders, and ordinary people. As Indonesia moved away from the strong grip of the Suharto regime, new social and political arrangements were played out in dangdut.

These brief summaries reveal the dialectical relationship between dangdut and broader narratives about social relations in modern Indonesia. This approach does not simply reveal the ways in which music is a vehicle for asserting or expressing essentialized notions of social identity. I agree with Waterman's critique of ethnomusicology that "by the 1980s and 1990s the notion that one could *explain* particular musical practices and forms by specifying their role in expressing or enacting identity had become commonplace in the ethnomusicological literature" (Waterman 2002, 19). Rather, I aim to show that dangdut as a political economy of contested symbols *mediates* meanings about social relations in modern Indonesian society.

Methodology

At Indonesian parties, wedding receptions, bars, and karaoke clubs, people sing. They dance. No matter where I was—in West Jakarta, Central Java, North Sumatra, South Kalimantan, or the eastern United States—I discovered that getting up in front of a crowd of people and singing classic dangdut songs was not only enjoyable but could also propel my research forward in unpredictable ways. I was perfectly happy to embarrass myself as an amateur singer because I was fairly certain that dangdut would open up a dialogue about the issues central to this study.

Dangdut Stories is based on interviews with musicians, composers, arrangers, producers, and fans; analysis of popular print media; lessons with musicians; musicological analysis; and participant-observation.[15] Interviews helped me answer questions about cultural production and reception. I have tried as much as possible to narrate the meanings of dangdut in my interlocutors' voices by including their own stories.[16] Lessons with musicians illuminated the basic technical knowledge and musical vocabulary to analyze songs with careful attention to insider perspectives. Participation and observation gave me the lived experience to interpret how social meanings of class, gender, ethnicity, and nation are constructed through symbolic practices in specific social environments.

My analysis of particular songs addresses musical sound, song lyrics, and performance style. People often made references to individual songs and musical production techniques to talk about the stylistic evolution of the genre, distinctions between artists, relationships with fans, and myriad other issues. Through an analysis of the relationship between lyrics and music sound, I began to understand the pleasure, humor, and irony of dangdut.

For my analysis of individual songs, I use "song guides" to illustrate elements of performance. A song guide is a graphic description of sonic and textual elements that corresponds to the temporal and formal organization of a song. I use song guides to show points of interest, and to explain the meaning or significance of sonic and textual elements. Each song guide emphasizes different musical elements because different elements take on significance in different eras.

In each chapter, I present analyses of songs in order to connect the music sound to modern Indonesian society. I have used original studio recordings of songs as examples, rather than local renditions of songs, or examples that never became popular, because these songs form the core dangdut repertoire; songs used as examples can be heard on the Oxford Web site. These songs are commonly sung in updated or localized forms that reflect the rhythms and pace of contemporary life. In chapter 8, I focus on regional songs to emphasize changes that have occurred after the fall of Suharto.

I conducted my research in urban areas of Jakarta, Bandung, and Surabaya, with short site visits to Banjarmasin, Banyuwangi, Denpasar, and Medan. I felt that a pioneering historical study of dangdut should begin in the cities because that is where dangdut initially took root. But, like any story, much has been left out. Even though dangdut is touted by critics, scholars, and some artists as Indonesia's national popular music, its meaning as "national" is not fixed. New forms and practices are developing every day in cities and towns across the archipelago. Further, dangdut has extended its reach from Indonesia to Malaysia, Singapore, Japan, and elsewhere. This leaves a great deal of research waiting to be conducted, not only on localized forms, but also on dangdut's expanding international reach.

Stories are linear: they have a beginning, middle, and end. However, they continue to evolve and their meanings change over time, and under different historical and material circumstances. Dangdut is embedded in social struggles over meanings of class, gender, ethnicity, and nation in modern Indonesia. But dangdut songs do not present solutions to social problems. Dangdut stories encompass the everyday realities of modern life, as well as imagined realms of pleasure, desire, and fantasy. Songs compel people to listen to these stories, no matter how mundane or trivial. Everyone has a story to tell, even though no one may ever hear it. These are the stories I will narrate in the following pages.

NOTES

1. The genre name is pronounced "dahng-DOOT" with a stress on the second syllable.

2. In 2006, there were two "American Idol" dangdut shows and both were broadcast on TPI; the Indonesian Dangdut Contest (Kontes Dangdut Indonesia, KDI) was the other.

3. Sociologists prefer the plural form "middle classes" in order to reflect the different and contradictory elements that constitute members of this socio-economic grouping in Indonesia. Heryanto (2003, 27) writes that "what all variants of the middle classes share in common (without which they cannot be designated as middle classes at all) are their orientation towards any combination of these: urban residence; modern occupations and education; and cultural tastes, which manifest most vividly but not exclusively, in consumer lifestyles." For further information about Indonesia's middle classes, see Dick 1985; Lev 1990; Robison 1996; Heryanto 1999 and 2003; and Gerke 2000.

4. Throughout the book, I emphasize the central role of dance and movement in dangdut aesthetics and practice. However, dangdut music is the focus of analysis in this study.

5. Genre is a key term in popular music studies (Negus 1996; Brackett 2000). A genre refers to a particular kind of music within a distinctive cultural web of production, circulation, and signification (Holt 2007).

6. (a) "Mabuk dan Judi" (Drunkenness and Gambling); (b) "Gubuk Derita" (Hut of Suffering); (c) "Hitam Duniamu Putih Cintaku" (Your World Is Dark, My Love Is Pure); (d) "Mandul" (Infertility); (e) "Gula-gula" (Mistress); (f) "Ratapan Anak Tiri" (Lament of a Stepchild); and (g) "Gelandangan" (Homelessness).

7. (a) "Hak Azasi" (Human Rights); (b) "Indonesia"; (c) "Perjuangan dan Do'a" (Struggle and Prayer); and (d) "Reformasi" (Government Reform).

8. Notable exceptions include Becker 1975; Heins 1975; Kornhauser 1978; Frederick 1982; Hatch 1985; Manuel and Baier 1986; Yampolsky 1989.

9. Both polls excluded Global TV, which broadcasts numerous music programs (including MTV Asia) that are not specific to genre, as well as the dangdut program *Salam Dangdut*. I conducted the first informal poll based on the weekly schedule, 5–11 June 2006. The second poll was reported in Irkham 2005.

10. Similarly, Indonesian studies in general have tended to focus on the public masculine discourse of nation-state building and modernization rather than the private or domestic feminine sphere of mass-mediated leisure, entertainment, and popular culture (Heryanto 2008, 7).

11. The March 11, 1966 Order (*Supersemar*), in which Sukarno gave Suharto full authority to restore order after the Indonesian killings of 1965–66, marks the end of Sukarno's Old Order (*Orde Lama*) and the beginning of Suharto's New Order (*Orde*

Baru). Suharto was named acting president by the People's Consultative Assembly (Majelis Permusyawaratan Rakyat MPR) on March 12, 1967. He was forced from power and officially resigned on May 21, 1998.

12. The Malay language is spoken in Malaysia and Indonesia as well as in East Timor, southern Thailand, Brunei, parts of the Philippines, and Singapore. Malay is one of the official languages of Malaysia, Brunei, Singapore and Indonesia. In Indonesia and East Timor, the language is called *Bahasa Indonesia,* which translates literally as "Indonesian language."

13. My findings are based on a review of over 400 articles about dangdut, representing 45 different publications, written between 1972 and 2006. I will use the term "popular print media" to refer to materials that can be grouped into the following four categories: newspapers and news magazines; magazines; tabloids (about music, film, and television); and media promotional publications.

14. Song titles include "Goyang Asoy" (Great Dance), "Goyang Dombret" (Dombret Dance), "Goyang Dangdut" (Dangdut Dance), "Goyang Gosip" (Gossip Dance), "Goyang Karawang" (Karawang Dance), "Goyang Inul" (Inul's Dance), and "Goyang Senggol" (Touching Dance).

15. Lessons with musicians included Husein Khan (*gendang;* Jakarta); Kang Uja (*gendang;* Bandung); and Yadi (keyboard; Bandung).

16. Interviews were conducted by the author in *Bahasa Indonesia* (Indonesian) unless otherwise noted. I have translated all of the interview excerpts included in the book.

Chapter 2

Mythologizing Melayu:
Discourse, Practice, and the
Stakes of Authenticity

> I wrote the song "Viva Dangdut" to document the history of the genre
> (he sings): "Dangdut is the sound of the drum, the rhythm played over
> and over again, Dangdut is the sound of the drum, So lively that it
> becomes the name of the music [genre]. This is Melayu music,
> Originally from Deli, And then influenced, By the West and India."
> (Rhoma Irama, pers. comm., 14 July 2005)[1]

In published interviews, speeches, and songs about the origins of dangdut,
Rhoma Irama maintains that the genre originates from Melayu music of Deli
("Melayu Deli") in North Sumatra.[2] Rhoma Irama "documents" in this song a
linear and natural development of dangdut from what he defines as an original
Melayu source. Based on a cultural lineage that extends from the pre-colonial
Deli sultanate, through "Melayu orchestras" (orkes Melayu) of the 1950s and
1960s, to dangdut of the 1970s, he constructs a continuous narrative around a
history of very chaotic and uneven development. Although the influence of
Western and Indian music was strong, the Melayu "sense of music" formed
the core element in dangdut:[3]

> We maintained the musical feeling of orkes Melayu. Listen to a song
> like "Badai Fitnah" (Raging Slander). The beat was Rock. The
> performance was Rock. We changed the instruments from acoustic
> to electric. We wore tight clothes, long hair, and high platform shoes.
> We turned somersaults onstage. The audience went wild. The sound
> was different but the "sense of music" was based on orkes Melayu.
> (Rhoma Irama, pers. comm., 14 July 2005)

With this rhetorical move, Rhoma Irama legitimizes dangdut by invoking the mythological past of Deli, the site of a sixteenth-century Islamic sultanate, to contextualize the present.[4] Deli is important for understandings of Melayu identity for two reasons: (1) the concern with royal lineage, and (2) the concern for a core culture based in Islam, in which a "sense of music" emerged from an ethnic group with shared ideas, beliefs, values, and symbols (Reid 2001, 304). This genealogizing grounds the heavily Islamic nature of Rhoma Irama's music in the religious past, and it links a Melayu kingdom (albeit a minor one) to the contemporary "king" of dangdut.

Elvy Sukaesih, one of the most important singers in the early development of dangdut, denies the historical connection between dangdut and Melayu music:

> If someone says that dangdut is Melayu, I will disagree because the Melayu beat and the dangdut beat are different. [she demonstrates the rhythms] Melayu *is* Melayu. Melayu refers to a type of music that existed in Deli [North Sumatra]. Listen to a song like "Burung Putih" (White Bird) or "Tanjung Katung" (The Katung Cape) [she sings] "the water is blue, a place to wash one's face." Dangdut lyrics are different. [she sings] "Who is that, the one that always tempts me? When he looks at me I feel a tremor in my heart." I want to set the record straight. Dangdut is not Melayu. It has more elements from India, and it is specific to Indonesia. (Elvy Sukaesih, pers. comm., 20 July 2005)[5]

Elvy Sukaesih's genealogy of dangdut emphasizes dichotomy and difference rather than historical origins and continuity. She rejects the notion that dangdut grew out of an "original" pre-colonial Melayu source, and instead places dangdut's formative location in the modern nation-state of Indonesia. It owes its style to Indian film elements, which infused the landscape of Indonesian popular culture during the 1950s and 1960s.[6] She focuses on the lyrical and musical elements of actual dangdut songs, which, on a very practical level, do not sound anything like Melayu Deli songs. Her example celebrates dangdut's earthy and immediate bodily presence—a moving tremor in the heart—rather than its origins in a detached romanticized past.

Competing claims about the origins of dangdut by dangdut "king" Rhoma Irama and dangdut "queen" Elvy Sukaesih raise questions about the history of the genre and the cultural politics that arise out of these debates, as explored in the following two chapters.[7] These culturalist claims have implications for defining contemporary notions of ethnic nationalism in Indonesia and Malaysia based on cultural traditions, language, religion, ethnicity, locality, and race. As

I will show, the category of Melayu can only be understood within a more flexible framework of cultural hybridity.

This chapter addresses the following questions: What is Melayu about dangdut? Is it possible to define a Melayu "sense of music" in dangdut? When did it become important to articulate Melayu with dangdut? Why would Melayuness become a point of contestation in contemporary times? For whom does this historical narrative matter? In contemporary debates about the history of Indonesian culture, what does it mean to claim that dangdut *is* Melayu?

Ethnomusicologist Philip Yampolsky states that "theories that attempt to establish a musical connection between regional Melayu music and the national music genre known as Melayu or Dangdut are, I believe, incorrect" because they have no musical features in common; their connection is "incidental" (1987, 45). My aim is not to show the invented or capricious nature of these claims.[8] Rather, I aim to show that the category of Melayu gets used in all sorts of ways to support a variety of ideological positions. Therefore, I will begin by contextualizing statements about a Melayu "sense of music" in dangdut.

Central to this discussion is the labeling of music as Melayu, a term that refers to "a confusing variety of configurations of human beings, locations, languages, customs, states and objects" (Barnard and Maier 2004, ix). I will not attempt to define Melayu music because the notion of "Melayu" in Indonesia is a free-floating concept that is constantly being redefined in different contexts and for various ideological purposes (Wee 1985, 13).[9] Indeed, this flexibility in defining Melayu makes it possible for Rhoma Irama to claim that dangdut is at its very core Melayu. Rather, I emphasize the ways in which musical practices are given meaning when people connect them to specific places during particular historical moments. I will focus on how people invoke or perform elements of music perceived to be indigenous to or strongly associated in origins with the Melayu region of Southeast Asia. These elements of music contrast with those identified with music indigenous to or having origins in India, the Middle East, Europe, and the United States. I argue that "Melayu" must be understood conceptually in terms of historical and cultural change, involving a high level of interaction among people of diverse and mixed ethnicities, especially in urban centers.

Rather than enumerating a set of elements that define Melayu identity, or privileging a source of Melayu origins that provides a historical basis for the development of a musical genre, I examine the aesthetic practices of *orkes Melayu* in specific locations involving specific actors within specific historical circumstances. These examples illustrate the blending of musical elements that was very much the norm in Melayu aesthetics. I will discuss *orkes Melayu* in three urban centers of Indonesia: Medan, Jakarta, and Surabaya. During the

1950s and 1960s, these urban centers were the principal loci for the composition, performance, and circulation of *orkes Melayu* music in Indonesia.

Melayu Deli

As Rhoma Irama's quote indicates, the "sound" (as opposed to the "sense" or "sensibility") of dangdut is quite different from Melayu songs in Deli, Sumatra. It is important to untangle *lagu Melayu* (Melayu songs) from the variety of Melayu orchestras that have existed since the late nineteenth century. *Lagu Melayu* can be sung in many ensemble configurations. *Lagu Melayu* can have regional affiliations and performance characteristics; *lagu Melayu Deli* refers to Melayu songs originating from or specific to the Deli region in North Sumatra.[10]

The songs of Melayu Deli, sometimes called "original" or "authentic Melayu songs" (*lagu Melayu asli*), were sung by professional female singer/dancers (*ronggeng*) who traded off singing verses with their male song/dance partners at dance parties. These songs were made up of preexisting verses and formulae that could be spontaneously arranged and adjusted to individual situations. Texts were generally in the four-line *pantun* form: the first two lines form the *sampiran* (hook or hanger) and the last two form the *isi* (contents). They are structured into the rhyme scheme abab, indicated with bold and italics as in figure 2.1. Songs were patterned into three rhythmic forms: *senandung* (slow quadruple meter); *mak inang* (moderate quadruple meter); and *lagu dua*, also called *joget* (fast triple meter or a duple meter with triple subdivisions) (Yampolsky 1996, 17). Songs were accompanied by a violin, one or two large circular frame drums (*gendang*), and a gong (*tawak-tawak*) (Goldsworthy 1979, 334).

These "original" *ronggeng* songs were culturally mixed in terms of their instrumentation and tonal and scalar construction. The violin was brought by Europeans, perhaps Portuguese, in the sixteenth century. Scales and melodies were "Melayu creations in a non-harmonic idiom, based on scales introduced

Kuala Deli airnya pun **jernih,** Tempat mandi si anaklah dar*a.* Tanah Deli tanahku yang **asli,** Tanah tempat hai tumpah lah dar*ah.*	The Deli river mouth where the water is clear, A place for a beautiful girl to bathe. Deli my original home, The place where I was born.
Tanjung katung airnya pun **biru,** Tempat orang mencuci lah muk*a.* Sedang sekampung lagipun **merindu,** Pondok pulang jauh lah di mat*a.*	The katung cape where the water is blue, Where people can wash their faces. People in villages also feel lonely, Their homes are far away.

FIGURE 2.1 *Pantun* form, "Kuala Deli" (Mouth of the Deli River) [public domain].

from Europe or elsewhere," possibly China and the Middle East (Yampolsky 1996, 17). Perlman writes that "In the Melayu ronggeng tradition, nominally classified as part of the post-Portuguese stratum, European-type diatonicism co-exists with Chinese-sounding pentatonicism and augmented 2nd tetra-chords of the hijaz type [from the Middle East]" (Perlman, 2001).[11]

Melayu and Dangdut

Only by narrating the history of cultural hybridity, and by focusing on the inclu-sivist nature of Melayu, does the connection to dangdut begin to make sense. Dangdut extends a dialogue among Melayu, Indian, Arab, and European cul-tures that has existed since the late 19th century in the urban environments of Jakarta (Batavia) and Surabaya.[12] Dangdut's Melayu ancestors are the traveling orchestras that traveled from Malaya (Malaysia) to Java in the 1890s under the names *stambul, bangsawan,* and *opera* (Cohen 2006). These orchestras played a mixed repertoire of Melayu, Chinese, Indian, Middle Eastern, and European music (Tan 1993, 73). In these ensembles, which were highly variable in their instrumentation, "Melayu" was a flexible and constantly evolving framework in which the interaction among Melayu, Chinese, Indian, Middle Eastern, and European elements was normative. The strong links among Malaya, Singapore, Batavia, Surabaya, Deli, and Riau were especially important for traveling theatrical and musical troupes that sought commercial opportunities throughout the Melayu region in the late nineteenth and early twentieth centuries.

Hybrid forms paralleled the evolution of new societies in the cities. People of distinct ethnic, racialized, and cultural identities speaking different lan-guages faced new socioeconomic realities as they confronted people of new identities—occupational, class, and cultural—and formed new alliances. Within this multiethnic, multilingual, and multicultural context, hybrid forms gave people a common "language" that helped them forge a common culture.

The recording industry marketed its wares widely across the region. In the 1930s, Sumatra, Malaya, and the Straits Settlements (SS) were a single market, at least for some 78-rpm record labels. The Gramophone Company Limited (later E.M.I.), in particular, listed the Melayu discs published on its label His Master's Voice (HMV) in both English-language catalogs for Malaya/SS and Dutch-language catalogs for the Dutch East Indies (DEI). And one finds a lot of Malayan Odeon records in Sumatra (Yampolsky, pers. comm, 18 February 2007). As late as the 1950s, it was more likely that a singer from Medan, North Sumatra, would perform in Malaya, Riau, or Singapore than in Jakarta (Nur Ainun, pers. comm., 20 November 2006).

Radio was the most important medium for disseminating recordings of popular music during the 1930s. *Lagu Melayu* were recorded and broadcast on radio by three main ensemble types (*orkes*) of the 1930s: *orkes harmonium, orkes gambus*, and *orkes Melayu*. Musicians from these three ensemble types were instrumental in establishing the foundation for dangdut, whereas musicians from *pop* (Western popular), *langgam* (regional popular), *kroncong* (string band), or any of the regional Melayu ensembles tended not to become active in dangdut. I will discuss these three ensemble types in the following section.

Orkes harmonium

Composer and singer Husein Bawafie locates the origins of dandgut in 1930s *orkes harmonium* in Batavia (Jakarta) ("Dangdut, Sebuah 'Flashback'" 1983, 13). Named after the harmonium, a small reed organ from Europe via India, *orkes harmonium* (or O.H.) included harmonium, violin, trumpet, *gendang* (small two-headed drum), *rebana* (frame drum), and sometimes tambourine.

Radio logs indicate that *orkes harmonium* played a mixed repertoire of Melayu, Arabic, Indian, and European music.[13] For example, radio logs show that a group led by S. M. Alaydroes performed the Melayu standards "Ma 'Inang" and "Sri Mersing" (*Archipel Programma*, 23 June 1938) while Alaydroes's "Modern Harmonium Orchestra" played Arabic songs as well as tangos (*Archipel Programma*, 27 May 1938). An *orkes harmonium* group led by S. Perang Bustami performed European marches (*Archipel Programma*, 30 October 1938).

The mixture that would later characterize dangdut was common in these ensembles. Bawafie notes that *orkes harmonium* groups played songs with Hindustani rhythms (*lagu-lagu berirama Hindustan*) as well as songs that mixed Melayu and Hindustani music (*irama Melayu à la Hindustan*) ("Dangdut, Sebuah 'Flashback'" 1983, 13). Musicians in Indonesia used the harmonium to accompany Hindi-language songs. For example, the 1932 catalogue of the Beka Company lists four Hindustani discs (eight sides) sung by Ebrahim Masrie (Beka 15525; 15580; 15526; 15581). Recorded in Surabaya in 1928, these are Hindi-language songs accompanied by a single harmonium in free rhythm.[14]

Samrah may have been another name for *orkes harmonium*; the instrumentation was similar (Ruchiat et al. 2000, 42; Soepandi et al. 1992). The term *samrah* (*samroh, samr*) probably derives from the Arabic *samra*, which means "nightly entertainment" (Arps 1996, 396). In the Javanese culture area (Central and East Java) and Madura, *samroh* can refer to women's singing of Arabic texts accompanied by *rebana* as well as a male *gambus* ensemble that accompanies dance (ibid.). Berg describes *samrah* as an evening of music and dance that is integral to Arab-Indonesian wedding events of Manado, North Sulawesi (2007, 92–138). A folk etymology links the term *samrah* with *"sambil musyawarah"* ("while joining people together") (Hendrowinoto et al 1998, 65–66). According to Munif Bahasuan, *samrah* refers to the occasions in Jakarta (Batavia) when Arabic and Indian-inspired music was played at Betawi parties.[15] *Samrah* groups accompanied Melayu dances as well as Betawi dances.[16]

After the war, the name *orkes harmonium* began to fade, although not completely (Takonai 2006, 183). Musicians added instruments, including saxophone and trumpet, to embellish the main melodies. In some cases, the harmonium was replaced by the accordion, and musicians eliminated the gong. These groups began using the term *orkes Melayu* (for example, O.H. Sinar Medan became Orkes Melayu Sinar Medan, or simply O. M. Sinar Medan).

Orkes gambus

The influence of Middle Eastern music was profound in *orkes gambus*, orchestras featuring the *gambus* (long-necked plucked fretless lute) or *'ud* (pear-shaped lute) and accompanied by small double-headed drums (*marwas*, pl. *marawis*). Immigrants from the Hadramaut region (Yemen) presumably brought the *gambus* and *marwas* with them to Indonesia (Capwell 1995, 82–83). They played for wedding parties and other community celebrations among Muslim patrons. The instrumentation included *gambus*, harmonium, violin, flute, string bass (stand-up bass or "bass *betot*"; *betot* = "to snatch, pull off"), *rebana*, and tambourine.

Orkes gambus, labeled "gambus Malay" or "gambus Melayu" on 78 rpm discs and in radio logs of the period, played a mixed repertoire. For example, a radio log for Surabaya in East Java lists S. Albar's (Syech Albar's) *orkes gambus* performing Arabic songs ("El iftitah marsch," "Lativil roeh," "Ellama," "Waslel habib," "Sadjija altarf") in addition to Melayu tunes ("extra Melayu"); (*Surabaya Programma*, 11 August 1937). Syech Albar and his orchestra also recorded a Hindustani tune entitled "Janasib I & II" (Fate I & II) around 1939 (Canary HS 258). For a radio program in 1938, Orkes Gambus Alwathoni, led by Md. Noer All Djawi, performed a European march ("Marsch"), a Melayu song ("Sedih hatikoe"; My Lonely Heart), and an Egyptian song ("Hedjaz Masrie") (*Archipel Programma*, 19 May 1938). Performers also combined styles in individual pieces. "Diwaktu soeboeh" (Dawn), described as a "gambus Melayu" song, begins with a freely metered *gambus* introduction similar to a *taqasim* (improvised instrumental introduction) and leads into a song with a rumba rhythmic framework, a Melayu melodic phrase and verse structure, and a Middle Eastern orchestral arrangement (Columbia TP 6).[17]

Orkes gambus also played Cuban-derived dance music, especially rumbas. Syech Albar, one of the most famous gambus musicians of the 1930s, made numerous recordings in Surabaya.[18] His 1937 recording of "Zahrotoel Hoesoen," labeled "modern Arabic vocal," is an Arabic song in a crooner vocal style accompanied by a rumba rhythmic framework played on a rebana, tambourine, and a clave or wood block. The song is accompanied by two gambus (one plays single notes and the other plays chords) and violin (HMV NS 278). The other side of the disc is entitled "Yoenadji," a tango, also classified as "modern Arabic vocal" (HMV NS 278). Rozen Bahar, who also led a band that performed Minang songs from West Sumatra, played rumbas including "Rumba Carioca" and "Ali Baba Rumba" (Archipel Programma, 12 March 1938). And the "Arab gambus" song "Kalamil Foead," recorded by a gambus orchestra led by B. Ihsan (West Sumatra), has a diatonic melody superimposed over a rumba rhythmic framework (Tjap Angsa AM 36).

Orkes Melayu

The term orkes Melayu (or orkest Melayu) began to appear in Indonesia in radio logs in the late 1930s. The Batavia (Jakarta)-based Orkest Melajoe Sinar Medan (directed by Abdul Halim) played Melayu songs harmonized by European instruments. They maintained Melayu musical characteristics, including a pantun verse structure, standard kinds of melodic phrases, and added words and phrases (for example, aduhai sayang ["ah, my darling"] and tuan ["sir"]) (Archipel Programma, 4 November 1938). An example of Melayu songs accompanied by the Special Singapore Malay Orchestra includes "Sayang Manis" (Sweetheart) and "Sinar Malacca" (Shining Malacca), accompanied by violin, flute, bass, piano, and gendang (Odeon A206109). The strident vocal style is similar to ronggeng performers, and an accompanying male chorus adds calls and yells to encourage the singer. In a 1940 recording of a Melayu Deli song called "Gunong Deli" (Deli Mountain) under the rubric of ronggeng Medan (ronggeng songs of Medan) (HMV P22811), the male and female vocalists trade pantun verses over a Melayu dance rhythm, and the song is harmonized by piano and accompanied by violin, bass, and gendang.

After independence in 1945, musicians brought a new creative sensibility to orkes Melayu, especially in the urban areas of Medan, Jakarta, and Surabaya. In addition to playing hybrid music, ensembles in Jakarta and Surabaya appropriated and transformed Indian film melodies, paving the way for dangdut. The 1950s represent a profoundly multicultural interplay of Melayu, Arabic, Indian, Latin American, and European sounds circulating in popular music. In the following section, I will describe and historicize the context of production in which musical elements were brought together and fused into *orkes Melayu* music of the 1950s.

It is important to distinguish between *orkes Melayu* in Medan, Jakarta, and Surabaya in the 1950s. This is particularly significant in relation to the Melayu Deli repertoire of songs, which was stronger in Medan because of its regional ties and geographical proximity to Deli. However, the Melayu repertoire of *orkes Melayu* in Medan (*orkes Melayu Deli*) was mixed. Latin rhythms permeated the music. For example, it was easy to fuse *senandung* and cha-cha rhythms (Roisam, pers. comm., 20 November 2006).[19] And it was common for *orkes Melayu* bands to have jazz musicians in them. Further, *orkes Melayu Deli* after 1950 was influenced by the new music coming from Jakarta via radio and film. Musicians in Medan blended the Jakarta-based music with their own *orkes Melayu Deli*. And Jakarta-based musicians played music of North Sumatra. So these were not two entirely separate entities. Jakarta-based singer Munif Bahasuan states:

> When I entered Sinar Medan in 1954–55 or so, we called it orkes Melayu moderen [modern orkes Melayu] because we used modern instruments: guitar, piano, winds (trumpet, saxophone, clarinet). But the songs were original Melayu [Melayu asli]. And composers created new songs in that style. Some of those composers were from Jakarta or Medan. The music was popular in Padang, and throughout Java and Sumatra, Riau, and even further to Kalimantan. (Munif Bahasuan, pers. comm., 16 July 2005)

One major distinction, however, is that the Jakarta-based singers in *orkes Melayu* began singing Indian film songs and using Indian vocal ornaments during the early 1950s, whereas *orkes Melayu* singers in Medan did not (Nur Ainun, pers. comm., 20 November 2006). Further, the Surabaya bands had a more Middle Eastern sound. The following section explores the Melayu "sense of music" in *orkes Melayu* of Medan and Jakarta, respectively, during the 1950s.

Medan: Lily Suheiry, Rubiah, and Ema Gangga

The composers and musicians in Medan were anything but pure in their approach to Melayu music. Lily Suheiry (1915?–1979), the leader of the Medan branch station of the Indonesian National Radio network (Radio Republik Indonesia, RRI), was born in Bogor, West Java, and raised in North Sumatra. To call him simply a Melayu Deli composer is incorrect. He received a Western music education from a German teacher at the Dutch colonial high school (Meer Uitgebreid Lager Onderwijs, or MULO; "Malam Amal" 1960, 3). He traveled with a *sandiwara* theatrical troupe called Bolero (named after the Latin dance form) and worked in Singapore before the war, but he insisted on settling in Medan (in 1941) rather than Malaya/Singapore (which were politically unified under Great Britain) to advance his career. At RRI Medan, Lily Suheiry had a large mixed orchestra at his disposal including trumpet, flute, clarinet, violin, piano, bass, *rebana,* drum set, and *kemongan* (gong). Lily Suheiry arranged versions of Minang songs to accompany dance. He composed orchestral suites that used European compositional techniques. He was active in film scoring and recording. Some of his songs were based on revolutionary themes, including "Pemuda Indonesia" (Indonesian Youth), "Untuk Pahlawan" (For Heroes), and "Marhaeni" (Female Proletarian). Under his direction, the RRI orchestra based in Medan played harmonized orchestral accompaniments of Melayu Deli songs, but he also composed new Melayu tunes for orchestra including "Selayang Pandang" (A Passing Glance), "Araskabu" (the name of a railway station in Medan), and "Teratai" (Lotus). In 1956, Lily Suheiry composed music for the musical film *Melati Sendja* (Jasmine in the Twilight, dir. Bachtiar Siagian). His songs were published in sheet music.

One of the main interpreters of Lily Suheiry's tunes was the female singer Rubiah (c. 1923–1992). Her Suheiry hits included "Bunga Tanjung" (Fragrant Flower), "Bayangan" (Reflection), and "Selendang Pelangi" (Multicolored Scarf). Rubiah was born in Selesai (East Sumatra). Her mother was from Banten (West Java), and her father was from the Tapanuli region (North Sumatra). During the Japanese colonial era (1942–1945), she traveled throughout the region with a *sandiwara* troupe. After the war, she settled in Malaysia, where P. Ramlee, the legendary Malaysian film star of the 1950s, employed Rubiah as a playback singer for Malaysian film star Kasmah Booty in films including *Racun Dunia* (Poison of the World, dir. B.S. Rajhans) (1950), *Djuwita* (Beautiful Girl, dir. S. Ramanathan) (1951), and *Sejoli* (A Couple, dir. B.S. Rajhans) (1951). She was also employed as a playback singer for other movies by the Shaw Brothers, a Chinese film production team based in Singapore. Rubiah moved back to Indonesia in the mid-1950s to continue her recording career. She made recordings with some of the top *orkes Melayu* bands in Jakarta (including O. M. Irama Agung, directed by Said Effendi) and worked as a playback singer for films. Through her recordings and films, she became popular in Singapore, Malaysia, and Indonesia.

Rubiah is venerated by contemporary musicians for her "original Melayu" (*Melayu asli*) sound. But what is striking about her playback singing and recordings is her versatility as a vocalist. As a playback singer for Kasmah Booty, Rubiah's vocal style is characterized by a sweet lilting vocal timbre and largely unornamented melodic phrases (except for vibrato at the ends of each phrase). Her sound complemented the smooth crooner vocal quality of P. Ramlee. On recordings, however, she could sound "Melayu asli" by singing with a more strident timbre, adding specific ornaments to tones in the middle of phrases, and improvising (for example, by interjecting standard phrases).[20] Her vocal style was not inflected with Indian elements.

Another important figure in the history of *orkes Melayu* in Medan is Ema Gangga (b. 1921?–199?). Ema Gangga was born in Jakarta (Batavia). Her mother sang in a *kroncong* band. As a girl, Ema traveled to Singapore, and worked in the traveling *sandiwara* troupe Dardanela (Batubara 1955, 13). After Japan attacked Singapore, she fled to Penang (Malaysia), East Sumatra, and finally Medan. In Medan, she sang with a *sandiwara* troupe set up by the Japanese to propagandize for the Greater East Asia Co-Prosperity Sphere (ibid.). After the war, she became the violin player for Lily Suheiry's orchestra at the regional branch of the national radio station (RRI Medan). In 1951–1952, Ema Gangga returned to Jakarta, where she joined O. M. Sinar Medan, directed by Umar Fauzi Aseran. She also launched a successful acting career. Her film credits include *Sekuntum Bunga di Tepi Danau* (A Flower at the Edge of the Lake; 1952, dir. Inoe Perbatasari), *Kuda Lumping* (Horse Trance Dance; 1953, prod. Samudra Film), *Debu Revolusi* (Dust of the Revolution; 1954, dir. Syamsuddin Syafei), *Paris Barantai* (1962, prod. Ifdil Film), and *The Big Village* (original English title; 1969, dir. Usmar Ismail). She continued to sing and play violin in bands during the 1960s.

Composer and bandleader Lily Suheiry, as well as female singers Rubiah and Ema Gangga, are celebrated in contemporary discourse for their *Melayu asli* identity. But their sound was modern and culturally hybrid. Suheiry composed for Western orchestra, with strong elements from Latin music and jazz. Rubiah and Ema Gangga performed in a variety of media and in a wide variety of vocal styles, depending on the medium and context of performance. All three worked in modern media of radio, recordings, and film, and their music circulated widely to people in Singapore, Malaysia and Indonesia. Their sound was designed to appeal to a wide market across the Melayu region. These examples show that the Melayu sense of music associated with Medan composers and singers was flexible, hybrid, modern, and highly mass-mediated.

Jakarta

Jakarta was the center for modern *orkes Melayu* recording in the 1950s. Recording was dominated by four Jakarta-based groups (and their leaders): Orkes Melayu Sinar Medan (Umar Fauzi Azran); Orkes Melayu Kenangan (Husein Aidit); Orkes Melayu Bukit Siguntang (A. Chalik); and Orkes Melayu Irama Agung (Said Effendi). Orkes Melayu Kenangan is shown in figure 2.2.

FIGURE 2.2 Orkes Melayu Kenangan, directed by Husein Aidit (far left), c. 1955. Female singers are (standing): Mardiana and Juhana Sattar; and (seated) R. O. Unarsih and Nurseha [courtesy of Zakaria].

Orkes Melayu assumed a symbolic role as national music in newly independent Indonesia.[21] Groups developed their own distinctive styles that set them apart from Malaysia, which had exerted a powerful influence on Indonesia through the music of film star, composer, and singer P. Ramlee. After independence, the newspaper *Aneka* published a report about *orkes Melayu* that asked: "What is the future of Indonesian music?" (Batubara 1954, 16). *Orkes Melayu* was now a viable national category alongside other forms of popular music including *langgam, kroncong,* and *seriosa* (semi-classical song accompanied by Western instruments). Batubara's essay made the following points: (1) *kroncong* was losing popularity to other forms of music, including *langgam,* Western music, and *orkes Melayu;* (2) *langgam* and *seriosa* were too similar to Western music; (3) *orkes Melayu* could accompany a simple form of dance (*joget*) that everyone could participate in; and (4) as a symbolic representation of the emerging nation, *orkes Melayu* seemed like a good choice: it was rooted in Melayu culture and language, yet it was flexible enough to represent a modern and distinctly Indonesian voice.

The modern *orkes Melayu* bands in Jakarta played dance music with a wide range of accompanying rhythms. Zakaria lists 13 rhythmic structures used in *orkes Melayu* between 1950 and 1960 (pers. comm., 12 July 2005). He divides these into four categories: *barat* (Western, which includes Cuban-derived rhythms); India (Indian); *padang pasir* (Middle Eastern); and Melayu (Indonesian/Malay), as shown in figure 2.3.

Many of these dance rhythmic forms were played by Jakarta's leading orchestra, O. M. Bukit Siguntang.[22] The instrumentation included violin, piano, acoustic guitar, string bass, woodwinds (flute, clarinet), brass (saxophone, trumpet), and percussion (*gendang kapsul* [a small double-headed drum shaped like a "capsule"] and maracas). The arrangements emphasized instrumental parts that embellished the vocal melody, often with a lead electric guitar, another solo instrument (clarinet, trumpet, violin), or small groups of melodic instruments in the ensemble (see figure 2.4). Singers included Suhaimi, Nur 'Ain, and Hasnah Tahar. Most of the musicians were trained in Western music and played, at one time or another, in the RRI Jakarta orchestra, led by Syaiful Bahri.

In live concerts, amplification was limited: one speaker projected the sound of the singer, who held the only microphone in the group. The primarily female singers stood while the male musicians sat. They played dance music, but photos from the period do not show people dancing. They also performed concerts for modern audiences in big cities.

Their songs included Melayu tunes as well as original pop-oriented compositions.[23] They played music for fast dances (rumba and *joget*), and slow dances (waltz and tango). They also recorded soundtracks for films, including *Sedetik Lagi* (One More Second, dir. Djoko Lelono) (1957). Their repertoire featured many dialogue songs, similar to Melayu *pantun*, but not necessarily in the *pantun* form. Jakarta composers wrote songs inspired by Indian film music, including "Kudaku Lari" (My Horse has Run Away, c. 1953), perhaps the first

Barat	India	Padang pasir	Melayu
Rumba	Kuracha	Masri	Ronggeng
Tango	Chalte		Joget
Calypso			Langgam Melayu
Cha-cha			Zapin
Samba			
Beguine			
Waltz			

FIGURE 2.3 Rhythmic Structures in *orkes Melayu*, 1950–1960.

FIGURE 2.4 *Orkes Melayu* at a party in Jakarta, c. 1955 showing *gendang kapsul* (left), accordion, trumpet, and violin [courtesy of Zakaria].

Indonesian recording adapted from an Indian film song.[24] And they used a drum in which the drumhead could be pressed to produce a "du-ut" sound.

Films from Malaysia, which incorporated Indian elements, were enormously popular in Indonesia. A 1952 report in the Indonesian newspaper *Sunday Courier* notes that the vocal quality used in modern Malaysian films and recordings of the 1950s was influenced by Indian film as early as 1952:

> The modern Melayu songs contain themes from Indian songs and these themes serve to enhance Melayu songs. In the Melayu songs of today we hear small ornaments that sound like the small steps of a happy child. This characteristic derives from the influence of Indian songs. (Sjamsulridwan 1952, 11)[25]

One of the star singers in O. M. Bukit Siguntang was Hasnah Tahar (b. 1933 in Singapore), whose biography illustrates her involvement across the Melayu region. Her mother was from Padang (West Sumatra) and her father was from Bogor (West Java) (Pelpie 1954, 17). Her family returned to Padang in 1948. She began her career singing songs of the Malay peninsular area (*lagu semenanjung*). Hasnah joined the acclaimed Padang-based *sandiwara* troupe Ratu

Asia, directed by Sjamsudin Sjafei. In 1950, she traveled to Jakarta with Ratu Asia and made her first recording with Irama Records in the early 1950s. She acted in films *Sekuntum Bunga* (PFN, 1951), *Rela* (PT Sangga Buana Film, 1953), and *Daerah Hilang* (Refic Film, 1956), among others.

Hasnah Tahar sang Melayu Deli tunes arranged for orchestra. [⊙] "Kuala Deli" (The Mouth of the Deli River) is based on a well-known song from Deli, as noted in the previous section. The rhythm follows a *senandung* pattern (slow quadruple meter). But in contrast to the strophic *pantun* verse structure presented earlier, this version is structured into two sections, labeled A (two phrases, four measures per phrase) and B (three phrases, four measures per phrase), as shown in figure 2.5. The song is framed by an introduction (intro) and an orchestral cadence (outro). The form of the song is: [intro—A-A-B-B-A´-B´—outro]. Each section is separated by an instrumental fill.

Musically, the sectionalization of these phrases is noteworthy because it shows the movement away from the standard accompaniment of *pantun* toward the use of two distinct song sections within a larger arrangement. Lyrically, the story connects time and place in three temporal registers: (1) an "original" homeland or birthplace (past); (2) a space of loneliness and reflection on the past (present); and (3) a place to die (future). The past and future are marked by flowing water, a sign of purity, life, and death. The present comes into focus only at the end of the song. Far away from the homeland and nature lays a space, perhaps a city, characterized by loneliness, dislocation, and yearning. These structuring devices point to an engagement with narrative structures rather than *pantun* poetic verses.

A: Kuala Deli airnya pun jernih, Tempat mandi si anaklah dara.	A: The Deli river mouth where the water is clear, A place for a beautiful girl to bathe.
[repeat verse A]	[repeat verse A]
B: Tanah Deli tanahku yang asli, Tanah Deli tanahku yang asli, Tanah tempat hai tumpah lah darah.	B: Deli my original home, Deli my original home, The place where I was born and will die.
[repeat verse B]	[repeat verse B]
A': Tanjung katung airnya pun biru, Tempat orang mencuci lah muka.	A': The katung cape where the water is blue, Where people can wash their faces.
B': Sedang sekampung lagipun merindu, Sedang sekampung lagipun merindu, Pondok pulang jauh lah di mata.	B': People in villages also feel lonely, People in villages also feel lonely, Their homes are far away.

FIGURE 2.5 "Kuala Deli" sung by Hasnah Tahar, c. 1952 (Irama M 348–19), accompanied by Orkes Melayu Bukit Siguntang, directed by A. Chalik. [public domain].

Another Hasnah Tahar song, "Disuatu Masa" (At Another Time), has text phrases reminiscent of *pantun*, but the entire text is structured into a narrative form; words at the beginning of phrases indicate time ("when"; "then"; "later") (see figure 2.6).[26] In this story, a woman tells her unfaithful lover that he will be the victim of a false and unsatisfying romantic relationship sometime in the future. The first verse (A) uses allusion and metaphor characteristic of *pantun* poetic forms. The singer compares a drop of "water on the taro leaf" to the evanescense of love, which can slip away in time without leaving a trace. Extending the *pantun* form further, verse A forms the "hook" or "hanger" (*sampiran*) while the remaining verses (A´-B-A´´) form the "contents" (*isi*). However, the song does not follow a *pantun* rhyme scheme or syllabic structure. Unlike *pantun* forms, in which verses are combined in performance spontaneously from a variety of sources, these verses are connected to each other through a fixed narrative structure.

The theme is love, as it is in most of Hasnah Tahar's songs, and she sings from the first-person point of view. The message of the song is presented in direct language, and it deals with a specific situation ("at another time"). As one report noted, her voice is full of passion: "For those of you whose heart has been broken, because your lover didn't show up, how can you not be moved when you hear the lyrics to 'My lover didn't come' ('Kasih tak Sampai') sung by Hasnah Tahar?" (Batubara 1954, 16). Tahar's emotional vocal quality was soft, sweet, and smooth, with little or no vibrato. Vocal ornaments are Melayu, in which the sustained tones at the middle and ends of phrases are

A: Ibarat air di daun keladi, Biarpun tergenang tetapi tak meninggalkan bekas, 'Pabila tersentuh dahannya bergoyang, Air pun tercurah tertumpah habis tak tinggal lagi.	A: Like water on the taro leaf, Although it gathers, won't leave a trace, When touched the branch moves, Even the water falls and none is left.
A': Begitu juga hatimu padaku, Cinta hanya separoh hati kau lepas kembali, 'Pabila bercerai telah jauh di mata, Engkau pun lupa tiada ingat sama sekali.	A': And so your heart is toward me, Your love is only partial and then lets go again, When we're separated and out of sight, You tend to forget about me.
B: Bila kau lihat pemudi yang lebih gaya, Cintamu pun segera berpindah kepadanya.	B: If you see someone more beautiful, Your affection immediately goes to her.
A'': Tapi biarlah kau cari yang lain, Kan kau buat sebagai korban cinta palsu hampa, Nanti disuatu masa kau juga 'kan merasa, Bagaimana sakitnya hati kecewa karena cinta.	A'': But it's ok if you find someone else, Then you will be a victim of false and empty love, Later at another time you also will feel, A broken heart and disappointment because of love.
[interlude]	[interlude]
[repeat verse A'']	[repeat verse A'']

FIGURE 2.6 "Disuatu Masa" (At Another Time) sung by Hasnah Tahar, c. 1955, (Irama M 310–8), accompanied by Orkes Melayu Bukit Siguntang, directed by A. Chalik. [public domain].

FIGURE 2.7 Transcription of vocal melody in first verse of "Disuatu Masa" (At Another Time) sung by Hasnah Tahar, c. 1955 (Irama M 310–8), accompanied by Orkes Melayu Bukit Siguntang, directed by A. Chalik.

embellished by appoggiaturas (circled) and turns (boxed), respectively, as shown in figure 2.7.

The orchestration of "Disuatu Masa" is typical of the modern *orkes Melayu* sound. [🔊] Instrumentation includes violin, clarinet, trumpet, saxophone, piano, guitar, bass, tambsourine, and a *gendang kapsul*. The Latin-based rhythmic framework, with its two eighth notes on beat four of each measure, is similar to cha-cha.

The form of the song is as follows: [intro—A-A′-B-A′′-interlude/B-A′—outro]. The AABA structure does not follow a standard 32-bar song form. Rather, each verse (A) has 8 measures, and the intervening B section comprises 4 measures. A 2-beat pickup serves as an introductory motive (*pengantar*) to lead into each verse. Rather than instrumental fills between verses, as is common in *pantun* performance practice, an interlude based on the B section is presented toward the end of the song. In this way, the entire narrative is presented continuously without short instrumental interruptions; the last A section (A′′) repeats the previous verse. A continuous heterophonic reinforcement of the vocal melody played on an electric guitar propels the song forward. These qualities give the song a more fluid urgent quality, compared to the repetitive *pantun* verse structure (consisting of verse-fill, etc.).

"Disuatu Masa" represents a creative departure in music played in Jakarta during the 1950s. Departing from *pantun* lyrics and performance practice, these songs began to tell stories in direct language. Western instrumental accompaniment, Latin dance rhythms, dynamic arrangements, and star singers characterized the new style. But it was the blending of these elements with Middle Eastern and Indian music that captivated audiences in the 1950s.

Many *orkes Melayu* leaders of Arab descent were active in the 1950s and 1960s in radio and recording in Jakarta: Said Effendi (Irama Agung); Umar Fauzi Aseran (Sinar Medan); Umar Alatas (Chandraleka); Husein Bawafie (Chandralela); and Husein Aidit (Kenangan). These individuals and groups formed a community of musicians who grew up together, shared similar musical training, played each other's music, and moved from one group to another.[27]

Singers who began their careers in *orkes Melayu* bands in the 1950s and 1960s, and then made the transition to dangdut in the 1970s, cited their own training in Qur'anic recitation (*tilawah*) as a major factor in becoming skilled dangdut singers. Ellya Khadam, Munif Bahasuan, A. Rafiq, Mansyur S., Elvy Sukaesih, and Rita Sugiarto all emphasized this point in our interviews. It was not specific vocal ornaments that they borrowed from Qur'anic recitation but vocal techniques of phrasing, diction, breathing, and pronunciation, as well as the ability to memorize and copy, or "play back," what they had heard in films and on recordings.

The use of vocal ornaments based on Qur'anic recitation set *orkes Melayu* apart from other popular music genres of the era. *Orkes Melayu* musicians generally were not active in *langgam* or *kroncong*, the two other dominant popular music genres of this period. Further, singers in *orkes Melayu* crossed over into the religious arena. For example, Ellya Khadam made recordings of Arabic language songs (*lagu padang pasir*) accompanied by *gambus*, flute, *rebana*, and tambourine.

Said Effendi (1925?–1983) was the star of Melayu music in Jakarta in the 1950s. Of Arab descent, from Bondowoso, East Java, he learned to sing as a student in a religious school (*madrasah*). He sang in Orkes Gambus Al Wardah.[28] Despite his parent's warnings, he was drawn to popular music. From 1943–1948, he traveled with *sandiwara* troupes including Warnasari Batu Tjita, Dewi Mada, and Fifi Young's Toneelkunst (Amir 1958, 2). In 1948, he began singing with Orkes Studio Jakarta, the orchestra based at RRI in Jakarta.

In the early 1960s, Effendi's songs "Sero[d]ja" (Lotus Flower) and "Semalam di Malaya" (A Night in Malaysia) became popular in Malaysia. Up to this point, Indonesian singers had imitated Malaysian singers, particularly P. Ramlee. For example, the singer M. Saugy was known as the "P. Ramlee of Indonesia." After Said Effendi became famous, however, Malaysian singers began imitating him. For example, in 1960, a contest was held in Malaysia to find the singer whose voice most closely resembled Said Effendi's (Achmad Zais won the contest).[29] Zakaria, a musician who was active during that era, has noted that this moment represents a shift in attitude among Indonesians about the relationship between Indonesia and Malaysia. Rather than feeling that their popular culture owed its inspiration to Malaysia (mainly through the music and films of P. Ramlee), Indonesians now felt that Malaysia was beginning to look to Indonesia for inspiration (Zakaria, pers. comm., 13 July 2005).

Said Effendi's band O. M. Irama Agung played Indian film music, too; for example, the introduction to the song "Rajuan Bina" (Irama M 386–32) is based on the reed instrument leitmotif that appears at the end of the classic Indian film *Nagin* (1955). The following example, "Seroja," shows the blending of Middle Eastern, Indian, and Western music in the popular music of the 1950s in Jakarta.

"Sero[d]ja" is from a film of the same name. *Seroja* was one of the first Indonesian films in which actors actually sang, a fact that made it comparable to films coming out of Hollywood: "Many films have been made with light stories and featuring actors (not singers) and voices supplied by playback singers as in India and Malaysia. Rarely are there films with light themes and songs such as those sung by popular singers in Hollywood such as Bing Crosby, Doris Day, and now Pat Boone, Elvis Presley, and Tommy Sands." ("Serodja," 1959, 19).[30]

Effendi's singing style touched listeners deeply, as noted in the following report:

> Those feeling sad will perhaps feel even sadder, whereas those in love will feel even more deeply in love. When the song is over, listeners will [either] take a deep breath, breathe a sigh of relief, or feel unsatisfied. (Amir 1958, 2)

Anom Pictures produced the film around the song. The plot is as follows: Effendi works at the home of the fussy Sulastri. He wants to be an entertainer and make it in the big city. While Sulastri is sympathetic at first, he eventually becomes tired of Effendi and throws him out of the house. Effendi is determined to become a singer, and after many obstacles, he succeeds (Kristanto 2005, 51). Some of Rhoma Irama's dangdut films of the 1970s would follow this general outline.

The image and subtle double meaning of picking flowers in the song "Seroja" is typical of Melayu *pantun*. But this song introduces characters and narrative tension ("Why is she gloomy?"), as shown in figure 2.8. The singer addresses his lover in this story directly ("you") and offers advice. He pleads with her and attempts to distract her by inviting her to pick flowers. Love, like stringing together flowers, must be done carefully and gently.

A: Mari menyusun seroja bunga seroja ah, Hiasan sanggul remaja putri remaja, Rupa yang elok dimanja jangan dimanja ah, Pujalah ia oh saja sekedar saja.	A: Let's arrange the lotus flowers, To beautify the hair of a young woman, Beautiful face, don't get carried away, Treat it as usual and nothing more.
[instrumental fill]	[instrumental fill]
B: Mengapa kau bermenung oh adik berhati bingung? Mengapa kau bermenung oh adik berhati bingung? Janganlah engkau percaya dengan asmara, Janganlah engkau percaya dengan asmara.	B: Why are you so sad and confused? Why are you so sad and confused? Don't trust your heart, Don't trust your heart.
C: Sekarang bukan bermenung zaman bermenung, Sekarang bukan bermenung zaman bermenung, Marilah bersama oh adik memetik bunga, Marilah bersama oh adik memetik bunga.	C: It's not the time to worry, It's not the time to worry, Let's go and pick some flowers, my love, Let's go and pick some flowers, my love.
[repeat verse A]	[repeat verse A]

FIGURE 2.8 "Seroja" (Lotus Flower) sung by S. Effendi, c. 1958 (Irama M 383–29), accompanied by Orkes Melayu Irama Agung, directed by S. Effendi. [courtesy of Ridho Bawafie].

The song's structure [intro—A-B-C-A—outro] is similar to Indian film songs, in which verse B is sung at a higher pitch level than verse A. Here, verse C begins an octave higher than verse A. This technique introduces a dramatic presentation that builds intensity as the song progresses. [◉]

"Seroja" has a strong Middle Eastern flavor. The male chorus at the beginning and the ending of the tune is a key feature of *gambus* songs. Effendi, trained in chanting the Qur'an as a child, ornaments the ends of words in an Arabic vocal style: the strident tonal quality of Said Effendi's voice in verse C (on the Arabic-derived word *zaman*), and the falling melody at the end of line 2 in verse C are typical features of *orkes gambus*. The lush string texture of the orchestral accompaniment and the heterophonic treatment of melody are key features of Egyptian popular music. The scale used in verse A and verse B is natural minor. In the song intro, the melody is embellished by a raised fourth degree and a raised seventh degree; the raised fourth degree appears again in verse C. These tones create hijaz tetrachords (g-a♭-b-c and c-d♭-e-f), emblematic of Arabic music. The rhythmic pattern, based on a triple meter similar to Melayu *joget*, is played on a *gendang kapsul*.

The musical qualities of "Seroja" presage the development of dangdut: love songs with gut-wrenching yet hopeful texts that blend vocal styles and musical elements of Melayu, Middle Eastern, Indian, and Western music. These "proto-dangdut" forms crystallized in the 1960s, as described in chapter 3.

The Stakes of Authenticity

What is the "Melayu sense of music" in these precursors to dangdut? On one hand, these forms brought together Melayu, Middle Eastern, Indian, and Western elements into a flexible and constantly evolving framework labeled "Melayu." In Medan, Lily Suheiry, Rubiah, and Ema Gangga played modern music for diverse audiences throughout the Melayu region. In Jakarta, musicians drew heavily on Middle Eastern and Indian music. Placed within this musical lineage, dangdut *is* Melayu.

But *orkes Melayu* did not spring from one original source in Deli, as proposed by Rhoma Irama. It was pieced together in different music "scenes" from a variety of sources and through a variety of media. Popular music genres in the urban environments of Medan and Jakarta (and Surabaya, described in the following chapter) were products of diverse and mixed ethnic groups gathering in and moving through the commercial "urban supercultures" of the Netherlands Indies (Reid 2001, 305).

Neither did *orkes Melayu* develop in a unilinear direction. Radio and recordings linked Medan and Jakarta with each other, as well as with the Middle East, India, Europe and the United States. The "sense" of the music owed as much to Malay-language texts as it did to Western-style orchestral arrangements, Middle Eastern vocal techniques, Indian melodies, and Latin dance rhythms.

To whom does this writing of history matter, and what ideological purposes does it serve? These questions took on great significance in the 1950s, as Indonesia and Malaysia became politically independent. In the early 1960s, especially during the political confrontation (*Konfrontasi*) with Malaysia, the category of Melayu was operative, but Indonesia had its own Melayu music, and North Sumatra was at the heart of it. These tensions between Indonesia and Malaysia in the political sphere help to explain why North Sumatra achieved such an important place in Indonesian music discourse after independence.

The core features of an ethnic group were "reinforced through reference to a specific past that [was] identified and interpreted, or reinterpreted, for current ethnic needs" (Andaya 2001, 316). Rhoma Irama has argued that, at its very core, dangdut is Melayu. His claims are based on a definition of Melayu in which the most important element is its link to the royal Islamic lineage of Deli in North Sumatra. Rhoma Irama emphasized the Melayu core of his music as a way of placing it into this lineage, which privileges Islam as the defining element of its identity.[31] However, *orkes Melayu* musicians looked in many directions for inspiration.

In this chapter, I have emphasized the hybrid and inclusive nature of *orkes Melayu*, which drew from diverse sources throughout the Melayu region, the Middle East, India, and the U.S. during the 1950s. I will continue to explore this thread in the next chapter on the major artistic developments and recording stars of *orkes Melayu* in the 1960s. The pronounced transnational nature of *orkes Melayu* musical development during this period allows us to further problematize dangdut as coming from an original source in North Sumatra. These developments took place within the commercialized urban music scenes of Jakarta and Surabaya, as described in the next chapter.

NOTES

1. Lyrics from the song "Viva Dangdut" are: "Dangdut suara gendang, Ditabuh-ditabuh berulang-ulang, Dangdut suara gendang, Sekarang ramai menjadi sebutan. Ini musik Melayu, Berasal dari Deli, Lalu kena pengaruh, Dari Barat dan Hindi."

2. The term "Melayu" was first used to refer to a settlement in southeast Sumatra that sent a mission to China in 644 (Andaya 2001, 319). The term "Melayu" rather than "Malay" foregrounds the earliest documentation of the term, and elides any affiliation with present-day nation-state borders (ibid.). For a good introduction to the discourse about Melayu culture, language, and identity, the reader is referred to Andaya 2001; Barnard 2004; Collins 2001; Milner 2008; Reid 2001; and Shamsul 2001.

3. This interview was conducted in the Indonesian language, but Rhoma Irama used the English phrase "sense of music."

4. In the 16th century, Deli was a very small polity. The nearest sultanates on the coast of Sumatra were or had been in Aru and Pasai; the major sultanate in Sumatra was in Aceh. During the 17th to the 19th centuries, Deli was an independent state, but was insignificant (Reid 2005, 13). Beginning in the 1860s, Deli was absorbed by the modern city of Medan, one of the major economic centers in the Indies.

5. Similar comments attributed to Elvy Sukaesih appear in the tabloid *Pos Film* in 1994 ("Elvy Sukaesih Tolak Anggapan Dangdut Adalah Melayu"); and Melzian 1994, 4.

6. Scholarship on the circulation and reception of Indian film outside India includes Abadzi n.d. (Greece); Armbrust 2008 (Egypt); Behrend 1998 (Kenya); David 2008 (Indonesia); Dhondy 1985 (England); Gopal and Moorti 2008; Hansen 2005 (South Africa); Larkin 2003 and 1997 (Nigeria); Parciack 2008 (Israel); and Ray 2000 (Fiji).

7. After several successful albums together, Rhoma Irama and Elvy Sukaesih decided to pursue solo careers in 1976. They have been competitive from time to time. For example, they led competing musicians' unions in the 1990s (Elvy Sukaesih/IKARDI and Rhoma Irama/PAMMI).

8. For example, Shamsul (2001) shows that essentialized concepts of Malayness were constructed within a colonial historiography, institutionalized in government and

education, and accepted by non-Malays as well as Malays themselves. Malay identity was based on three pillars of Malayness: language, ruler, and religion (*bahasa, raja, dan agama*).

9. Melayu (or Malay) people inhabit different social, spatial, and temporal realms, which contribute to "varying degrees of Malayness" in the Melayu region (Wee 1985, 13). Notions of these different degrees of identity tend to be diferent in Malaysia, Singapore, and Indonesia. For example, Wee notes that definitions of Melayu identity in Malaysia and Singapore tend to be more fixed than in Indonesia (ibid.).

10. *Lagu Melayu* developed throughout the Melayu region; I am limiting my discussion to lagu Melayu in Indonesia.

11. In Malaysia, the songs incorporated elements from China, the Middle East, and India, among others (Matusky and Tan 1997, 325).

12. Batavia is the former Dutch name for the city/area now called Jakarta.

13. These performances were broadcast as part of the *Archipel Programma*, the programming sent out over the transmitters of the government-run radio network NIROM (*Nederlandsch-Indische Radio Omroep Maatschappij*) to its "eastern" (*ketimuran*) audience. (Different programming was sent out to the European audience in the colony.) NIROM published a program guide, *Soeara Nirom*, that listed the *Archipel Programma* and also the specific local programming for certain major cities (e.g., Surabaya). I am grateful to Philip Yampolsky for sharing his collection of 78rpm recordings, as well as the *Archipel Programma* radio logs. For the history of the recording industry during this era, see Yampolsky's forthcoming work.

14. I have only seen one of these discs (two sides) and the titles: "Thoo Gair Nahee Mai Gair Nahee" and "Sakee Thoo Deevai Jamai" (Beka B15580).

15. Betawi is the Indonesian name for the Dutch "Batavia," the former name for Jakarta.

16. Melayu dances included "Burung Putih" (White Bird) and "Pulau Angsa Dua" (Angsa Dua Island); Betawi dances included "Lenggang-lenggang" (Swaying-Walking) "Kangkung Kicir-kicir," and "Jali-jali" (Hendrowinoto et al. 1998:65–66). *Orkes harmonium* also played a mixed repertoire for theatrical productions of *sandiwara* (by the troupes Dardanela and Dahlia, for example).

17. Song titles, names of performers, and names of performing groups and their directors are spelled as they appear in published sources (record labels and jackets, radio program guides, and radio listings in newspapers). Inconsistencies and spelling variants are common (Yampolsky 1987, 28–31). Additional discographical information is listed under song title in the References.

18. Syech Albar's connection to dangdut lives on through his family. His son is Ahmad Albar, a pop star of the 1970s who made forays into dangdut. His wife, after the death of Albar, married Djamuluddin Malik, who is the father of dangdut singer Camelia Malik. His grandson married Elvy Sukaesih's daughter Fitria.

19. A grandson of the sultan of Deli, T. Nazli, and Muis Radjab used calypso and cha-cha rhythms to modernize local Melayu music ("Dangdut, Sebuah 'Flashback,'" 1983, 13)

20. For example, *aduhai sayang* ("oh, my darling") and *hatiku lah rindu* ("my heart yearns").

21. A. K. Gani, a member of the Indonesian Islamic Union Party (Partai Syarikat Islam Indonesia, PSII) used the word "Melayu" to describe music at a *kroncong* festival in 1938 as a music that had the potential to raise nationalist sentiment ("Satria Berdakwah" 1984, 28).

22. The name Bukit Siguntang refers to a small hill in the modern city of Palembang that is presumed to be the sacred site of the ancient kingdom of Srivijaya (Reid 2001, 298).

23. Melayu tunes included "Kuala Deli" (The Mouth of the Deli River), "Hasratku" (My Desire), and "Kasih Sekejap" (Temporary Love); original pop-oriented compositions included "Burung Nuri" (Parrot), "Kasihku" (My Love), and "Bertamasja ke Pulau" (An Excursion to the Island).

24. Irama M 313–11, sung by Hasnah Tahar, accompanied by Orkes Melayu Bukit Siguntang, directed by A. Chalik.

25. Philip Yampolsky alerted me to this source, for which I am grateful.

26. This song was later recorded by the band D'Loyds with different lyrics under the title "Cinta Hampa" (Empty Love).

27. For example, O. M. Kenangan, directed by Husein Aidit, was an extension of O. M. Sinar Medan. O. M. Kenangan included several *gambus* players from Orkes Gambus Al-waton.

28. Hussein Bawafie notes that in Orkes Gambus Al Wardah, directed by Mochtar Lutfi, for every two Arab-style pieces, they played one Hindustani piece ("Dangdut, Sebuah 'Flashback,'" 1983, 13).

29. The popularity of "Seroja" was noted in an article about the prizewinner of a contest to identify the singer who could sing the best version of "Seroja" ("Bintang 'Serodja,'" 1959).

30. Said Effendi sang 8 songs in the film: "Bimbang dan Ragu" (Worried and Hesitant); "Asmara Dewi" (Dewi's Love); "Potong Padi" (Harvest the Rice); "Nasib Tak Beruntung" (Unlucky Fate); "Utjapan Kasih" (Words of Love); "Hati Terluka" (Wounded Heart) (all composed by Effendi); "Hanja Untukmu" (Only for You) (comp. R. Tobing); and "Seroja" (composed by Husein Bawafie). ("Serodja," 1959, 19).

31. Even at the beginning of his career, Rhoma Irama had insisted on being called a star of "contemporary Melayu music" (*musik melayu kontemporer*) and not a star of dangdut (Navis 1976, 16).

Chapter 3

A Doll from India, Mr. Mahmud, and the Elvis of Indonesia

The anti-imperialist regime of Indonesia's first president Sukarno denounced the allegedly harmful influence of American and European commercial culture (Frederick 1982; Hatch 1985; Sen and Hill 2000). For example, during a speech in 1959, Sukarno characterized the grating sound of American pop music as "ngak-ngik-ngok" (Setiyono 2001). Popular music bands with English-sounding names were compelled to change their names to Indonesian ones to erase any influence of American music. Sukarno even imprisoned members of the American and British-influenced pop music band Koes Bersaudara (Koes Brothers) in 1965 (ibid.).

American films were subject to similar treatment. The Committee for Action to Boycott Imperialist Films from the USA (PAPFIAS) boycotted American films in 1964 (Biran 2001, 226). However, despite the Sukarno regime's efforts to ban American films and music from entering Indonesia, the late 1950s and early 1960s was a remarkably fertile period in the development of Indonesian popular music. Although popular music was limited by government regulation on the national radio network (Lindsay 1997, 111), hundreds of illegal student-run radio stations broadcast prohibited recordings in Jakarta (Sen 2003, 578). Recordings of Pat Boone, Connie Francis, Elvis Presley, Ricky Nelson, as well as Tom Jones and the Beatles constituted an important element of the sound archive used by Indonesian composers and musicians.

Although Sukarno closed Indonesian borders to cultural commodities from the United States and Europe, he opened the door to popular music from India and the Middle East.[1] Sukarno allowed the import of films (musicals) from India during 1950–1964. Films from Malaysia, which incorporated Indian stories and plots, were enormously popular in Indonesia. What does it mean in the context of Indonesia in the 1950s and 1960s to have such a profound multicultural interplay of Melayu, Middle Eastern, Indian, European, and American sounds circulating in popular music?

In this chapter, I focus on the main individuals, musical pieces, musical elements, and processes of "translating songs" from India that shaped the proto-dangdut genre during this period. I approach the origins of dangdut as a global dialogue of cultures, in which popular musics of India, the Middle East, Europe, and the United States were appropriated, translated, transformed, and blended with a localized Indonesian sensibility in the urban centers of Jakarta and Surabaya during the 1950s and 1960s.

The first generation of dangdut stars, including Ellya Khadam, Munif Bahasuan, and A. Rafiq, began singing in *orkes Melayu* bands during the 1950s. In this chapter, I will use these singers and their songs to illustrate the link between *orkes Melayu* and dangdut.

Jakarta: Orkes Melayu à la India

As poet, cultural critic, and founding editor of *Tempo* magazine Goenawan Mohamad writes, Indian films brought something new and exciting to Indonesian audiences of the 1950s:[2]

> In our small village, at that time, a movie theater had just opened.
> People were no longer watching, over and over, Captain America
> [American films]. Now came something more sparkling and fitting
> with stories about kings and princes: Indian film. Certain Bombay
> stars were considered hot in our homes: the beautiful Shakila, the
> handsome mustachioed Mahipal, and Raj Kapoor, who pedicab
> drivers and school kids used to call "Rai Kapur." Hindi language even
> entered the vocabulary of our local cafes: *nehi* became "no," and
> *sukriya* became "thank you." (Mohamad 1984, 15)

The dialogue in these Hindi movies was subtitled. But even without subtitles, spectators could relate to the rich visual imagery, straightforward themes, and the "six songs and three dances" formulae of most Indian films.

Further, the Latin-based rhythms common in Indian film songs were familiar to popular audiences who had been listening to rumbas and tangos in their own Melayu-based popular musical forms that were available on records and radio as early as the 1930s. And Indian film music, which drew heavily on American rock 'n' roll, transported American-inflected music, which had limited distribution in Indonesia at the time.

One of the main elements that distinguished *orkes Melayu* bands from one another in Jakarta during the 1950s was whether they played Indian film songs. It was not only the song repertoire that differentiated these groups, but the instruments, style of singing, lyrics, and generational affiliation of audiences, as illustrated in the following statement by A. Karim Nun, director of the music group Orkes Melayu Dana Seloka (Jakarta):

> In Jakarta, compared to a number of orkes Melayu bands including
> Bukit Siguntang (directed by A. Chalik), Sinar Medan (directed by
> Umar Fausi) and others, Orkes Dana Seloka has its own flavor. Orkes
> Dana Seloka just plays the original style [*asli*] and not the tunes that
> blend Melayu with India. And in general our lyrics are in the form of
> pantun and older lyrical forms. Of course, the younger generation must
> have its own style and a form that is youthful and modern because the
> spirit of youth is a dynamic spirit ("A. Karim Nun" 1955, 15).

Munif Bahasuan, a pioneer of dangdut, sang arranged versions of Melayu songs that came originally from North Sumatra.[3] But as a member of the band Orkes Melayu Sinar Medan he sang what he calls "translated Indian songs": Indonesian lyrics sung to Indian film song melodies. These translated Indian songs established a common "language" for Betawi, Arab, and Indian communities in Jakarta[4]:

> The main audience for orkes Melayu in the 1950s was Betawi. They
> wanted an Islamic-sounding music. Indonesians of Arab descent loved
> gambus. Indian communities liked orkes harmonium that played
> Melayu songs à la India. Betawi people didn't listen to much Indian
> music because they didn't understand the language. They understood
> the Arabic songs. So, the Indian songs had to be translated first. Orkes
> Melayu Sinar Medan was already playing translated Indian songs in
> the 1950s. (Munif Bahasuan, pers. comm., 16 July 2005)

By the early 1960s these translated Indian songs laid the groundwork for dangdut, even though the naming of the genre was still a decade away. Composers created songs inspired by Indian film songs, and they also adapted Indonesian lyrics to Indian film song melodies, as I will describe in the following section.

Ellya Khadam

Ellya Khadam (1929?–2009) is considered a pioneer in the dangdut genre (see figure 3.1). As a young girl, she sang Melayu and Arabic songs. She was skilled at chanting verses from the Qur'an (*tilawah*). Ellya began singing Indian songs as a member of Abdul Kadir's (A. Kadir) group Sinar Kemala in Surabaya. Known variously as Ellya Agus, Ellya M. Harris, and Ellya Alwi, Ellya Khadam dressed in Indian clothes and tried to emulate the dance and facial movements of Indian film stars. She also imitated the vocal style and ornaments heard in Indian film songs. As a freelance artist with various bands in the 1950s, she performed in Singapore, Malaysia, and Indonesia.

Ellya was a prolific composer. Her compositions include "Termenung" (Daydreaming), "Kau Pergi Tanpa Pesan" (You Left without a Word), "Pengertian" (Understanding), "Janji" (Promise), and "Mengharap" (To Hope). Hindi film music was the wellspring for many of her most famous songs including "Boneka dari India" (Doll from India) and "Termenung," as illustrated in the next section. She described her love of Indian music as follows:

> I used the ornaments [cengkok] I had learned from listening to Indian music records. I loved Indian songs because they were different. They were so emotionally moving and seductive. They captured the sound of people in love. (Ellya Khadam, pers. comm., 18 July 2005)

In "Boneka dari India," composer and vocalist Ellya Khadam set the stage for dangdut. The reference to India is clear from the title of the song. In this song-story, a girl receives a doll as a birthday present from her father who has just returned from India (see figure 3.2). The doll's attractive costume, winking eyes, and swaying movements picked up on images in Indian films that were so popular during the period.

The accompaniment of "Boneka dari India" is an *orkes Melayu* ensemble including accordion, mandolin, bass, *gendang kapsul,* and additional percussion (tambourine and maracas). [◐] There is also a vibraphone, an instrument often used in Indian film music. Particularly important for the future of dangdut is the long introduction and interlude, the flute played in the interlude, as well as the accompanying drum pattern. As in Melayu songs, the singer ends the verse with a stock phrase, in this case *oh sayang* ("oh, my love").

The form of "Boneka dari India" is: [intro—A-interlude-B-A´-interlude-B'- A—outro]. The intro, interlude, and outro are built into the composition.

Chalte

Perhaps the most distinctive element of early dangdut prototypes such as "Boneka dari India" was the rhythmic pattern played on *gendang kapsul,* a medium-size two-headed drum that could approximate the sound of the two-drum set (*tabla*) heard in Indian film songs (see figure 2.4).

FIGURE 3.1 Ellya Khadam and A. Kadir (with tambourine) accompanied by Orkes
Melayu Sinar Kemala, c. 1969 [courtesy of A. Kadir].

A: Hatiku gembira riang tak terkira, Mendengar berita kabar dan bahagia.	A: My heart is very happy beyond belief, To hear the happy news.
Ayahku kan tiba datang dari India, Membawa boneka yang indah jelita, oh sayang.	My father will come home from India, And bring a beautiful doll, my love.
[interlude]	[interlude]
B: Boneka cantik kumimpi-mimpi, Menjadi idaman sepanjang hari.	B: A beautiful doll I dream about, To idolize all day long.
Kini kudapat boneka baru, Untuk hadiah ulang tahunku.	Now I have a new doll, For my birthday present.
A': Bonekanya indah pandai main mata, Hatiku gembira riang tak terkira.	A': The beautiful doll is good at winking, My heart is happy beyond belief.
Kuayun kubuai kudendangkan sayang, Tidurlah hai si buyung juwitaku sayang, oh sayang.	I swing her and stroke her and sing to her, Go to sleep my little angel.
[interlude]	[interlude]
B': Boneka sayang berbaju biru, Boleh dipandang tak boleh diganggu.	B': My doll is dressed in blue, You can look but don't touch.
Boneka cantik dari India, Boleh dilirik tak boleh dibawa.	Beautiful doll from India, You can look but you can't take her with you.
[repeat verse A]	[repeat verse A]

FIGURE 3.2 "Boneka dari India" (Doll from India) sung by Ellya Khadam, c. 1962–1963 (Irama EPLN 15), accompanied by Orkes Melayu Kelana Ria, directed by Munif Bahasuan and Adi Karso. [courtesy of Ellya Khadam].

In Indonesia, the accompanying rhythm was called *chalte* or *calte*. According to composer and band leader Zakaria, the *chalte* rhythm is the distinguishing mark of dangdut. He makes the point that dangdut already existed in the 1950s, since the drum rhythm was already present:

> The dangdut beat chalte has been present in our music since the 1950s. Dangdut refers to a drum rhythm, not a song [a reference to the song "Dangdut" composed by Rhoma Irama]. It's a mistake to think that dangdut only emerged when people started using that term. (Zakaria, pers. comm., 12 July 2005)

There are five main drum syllables that constitute the basic chalte pattern (Simatapung 1996, 41).[5] Three drum syllables "dang," "du-ut," and "dut" are realized on the large drumhead using the player's left hand. "Dang" is produced by resting the heel of the left hand very slightly against the head and striking the middle portion of the drumhead with either the middle or index finger. This technique results in a slightly dampened low-pitched sound. With the heel of the left hand placed slightly against the middle of the drumhead, the player can produce the "du-ut" sound by first striking the head with the middle or index finger and then either (1) pressing down on the head or (2) pressing down and moving the left hand forward. Tightening the drumhead, reducing the space inside the drum, causes air inside the drum to vibrate more quickly and results in a higher-pitched sound. As the player strikes and then presses against the drumhead, he produces the characteristic ascending tone that gives the genre its name. The high-pitched "dut" sound is produced by striking the top edge of the large drumhead with the middle or index finger.

The drum syllables "tak" and "tung" are produced on the small drumhead using the player's right hand. "Tak" is produced by striking the drumhead with the index finger toward the inside rim of the drum. The player then dampens the sound. "Tung" is played in the same position, but the sound is not dampened.

The *chalte* pattern has both rhythmic and tonal elements. I have used a five-line staff to show the five drum sounds (see figure 3.3). These are relative and not absolute pitch levels. Sounds produced by the left hand are indicated with stems pointing downward, and sounds produced by the right hand are indicated by stems pointing upward. Parentheses indicate optional sounds.

The origin of the *chalte* pattern cannot be determined with any certainty. It resembles drum patterns of India (Manuel 1988, 211), Malaysia (Chopyak 1986, 123; Simatupang 1996, 40–45; Tanaka n.d.), and Cuban-based music, as illustrated in figure 3.4.

The similarities to *inang* indicate possible roots in Melayu *ronggeng*, described in chapter 2 (Tanaka, n.d.). In Malaysia, *inang* can refer to a dance, as well as various accompanying rhythmic patterns, and a style of performance (Chopyak 1986, 123–124). The *inang* pattern is one of three basic patterns used in *ronggeng asli* ("traditional *ronggeng*") music in North Sumatra (Yampolsky 1996) and Malaysia (Tan 1993, 147). Chopyak notes that the rhythmic patterns of *inang* are most often used in Malaysian dangdut (1986, 130).

Similarities between *chalte* and the Melayu *masri* rhythmic pattern indicate a Middle Eastern connection. *Masri* refers to a type of music and dance that was also part of the *ronggeng asli* tradition (Chopyak 1986, 120; Tan 1993, 150). Malaysian musicians have noted the Middle Eastern influence on *masri* melodies (Chopyak 1986, 121). In *bangsawan* theater, masri is used to accompany plays of Middle Eastern origins (Tan 1993, 150).

drum syllable: dut   dang du-ut   dut   dang   du-ut

FIGURE 3.3 *Chalte* rhythmic pattern.

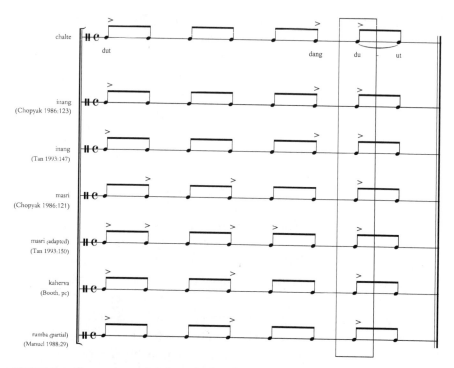

FIGURE 3.4 Comparison of *chalte* and other drum patterns.

The strong connection between the *chalte* pattern and film music from India is shown in the rhythmic pattern as well as the naming of the pattern. The *chalte* rhythmic framework is similar to the *kaherva (kaherawa)* rhythm often used in Indian film music (Manuel 1988, 211). Greg Booth notes that "musicians describe this rhythm as having 4 or 8 beats, but the distinguishing feature is the bass accent (in an 8-beat cycle) on beats 1 and 7, with a light accent on beat 4. This produces the 3+3+2 structure with accents at the beginning of the first and last unit" (Greg Booth, pers. comm., 15 June 2007).

There is no Indian rhythmic framework *(tala)* called *chalte* in Indian music. In Hindi, *chalte* is part of the verb *chaina,* which means roughly "to go." There is a very famous song called "Chalte, Chalte," which could be translated as "I was walking along" or "as I was going through life." It is the verb in the sentence "I am going/leaving now" but one can also *chalte* a car if one is the driver (Greg Booth, pers. comm., 15 June 2007). In this sense, *chalte* can be considered the driving rhythmic pattern that propels dangdut. The term *chalti* is used among Indo-Caribbean "local classical" ("*tan*-singing") musicians, including those who know some Hindi (Peter Manuel, pers. comm., 6 November 2006).

Further, musicians have noted the similarities of the *chalte* pattern to Cuban rumba, which played a major role in popular music of the 1930s as well as in rhythms heard in films from India and Malaysia during the 1950s (Munif Bahasuan, pers. comm., 16 July 2005).

Therefore, if we understand Melayu as a hybrid category that encompasses Melayu, Indian, Middle Eastern, and Latin American elements, we can understand the Melayu nature of *chalte,* the basic pattern used in dangdut. This cultural development, based on a process of assimilation, in which similar elements were woven together and given an original name (for example, *chalte*), is much more convincing than the model that names a source of origin for dangdut.

In the late 1960s, Orkes Melayu Purnama (O. M. Purnama) initiated the change from using *gendang kapsul* to the set of two small drums that constitute *gendang* in dangdut (sometimes called *gendang tamtam*). Figure 3.5(a) shows Awab Haris, codirector of O. M. Purnama, playing the "right hand" drum of the tabla (*dayan*), and a frame drum with his left hand (Sarsidi 1995b, 7).[6] Figure 3.5(b)

(a)

FIGURE 3.5 Precursors to the *gendang* in dangdut: (a) Awab Haris playing two drums, *Dang Dut* 1 (3), June 1995, 7; [courtesy of Zakaria] (b) A. Kadir playing bongo [courtesy of A. Kadir].

(b)

FIGURE 3.5 *Continued*

shows A. Kadir playing the bongo. The process of Awab Haris adapting the tabla sound to dangdut by combining the qualities of a tabla and a bongo is described in the following quotation:

> The mursali [thin layers of black paste called sihai or shai] on an Indian drum is placed on the top of the skin, but Awab moved it to the underside. The mursali skin was then applied to the top of a bongo, replacing the plastic covering, in order to get the characteristic sound used in dangdut. (Sarsidi 1995b, 7)

Comparison of melodic and rhythmic elements

The next section further illustrates the process of translating rhythmic and melodic elements from Indian film music.

The source for one of Ellya Khadam's compositions "Termenung" is the film song "Chhup Gayaa Koii Re Duur Se Pukaar Ke" (which I will refer to as "Chhup Gayaa Koii Re") composed by Hemant Kumar and sung by Lata Mangeshkar in the Indian film *Champakali* (1957, dir. Nandlal Jaswantlal). In both songs, a woman expresses her longing for a lover who is far away, as shown in the following translations of the first verse of each song (see figure 3.7).[7]

The transcribed melody, which forms the A section ("song A"), may be described as a refrain; indeed, in Indian film songs of the 1950s, it was typical to begin with a refrain followed by an interlude, followed by the verse at a

FIGURE 3.6 Comparison of "Chhup Gayaa Koii Re Duur Se Pukaar Ke" sung by Lata Mangeshkar and "Termenung" (Daydreaming) sung by Ellya Khadam (Irama LG 631–03) (first verse).

higher pitch level (which would be "song B").[8] Dangdut songs did not adhere to this framework of opening with the refrain. But dangdut did retain the contrasting A and B melodies, in which the second verse centers around a higher pitch level.

The transcription of the two songs (transposed to G mixolydian; G-A-B-C-D-E-F-G) shows that the melodies are practically the same (see figure 3.6). [⬤ and ⬤] Ornamentation is extensive in both parts. Yet, why do the two versions sound so different? First, Lata Mangeshkar's vocal timbre is thinner than Ellya Khadam's. Second, the quarter-note pulse in "Chhup Gayaa Koii Re" is faster than "Termenung" (152 compared to 106). Third, the harmonic foundation in "Chhup gayaa Koii Re" is only suggested (by the bass), giving it a dreamy quality, whereas harmony is boldly stated in "Termenung" (on the piano). Fourth, the song is harmonized differently, as indicated in the transcription. Finally, although harmonic rhythm is the same (one chord per measure), the harmonies differ in these versions in all but three measures (measures 1, 2, and 5).

In figure 3.8, a comparison of percussion parts shows the similarities between the *kaherva* pattern in "Chhup Gayaa Koii Re" and the *chalte* pattern in "Termenung." The "du-ut" sound can be heard clearly in "Termenung" and additional percussion (triangle, cowbell, and tambourine) enhances the lively mood.

The melody for "Termenung" is a direct copy of "Chhup Gayaa Koi Re Duur Se Pukaar Ke." The flute is another prominent feature of both songs; indeed, the idea to use flute in *orkes Melayu* came from Indian film songs. However, the vocal style, tempo, underlying harmonies, and accompanying instruments create a different mood altogether. This "translated Indian song" represents a clear link to, as well as a creative departure from, the music of India.

"Chhup gayaa koii re duur se pukaar ke"	"Termenung"
chhup gayaa koii re someone has gone and hidden,	*dalam aku termenung* whenever I'm lost in thought,
duur se pukaar ke after calling me from far,	*hatiku selalu* my heart always,
dard anokhe haay a (sweet) pain in my heart,	*teringat padamu* longs for you,
de gayaa pyaar ke that he left in my heart.	*hai kekasihku* oh, my darling.

FIGURE 3.7 Comparison of song texts in "Chhup Gayaa Koii Re Duur Se Pukaar Ke" and "Termenung" (Irama LG 631–03) (first verse).

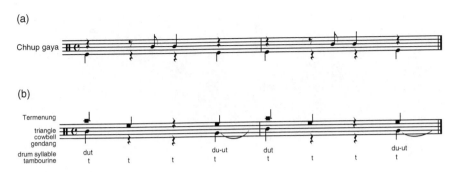

FIGURE 3.8 Comparison of percussion accompaniment in "Chhup Gayaa Koii Re Duur Se Pukaar Ke" and "Termenung."

Another star performer, composer, and band leader in the proto-dangdut era of the 1960s was Munif Bahasuan (see figure 3.9). His father was born in the Hadramaut region (currently the Republic of Yemen). In 1901, at the age of 12, Munif's father came with his parents, spice traders, to central Jakarta. Munif's mother was from Gresik in East Java. The family did very well economically and they developed cosmopolitan tastes. His older sister would delight the family by playing piano pieces by Mozart and Beethoven.

Munif Bahasuan (b. 1935) was a talented singer. At home he would often sing at parties accompanied by *orkes gambus*. He began singing with Muchtar Lufti's *gambus* group at RRI Jakarta and he also sang Egyptian popular songs with Orkes Gambus Al Wardah.

Munif Bahasuan, as well as many of the musicians who played in Orkes Gambus Al Wardah, joined Orkes Melayu Sinar Medan in 1955. He made his first recording with A. Kadir's Orkes Melayu Sinar Kemala in 1957. Munif Bahasuan and fellow musician Adi Karso formed their own band, Kelana Ria, in 1959, with Ellya Khadam, M. Mashadi, M. Lutfi (Mashadi's older brother), and Juhana Sattar. But even after proving himself as a singer and band leader, he had to use the name "M. Fauzi" to hide his identity from his family, who did not approve of his chosen profession. Stylistic experimentation and compositional variety characterized the music of Kelana Ria:

> In Kelana Ria there were lots of composers and styles. For each LP recording we needed 12 songs. I invited other singers to join us. Mashabi was the most creative—his songs were Melayu a la India. My songs were more influenced by Latin music, like "Bunga Nirwana" (Nirwana Flower). We played songs a la India, a la Arab, a la Latin, and songs a la Melayu (Munif Bahasuan, pers. comm., 16 July 2005)

FIGURE 3.9 Munif Bahasuan, accompanied by Orkes Melayu Chandralela, c. 1969 [courtesy of Munif Bahasuan].

Munif Bahasuan brought a cosmopolitan flavor to the music. One of his first recordings was a version of the international hit "Ya Mustafa," originally recorded in 1958 by Lebanese singer Bob Azam, who also recorded a version in French. The text includes the humorous bilingual opening line in French and Italian: "Chérie je t'aime, chéri je t'adore—como la salsa del pomodoro" ("Darling, I love you, darling, I adore you—like tomato sauce"). The song became such a hit for Munif that he recorded several more songs with "Ya" in the title ("Ya Mahmud" and "Ya Hamidah"). In "Ya Mahmud," he sings in English: "I love you Mr. Mahmud, Come to me Mr. Mahmud." There is also a section in Arabic.

Munif Bahasuan's song "Patah Kasih" (Broken Heart) demonstrates the proto-dangdut element of a moderate to fast tempo dance rhythm combined with a text about suffering and loss, as shown in figure 3.10.

The form of the piece is: [intro—{:A-B-refrain-interlude:}—outro]. The B section is sung at a higher pitch level than the A section. The rhythmic framework is *masri*, which has Middle Eastern connotations, as described earlier. [◐]

"Patah Kasih" has the rich texture and sophisticated orchestration characteristic of Middle Eastern popular music, especially the large Egyptian orchestras of the era (*firqah*). Elements that link "Patah Kasih" with Middle Eastern popular music include the following elements:

A: Cukup sudah 'ku derita rintihan jiwa, Karena kau juga pembuat gara-gara, Engkau memperkosa cinta mesra nan murni, Sehingga berpisah paduan kasih sayang.	A: Enough already I have suffered this heartache, Because you are such a troublemaker, You destroyed a pure love, That broke up our relationship.
[instrumental fill]	[instrumental fill]
B: Jutaan bintang-bintang nan dahulu bersakti, Tak percaya lagi hilang di langit tinggi, Kau bermain janji hingga berpisah diri, Kau bermain cinta sehingga ku derita.	B: Thousands of stars that used to be magical, They can't be trusted, lost in the sky, You played with promises and it broke us up. You played around with love and now I suffer.
Refrain: [Rintihan jiwa lara, hatiku tambah duka, Rintihan jiwa lara, hatiku tambah duka.] 2x	Refrain: [My soul suffers, my heart is full of sadness, My soul suffers, my heart is full of sadness] 2x
[instrumental interlude]	[instrumental interlude]
[repeat verse A]	[repeat verse A]
[instrumental fill]	[instrumental fill]
[repeat verse B]	[repeat verse B]
[Refrain]	[Refrain]
Female chorus: repeat refrain Male voice: Ah…	Female chorus: repeat refrain Male voice: Ah…

FIGURE 3.10 "Patah Kasih" (Broken Heart) sung by Munif Bahasuan, c. 1960 (Mustika AM 15), accompanied by Orkes Melayu Sinar Kemala, directed by A. Kadir [courtesy of Ridho Bawafie].

- stepwise sequenced melodic phrases played by bowed strings;
- swinging heterophonic melodies played on the violin and piano;
- variation between small and large sections of the orchestra;
- accordion "commenting" (Ar., *lazimah*; pl. *lawazim*) on the main vocal melody;
- female vocal chorus and male chanting at the end of the song.

The preceding examples show the influence of Indian film music and Middle Eastern popular music on composers and singers in Jakarta who would become pioneers of the dangdut genre. Equally important to the early history of dangdut is the Surabaya-based band Sinar Kemala described in the following section.

Surabaya: A. Kadir and Sinar Kemala

Based in the bustling Arab quarter of Ampel in Surabaya, near the mosque of the pilgrimage complex of Sunan Ampel, Abdul Kadir (A. Kadir) formed the band Sinar Kemala ("Radiant Stone of Magical Powers") in 1952–1953. Members of the band pointed to its origins in Orkes Gambus S. Albar (Syech Albar; see chapter 2), and its successor, Orkes Gambus Alfan. Orkes Melayu Sinar Kemala was the largest orchestra of the 1960s, expanding to 15–25 musicians (including 4–6 singers) at its peak in 1969. The band distinguished itself from bands in Medan and Jakarta by having a large number of violinists (4–6, compared to 2–4 in Medan and Jakarta). Additional instruments included accordion, piano, guitar, mandolin, string bass, clarinet, flute (bamboo *suling* and Western), trumpet, trombone, and percussion (bongo, *gendang*, tambourine, maracas).

The music tended more toward a Middle Eastern sound than the Medan or Jakarta bands. Orchestral arrangements reflected a strong Middle Eastern influence, particularly from Egypt and Lebanon. Singers and composers were especially influenced by Egyptian singers Umm Kulthum, Mohammed Abdel Wahab, Abdel Halim Hafez, and Lebanese singer Fayruz.

Sinar Kemala songs reflected Islamic themes and Arabic words more than groups in Medan or Jakarta; for example, "Keagungan Tuhan" (The Greatness of God), "Perintah Illahi" (Divine Law), "Insjaflah" (Be Aware). Singers' names reflected a Middle Eastern orientation: Nurkumala, Nur A'in, Latifah, and Ida Laila, among others. The highly ornamented vocal part bore similarities to Qur'anic recitation style.

Sinar Kemala performed in modern Western attire: male band members dressed in Western suits and female singers in elegant dresses (see figure 3.11). They were a commercial band, hired to perform for family celebrations and concerts. They played Western popular songs as well as Latin dance music. Although their repertoire consisted of dance music, people in the audience did not dance. Rather, the band presented semi-dramatic choreographies by female dancers who enacted the characters depicted in the songs. They portrayed characters from the Arabian Nights, which were also common in the earlier Surabaya *stambul* theater (Cohen 2006). For example, the character Cleopatra appears in a photo of the band from 1969 (see figure 3.11).

Indian films entered Indonesia around 1952, but only began to influence the popular music of Surabaya after 1955, which was several years later than the Indian film influence on the music of the Jakarta-based O. M. Bukit Siguntang. From the early 1960s onward, O. M. Sinar Kemala reflected a heavy Indian influence, especially during the late 1960s.

A. Kadir nurtured the careers of star singers including Ida Laila (b. 1935), Ali Alatas (b. 1948) and Achmad Rafiq (A. Rafiq, b. 1949). Ellya Khadam and Munif Bahasuan, mentioned in the previous section, traveled from Jakarta to make some of their earliest recordings with Sinar Kemala. Ellya Khadam credits A. Kadir with teaching her to sing Indian film songs. The composer Achmadi,

FIGURE 3.11 Orkes Melayu Sinar Kemala and guest musicians in 1969. Front, L to R: Malik (accordion, piano), A. Karim (tambourine), Umar (vocal), S. Effendi (vocal), Fuad (maracas), Husein (accordion). Back, L to R: Ghozali (emcee), Ida Laila (vocal), Nur Kumala (vocal), Munif (vocal), Khadam (trombone), Bik Nu (dancer in Cleopatra costume), (unidentified), Ellya Khadam (vocal), A. Kadir (leader and vocal), Juhana Sattar (vocal), Wakid (guitar), Salim (emcee), Saleh (trumpet), Mahmud (clarinet), Ali (clarinet), an unidentified coordinator/manager, and Muzh (*gendang*) [courtesy of A. Kadir].

who went on to form Orkes Melayu Awara, and the violinist Fauzi who formed Orkes Melayu Sinar Mutiara, began their careers with Sinar Kemala.

Singer A. Rafiq, who would become one of dangdut's first recording stars, marks the transition from A. Kadir's Sinar Kemala to dangdut. A. Rafiq, born in Semarang in 1949, grew up in a religious family, with ancestors from the Middle East, India, and Turkey. Like Ellya Khadam and Munif Bahasuan, A. Rafiq was adept at Qur'anic recitation as a child. The family strongly disagreed with his choice of a career in music, but he pursued it anyway. He left Semarang to join Sinar Kemala in Surabaya and recorded with the group in the late 1960s. In 1969 he moved to Jakarta, where he became a star of radio, film, and television.

A. Rafiq brought a physical and dramatic visual element to dangdut: "I had a cinematic quality on stage using movements that made people imagine they were watching a film" (A. Rafiq, pers. comm., 18 July 2005). A. Rafiq combined movements from Indian film, Chinese martial arts, Melayu dance (*zapin*), and American rock 'n' roll:

> When I was young, I was called the Elvis of Indonesia. But I only sang dangdut. My movements, my manners, my stage show, my costume, it was all modeled on Elvis. Even Errol, the one known as Elvis of Indonesia, said to me "You're the real Elvis, not me!" But he sang all of Elvis' songs, so he is the real Elvis of Indonesia. But if I had not sung dangdut, I would be the Elvis of Indonesia. (A. Rafiq, pers. comm., 18 July 2005)

FIGURE 3.12 A. Rafiq posing in one of his stage outfits [courtesy of A. Rafiq].

A. Rafiq brought a hip and recognizable fashion style to dangdut with a distinctive kind of flared pants (bell bottoms) referred to as "A. Rafiq pants" (see figure 3.12). In conjunction with his Elvis-like movements, manners, stage show, and costume, A. Rafiq sang and composed songs with primarily Indian melodies. For example, "Pandangan Pertama" (When I First Saw You) is based on the song "Cheda Mere Dil Ne" in the film *Asli Nagli*, sung by Dev Anand (1962). But his biggest hit, "Pengalaman Pertama" (First Experience) was his own invention based on "marrying different styles" (A. Rafiq, pers. comm., 18 July 2005).

Indian music remained a strong presence in the music of Ellya Khadam, Munif Bahasuan, and A. Rafiq. They continued to flourish as popular music stars throughout the 1970s. But as we approach the era of New Order Indonesia, and *orkes Melayu* begins to give way to dangdut, American popular music exerted a major influence on Indonesian music, as shown in the following section.

Pop Melayu

In the mid-1960s, Melayu music in Jakarta branched off into two directions: American-influenced *pop Melayu*, and Indian and Middle Eastern-influenced *orkes Melayu*. The influence of American singers and bands was greatest on the music of *pop Indonesia*, which flourished during this period.

Pop *Melayu* bandleader Zakaria (b. 1936) aimed to create songs that would appeal to fans of Melayu music as well as fans of *pop Indonesia*. In 1962, he formed a group called Pancaran Muda ("The Image of Youth") (see figure 3.13). Zakaria worked on songs and new arrangements with pop and jazz pianist Syafii Glimboh, as well as entertainer and composer Bing Slamet and violinist Idris Sardi.

The Sukarno government, which had vigorously encouraged Indian film imports during the late 1950s and early 1960s, changed course by ceasing to allow imports during 1964–1966. As Indonesia became more isolated politically, songs with an Indian flavor (*berbau India*) were reportedly banned at the time from being played on the radio (Barakuan 1964, 21). The central government was trying to divert attention from Indian culture and refocus it on Indonesia. In 1964, Zakaria's Pancaran Muda walked a fine line between the acceptable Melayu music and music with an Indian sound. As one report stated: "This band succeeded in the Dwikora era, a period when many Indian songs were banned" ("Dangdut, Sebuah Flashback" 1983, 15; see also "O.M. Chandralela" 1964, 21). *Dwikora* (*dwikomando rakyat*), a slogan of the Sukarno

FIGURE 3.13 Pancaran Muda c. 1964. Back Row, L to R: Slamet, Yayung, Malik,
R. Sunarsih, and Ilin Sumantri; Front Row, L to R: Gatot, Rustedjo, Umar Tam Tam,
Diding, and Zakaria [courtesy of Zakaria].

era, refers to the people's two mandates of 1964: crush Malaysia and defend
the revolution. The Indian-inspired song "Keagungan Tuhan" (The Greatness
of God) composed by Malik B. Z. in 1965, was not released until 1966 because
the Communist party opposed its religious theme.[9] Launched by the national
recording company Lokananta, after Suharto came to power, the song became
a huge hit throughout Indonesia and it was eventually translated into Urdu,
Hindi, and Arabic.

The New Order: Suharto Comes to Power

There was a vacuum in popular music recording for several years after the military coup and subsequent regime change from Sukarno's "Old Order" to
Suharto's "New Order" in 1966–1967. Deregulation of film imports began on
3 October 1966 (Said 1991, 78). Ellya Khadam's "Kau Pergi Tanpa Pesan" (You
Left Without a Word) in 1967 was considered a "comeback" for Melayu music
à la India. Previously criticized by Sukarno as an imperialist symbol of

capitalism, American popular music was encouraged under the new president Suharto. *Pop Indonesia* and rock were geared primarily to an emerging middle- and upper-class youth culture. *Pop Indonesia* offered accessible lyrics (in Indonesian), sweet and smooth timbres, and sentimental love songs. Recordings of *pop Indonesia* boomed in the late 1960s.

In Jakarta, *orkes Melayu* waned in popularity, while the combination of pop and Melayu ascended in popularity. *Pop Melayu* bands had a modern sound. Musicians could read music scores. They had financial backing that allowed them to purchase fine-quality instruments. Whereas *orkes Melayu* bands performed with only one microphone for the singer and one or two speakers for amplification, *pop Melayu* bands had a microphone for each person and multiple speakers. *Pop Melayu* bands played at national events. For example, Pancaran Muda played at the wedding celebration of Sukarno's daughter Megawati Sukarnoputra in 1968.[10] Figure 3.14 illustrates a comparison of *pop Melayu* and *orkes Melayu, 1967–1974*.

Conclusion

The "translated Indian songs" played by *orkes Melayu* groups in the 1950s and 1960s would later be called dangdut. The marriage of Indian, Middle Eastern, and American music described in this chapter grew into dangdut. So, while the genre was not yet crystallized, or named, many of the main elements were in place for this "proto-dangdut," as illustrated below.

- Indonesian lyrics;
- Melayu, Middle Eastern and Indian-derived vocal ornaments;
- song structure consisting of instrumental intro, A section (possible repeat), B section (possible repeat), interlude, A section, instrumental outro;
- few chords (usually between three and five);
- *chalte* rhythmic framework played on *gendang* and other percussion (bongo, maracas, tambourine);
- fills, played by the drummer, in accordance with the arrangement of the song;
- moderate to fast tempo dance pieces;
- bass lines moving in tandem with the drum rhythm;
- flute and plucked stringed instruments featured in the interlude sections;
- lyrics with a narrative quality;

- themes based on love and relationships;
- dance movements and costumes linked to film.

It would take developments in the 1970s, particularly the influx of rock elements from the United States and Great Britain, as well as the tremendous influence of cassette culture, to secure dangdut's place as a dominant force in Indonesian popular music. All of these stylistic elements would merge under the rubric of "dangdut" in Rhoma Irama's music, described in the following chapter.

	Pop Melayu	Orkes Melayu
Singer	Lilis Suryani, Titing Yeni, Titik Sandhora, Muchsin Alatas, Ida Royani, Benyamin, Wiwiek Abidin, Oma Irama, Elvy Sukaesih	Ellya Khadam, Juhana Sattar, Ida Laila, A. Kadir, Munif Bahasuan, A. Rafiq, Mashabi, Oma Irama, Elvy Sukaesih
Bands	Pancaran Muda, Eka Sapta, Zaenal Combo, Bimbo, D'Lloyd, Mercy's	O.M. Chandraleka, O.M. Chandralela, O.M. Purnama, O.M. Sinar Kemala
Composers	Zakaria, Zaenal Arifin	Husein Bawafie, Ilin Sumantri, Umar Alatas, Ellya Khadam, A. Kadir
Influences	Bing Slamet, Idris Sadri, American pop, The Beatles, Tom Jones, Frank Sinatra, Jazz	*Lagu Melayu*, Indian film, Middle Eastern pop, American pop
Lyrics/themes	Love, sentimentality	Heartache, loss, suffering
Instruments	Electric guitar, electric bass, mandolin, strings, saxophone, clarinet, electric organ, percussion (*gendang*, tambourine, maracas)	Acoustic or electric guitar, upright or electric bass, mandolin, accordion, saxophone, clarinet, flute, percussion (*gendang*, tambourine, maracas)
Performance occasions	Concerts, parties, national events	Local parties
Radio	RRI, *radio amatir*	*Radio amatir*
Recording companies	Remaco, Metropolitan (Musica), Dimita, Canary	Irama, Remaco, Dimita, Lokananta
Performance style	Modern, progressive; musicians and singers stand	Indian, filmic; musicians sit (singers stand)
Audience	Middle and upper classes	Underclass and middle classes
Vocal style	Sweet, smooth, Western pop, Melayu	Ornaments (Melayu, Indian, Middle Eastern)
Tempo	Slow to moderate	Moderate to fast
Song structure	32-bar song form; verse-refrain, with short introductions and abbreviated or no interludes	Variable, extended forms with long introductions and interludes

FIGURE 3.14 Comparison of *pop Melayu* and *orkes Melayu*, 1967–1974.

NOTES

1. A similar mode of alignment/non-alignment characterized the sphere of politics. Sukarno hosted the 1955 Asia-Africa conference, where the leaders of newly independent Asian and African countries joined together in a non-aligned movement that aimed to solidify political and economic links among participating nations.

2. Film music could be heard on radio as well. From Jakarta, musicians could pick up the signal of radio stations based in Ceylon (Sri Lanka) in the mid-1950s (Rhoma Irama, pers. comm., 14 July 2005).

3. These included "Selendang Songket" (Songket Scarf), "Ibarat Air di Daun Keladi" (Like Water on the Taro Leaf), and "Yale-yale," among others.

4. The Betawi ethnic group constitutes the original inhabitants of Batavia, the Indonesian name for the Dutch "Batavia," the former name for Jakarta (Loven 2008).

5. Simatupang's description of the chalte pattern is excellent; I have adapted the naming of the "du-ut" sound from his description. The following explanation is based on Simatupang as well as my lessons with drummers Husein Khan (Jakarta) and Kang Uja (Bandung).

6. There is not a fixed or consistent practice for tuning drums. For dangdut recordings, drummers often tune the small drum to the tonic pitch of the song. In live performances, they tune the small drum to the tonic most frequently used by that particular group.

7. I am grateful to Sreyashi Dey for a translation of the first verse of "Chhup Gayaa Koii Re."

8. Indonesian composers refer to different melodic sections or verses as "song A," "song B," etc. I will indicate these sections in the song text examples as "A," "B," etc.

9. Malik B. Z., pers. comm., 10 July 2008.

10. Megawati would later serve as president of the Republic of Indonesia from 2001 to 2004.

Chapter 4

Music and *Rakyat:*
Constructing "the People"
in Dangdut

New socioeconomic and political realities stimulated the rise of American and British popular music after Suharto came to power in 1966–1967. The coup that ushered in the New Order opened Indonesia to sustained industrial expansion, Western-style capitalism, intensified commodification, and a culture of consumerism. New electronic technologies enabled music to travel in the form of cassette recordings to regions far from the urban centers of production. Innovative forms of promotion—films, billboards, and magazines—generated interest in the social lives of entertainers and celebrities. New ways of presenting music in public concerts, festivals, and outdoor fairs in big cities promoted emerging forms of rock and pop. Regulations on radio broadcasting were lifted, and hundreds of private stations, many of them student-run, reemerged during the late 1960s (Lindsay 1997, 112). And a new ethos of consumerism in Indonesia gave more people the motivation, as well as the resources, to buy commercial products associated with popular music.

In the early 1970s, the Indian-based music played in *orkes Melayu* described in chapters 2 and 3 crystallized into "dangdut." The notion of dangdut as the music of "the people"—the majority of society (*rakyat*)—emerged during this era, and it has been a persistent theme ever since (Paramida 2005, ix). *Rakyat* can be defined in several ways. During the revolutionary period (1945–1949), the term *rakyat* referred to the followers (subjects) of a leader—in this case, Sukarno, who was the voice of the people (literally, an "extension of the tongue of the people," *penyambung lidah rakyat Indonesia*) (Anderson 1990, 62). According to anthropologist James Siegel, the *rakyat* ceased to exist in the New Order because Suharto did not speak either for or to them (Siegel 1998, 4).

Nevertheless, popular understandings of the *rakyat* still exist as "the innocent, morally superior, economically unprivileged but politically sovereign figures who often suffer from injustice inflicted by the rich and powerful" (Heryanto 1999, 162).

During the 1970s, people who listened to dangdut occupied the lower stratum of the political and economic structure, and were described in magazine and newspaper articles of the period as: "little people" (*rakyat kecil*); "common people" (*rakyat jelata*); "poverty-stricken people" (*rakyat jémbél*); "underclass group" (*golongan bawah*); "marginalized group" (*kaum marginal*), "those who have been pushed aside" (*pinggiran*), and constituting "the middle class and below" (*kelas menengah ke bawah*).

The articulation of dangdut and *rakyat* operates on three intertextual levels, which I will call (1) dangdut *is* the *rakyat;* (2) dangdut *for* the *rakyat;* and (3) dangdut *as* the *rakyat*. First, as described in sociological terms, dangdut *is* the music of the *rakyat*. At this level, the public is a noun that can be enumerated, described, and mobilized. In a largely ahistorical argument that mirrors Rhoma Irama's statements about Melayu music in chapter 2, dangdut has been constructed as a natural reflection of the *rakyat,* as opposed to *pop Indonesia,* rock, jazz, or other forms in which musical elements are largely imported from Europe or the United States. In this narrative, dangdut grows naturally out of its consumers' socioeconomic and cultural conditions, and it represents their interests, tastes, and aspirations. Dangdut audiences are perceived as a stable group of dedicated and fanatic fans. However, it is difficult to reconcile this view of representation with dangdut's production and circulation, which are thought to be controlled by a small and manipulative music industry that is largely run by people outside the group (non-*rakyat*). Further, the early forms of dangdut were based on instruments, timbres, and song forms from a variety of imported genres, as described in chapters 2 and 3. This fact complicates essentialized notions of music originating from and belonging to a definable indigenous group.

The second level, "dangdut *for* the *rakyat,*" describes the ways in which influential social actors and commercial institutions have actively constructed audiences and meanings about the *rakyat*. Dangdut's audience did not exist prior to the creation of dangdut, as a group whose class interests were subsequently reflected in a musical genre.[1] Dangdut does not belong to a class, as a category or attribute of that class. Rather, dangdut acts as a structuring agent that helps to produce meanings about the *rakyat* in Indonesian society. In this sense, a social process took place around the music involving new aesthetics, politics, and economics of the media industries (cassettes, film, and radio). Under these conditions, dangdut superstar Rhoma Irama composed populist messages with a danceable beat that appealed to an urban Islamic underclass and primarily male youth audience. In terms of his lyrics, musical sound, performance style, and visual imagery, Rhoma Irama actively shaped rather than simply reflected meanings about the *rakyat*. In this section, I examine the ways in which Rhoma Irama addressed a public in particular ways.

Third, I analyze popular print publications, in which representations of dangdut *as* the *rakyat* were produced with great frequency and in a variety of popular print media. The *rakyat* is not a singular unified category, and neither is dangdut's audience, but the term signifies the juxtaposition of class-based and nation-based meanings that characterize the discourse about dangdut during the 1970s. I describe the ways in which popular print media "speaks for" people, and the relations of power that define those discourses. In popular print media, dangdut's audience was largely absent as the author of its own representation. In this way, popular print media played a large role in presenting what it was possible to think and know about the *rakyat*. I contend that middle classes and elites had long participated in dangdut as a discursive practice, if only as a way to distance themselves from the people and culture associated with the music. By taking this approach, I seek to provide a critical understanding of Indonesian music and media and the construction of popular music audiences within the changing social and historical conditions of modern Indonesia. The ways in which dangdut has been articulated with the multiple and shifting meanings of the *rakyat* can help us understand how mass-mediated popular music has been instrumental in constructing the nature and function of "the people" in modern Indonesia.

Dangdut *Is* the Rakyat

In this formulation, dangdut's popularity, and the articulation of music with the underclass majority of society, is based on its: (1) historical roots in the melodies, rhythms, and vocal style of Melayu popular music (*orkes Melayu*); (2) Indonesian-language lyrics; (3) relatively simple styles of dance (*joget* and *goyang*); (4) straightforward and easily comprehensible lyrics; and (5) song texts that deal with the everyday realities of ordinary people.

Stories about dangdut as the blood, soul, and voice of Indonesians proliferated during the 1970s. For example, according to Rhoma Irama:

> Dangdut has become so popular because it is so basic to the soul of indigenous people (*jiwa pribumi*). Because no matter how proud we are, our hearts are infused with Melayu blood (*darah Melayu*).
> (quoted in Mousli 1980b, 34)

In 1979, cultural critic, religious leader, and poet Emha Ainun Nadjib (Emha) admonished Indonesians for losing their collective "dangdut soul" (*jiwa ber-dangdut*) (Emha 1979), with a reference to dangdut as "soul music." Writing for an educated middle-class and elite readership hailed by Western narratives of modernity (*modernitas*), Emha noted that despite their desire to progress (*maju*), all Indonesians are deep down "very dangdut" (*dangdut sekali*). As American products flooded the Indonesian market, Emha asked "what are we if not a bunch of brown-skinned Western clothes-wearing people with a dangdut mentality?" Modernity might look good on the outside, but it disguised the everyday problems that faced most Indonesians, and it threatened to exacerbate social inequalities. However, by looking inward, and by reflecting on their own cultural history, people could reclaim their true selves, and that reclamation could help them reject the pervasive and negative effects of modernity. Dangdut was at the heart of this soul-searching process.

Dangdut was not only deeply embedded in Indonesian souls, but its power was located in the physical bodily production of vocal sound. Commentators noted that the popularity of Rhoma Irama was due to the timbre of his voice, which reflected suffering. His voice was described as:

> ...not smooth, and not rough either like rock singers, but leaning towards warm or quivering—with small waves of emotion, reflecting honesty and, I don't know how, a feeling of suffering. This is the active kind of voice that absorbs and transports the listener, always seeming to want to reveal the singer's deepest feelings. He not only sings love songs and songs about the underclass, which are his largest audience. But he also sings about their wishes and desires. ("Satria Berdakwah" 1984, 28)

In contrast, Indonesian popular music (*pop Indonesia*) and rock did not have the historical roots or musical features that linked them to the *rakyat*'s suffering. Modeled on American pop, the sweet syrupy vocal style, slow tempos, and lack of humor in *pop Indonesia* did not resonate with the desires and aspirations of the urban underclass.

Dangdut developed in economically and socially marginalized urban neighborhoods in the late 1960s and early 1970s including Bangunrejo (Surabaya), Sunan Kuning (Semarang) and Planet Senen (Jakarta). Planet Senen began as a junkyard where homeless would gather.[2] Singer Meggy Z. recalls:

> It was considered a black place [*daerah hitam*], a place without a master/without rules. When I went to Planet Senen, I often saw dead

bodies on the side of the road. People who hung out there included the homeless, market sellers, contract laborers, prostitutes, criminals, gamblers, and artists. Every night musicians would gather on a small wooden stage to entertain. Anyone could come and play, and anyone could listen. There was a lot of inspiration there. (quoted in Agus 2000, 6)

Musicians who would become recording stars in the 1970s and 1980s went there for inspiration; composer Asmin Cayder remembers singers including Rhoma Irama, Mukhsin Alatas, Husein Bawafie, and Mashabi (Agus 2000, 6). They named their bands Chandralela and Chandraleka, after the Indian films they watched. Chandralela, formed in 1957–1958 and directed by Husein Bawafie, combined the Sanskrit word meaning full moon (*chandra*) and the Arabic word meaning night (*lela* or *laila*). Their instruments included guitar, mandolin, accordion, *gendang, suling,* and other instruments that could be easily transported. Chandraleka, formed in the early 1960s and directed by Umar Alatas, took its name from the Tamil film *Chandralekha* (1948). Both bands were loosely organized. Musicians moved freely between groups, looking for opportunities wherever they could find them. Dangdut grew up among this community:

Between the musicians and the inhabitants of Planet Senen there was a kind of relationship based on mutual need. Musicians needed money, prostitutes needed work, food stand owners needed lively customers, and people needed entertainment. (Giman, quoted in Gumelar 2000, 9)

Dangdut appealed to *becak* (pedicab) and *bajaj* (motorized cab) drivers, soup and cigarette peddlers, market sellers and traders who lived in the streets, alleys, and slums of Jakarta and other urban areas. Urban industrial workers—those who worked in the most dangerous, dirty, and difficult working environments (Heryanto 1999)—did not live in the soft dreamy music of *pop Indonesia.* Dangdut's raw percussion-driven sound accommodated the gritty urban soundscape that surrounded its listeners. However, the music always had a commercial quality: "There were no bars to hear dangdut, so this is where musicians played, and they played for money. Food sellers, cigarette vendors, prostitutes, and thieves (*tukang copet*) could make money there" (Agus 2000, 6).

Stories about the origins of the name *dangdut* relate directly to its underclass roots. In the early 1970s, rock musician Benny Subardja, a member of the rock band Giant Step, characterized dangdut as *musik tai anjing* ("dog shit music") (Frederick 1982, 124 n60). Editors at the music magazine *Aktuil,* which

I will discuss later in this chapter, reportedly coined the term as a derogatory label for the music's characteristic and persistent drum pattern "dang-dut."[3] Rhoma Irama states that "the name 'dangdut' is actually an insulting term used by 'the haves' toward the music of the poor neighborhoods [where it originated among the "have-nots"]. They ridiculed the sound of the drum, the dominant element in orkes Melayu. Then we threw the insult right back via a song, which we named 'Dangdut.'"[4] In that tune, composed in 1973 and alternately known by the Hindi-sounding title "Terajana," he turned a negative slang term used to demean the underclass into a marker of positive self-definition.

The term was used to distinguish dangdut from *orkes Melayu*, especially the music of North Sumatra: "The name orkes Melayu was too specific to Sumatra, too reminiscent of Deli. So we just decided to stick with 'dangdut.' Even though it was derogatory, it eventually caught on" (Meggy Z., pers. comm., 12 July 2005). The name "dangdut" gained widespread circulation via radio in 1973–1974 by Bung Mangkudilaga, a radio disc jockey and dangdut promoter at Radio Agustina in Tanjung Priok, Jakarta (Meggy Z., pers. comm., 12 July 2005; Mansyur S., pers. comm., 12 July 2005; Dadang S., pers. comm., 15 July 2005). Mangkudilaga ran a daily radio program called "Dangdut Soup" ("Sop Dangdut"), reflecting the ordinary quality of the music and the soup-like mixture of elements that constituted it. Radio stations recognized this growing market of urban consumers. Other radio stations that played the music included Amatir, Cendrawasih, Agustina Junior, and Ramajaya. Largely due to the success of Ellya Khadam's recordings, the Indianized *orkes Melayu* sound became a significant force in the music industry. In 1972, Ellya Khadam's albums sold more than her competitors in the *pop Indonesia* genre ("Pesta Bumi Musik" 1973, 17). The *pop Indonesia* "aristocrats" in the music business (*priyayi musik Indonesia*) began "lowering themselves" (*ikut turun ke bawah*) to sing Melayu music ("Fokus Kita" 1975, 3). For example, The Mercy's (from Medan) recorded "Injit-Injit" (Children's Game), "Joget Gembira" (Joyful Dancing), and "Kembalilah" (Come Back). In 1975, dangdut claimed 75 percent of all recorded music, produced by such former pop hit-makers as Koes Plus, D'Lloyd, and Bimbo ("Panen Dangdut" 1975, 48). But it was a talented, restless, brilliant, and charismatic young man named Rhoma Irama who transformed the music industry in the mid-1970s.

Dangdut *for* the Rakyat: Rhoma Irama

Musician, composer, record producer, film star, and Islamic proselytizer Rhoma Irama occupies a central place in the history of dangdut. Composer of

hundreds of songs and star of over 20 films, Rhoma Irama has been a dominant force in Indonesian music and popular culture since the early 1970s.
Using popular print media to defend the genre against claims that it was
backward and unsophisticated, he paved the way for dangdut to become
Indonesia's most popular music.

Rhoma Irama was born on 11 December 1946, in Tasikmalaya, West Java.
His father, R. Burdah Anggawirja, was an army officer and his mother, Tuty
Juwairyah, was a housewife. His birth story has been told many times: while
his mother was giving birth, his father ventured out to watch a *sandiwara* troupe
named Irama Baru ("the new rhythm"); hence, the name "Irama." After making the pilgrimage to Mecca in 1975, Oma changed his name to Rhoma Irama
(R. H. stands for "Raden Haji"; *raden* is an aristocratic title and *haji* refers to a
male who has made the pilgrimmage).

His family moved to Jakarta around 1950, and young Oma began singing
and playing the guitar. In the early 1960s, he was drawn to the sound of
American and British pop and rock 'n' roll and he sang in the cover bands
Gayhand and Tornado. These bands played at parties in the well-heeled
neighborhoods of Jakarta; young Oma also performed as a singer in *orkes
Melayu* bands in the poorer neighborhoods. He finished high school in
Jakarta and entered university but never finished. Word quickly spread about
the talented young singer who could sing Western pop, Indian film, and
Melayu songs. He made his first recording with the *orkes Melayu* band
Indraprasta, led by Murad Harris (M. Harris). In 1967 he recorded duets with
Elvy Sukaesih and O. M. Purnama. In 1970–1971, he formed the band Soneta
to play his own compositions; by 1975, he had created a new sound for popular
music.

During the 1980s, he established a second career as a religious preacher
who delivered his sermons to the people through exhortations, instruction, and
commands. He anchored his sermons with Arabic quotes from the Qur'an,
and illustrated his points with lyrics from his songs. During this period, the
line between his music and his sermons was often negligible.

Rhoma Irama has garnered attention both at home and throughout the
world as the "King of Dangdut" (*Raja Dangdut*). His songs have been the subject of scholarly articles (Frederick 1982; Yampolsky 1991; Pioquinto 1998) and
world music books and textbooks (Taylor 1997; Broughton and Ellingham
2000; Sutton 2002, 319–321; Capwell 2004, 165–166). During my fieldwork in
2005–2007, his songs were more frequently played in live performances, as
well as radio and television broadcasts, than those of any other single dangdut
composer. At this writing, he continues to perform throughout Indonesia and
abroad. He has gained national and international media attention in recent

years for his efforts to ban singer Inul Daratista, and for his involvement in drafting an anti-pornography bill that has drawn the ire of feminists and fans alike (see chapter 7). I will discuss his musical development in the following sections.

Drawing on a wide variety of musical sources, Rhoma Irama used dangdut as a vehicle to shape people's political and moral ideas. Using the colors of the Indonesian flag, he emphasized the power of his music in the following quote:

> My principle is that music has to be able to shape the people. If we want them red, they'll turn red. If we want them white, they'll turn white. In order to do that, we need harmony between the lyrics, the feeling, and the performance so that our aims/goals will reach them. When they go home after one of our shows, they'll think back to what we said. We need music that can entertain in order to motivate people and educate people. Drunks will stop drinking. Rude people will become pleasant. Non-believers will become believers. All from music. (pers. comm., 14 July 2005)

Rhoma Irama made the urbanized, mass mediated, and commodified dangdut into a form of popular Islam, one that was pragmatic and performative. He explained the pragmatic nature of shaping religious messages (*dakwah*) into a commercial form in order to bring them to the masses:

> In the 1970s, the idea to make dakwah songs was considered strange by recording companies and producers. They refused to record dakwah songs because they claimed they would not be commercially popular. They said we had to follow the taste of the people who only liked to hear love songs or party music. Indeed, the orientation of cassette producers was to find the largest profit possible. I accepted their position. So we had to make dakwah songs that had a commercial goal. If dakwah could not attract people in a commercial way then dakwah would not reach the people. (pers. comm., 3 October 2008)

In contrast to the previous section, which focused on the ways in which dangdut reflects the people's desires and aspirations, the following section will examine how dangdut was used as a medium for shaping attitudes about morality, gendered relations, and national community. What kinds of messages are embedded in Rhoma Irama's songs? How does he address his audience? What are some of the ways that Rhoma Irama's messages have been received? My analysis constructs an interpretation of Rhoma Irama's lyrics, music sound, performance style, and visual imagery (on cassette covers and in promotional material, tabloids, and films).

Song texts

In the following section, I analyze a corpus of 307 songs, all of which appear on albums or film sound tracks composed by Rhoma Irama. While this may not represent the entire corpus of his prolific compositional output, it constitutes a large sample for a topical analysis of his song texts.[5] Each song has a clearly defined topic, often identified by its title; for example, "Hunger" (Lapar); "Failed Relationship" (Kegagalan Cinta) and "Human Rights" (Hak Azasi). However, most songs further express a specific position on the topic at hand, and so my analysis considers not only the song title, but the full text of each song.[6]

Out of 307 songs, 150 songs express instructive messages about what it means to behave properly as a human being, organized into the following categories: moral behavior, with a strong religious emphasis (57); moral behavior, with no explicit mention of religion (29); and male-female love and relationships (20). In addition, songs in the following categories include messages, but the message is not explicitly stated: society and politics (24); and everyday life (20). In the following section, I will discuss each of the above categories and provide three titles for each to lllustrate the type of message within those categories.

MORAL BEHAVIOR, WITH A STRONG RELIGIOUS EMPHASIS. After returning from the religious pilgrimage (*hajj*) to Mecca in November 1975, Rhoma Irama changed the moral fabric of his band Soneta. For example, he insisted that bandmembers stop drinking alcohol and having sexual relations outside marriage. Members were kicked out of the band for not adhering to these rules. In addition to changing the lyrics and music, he made "alterations in hair style (shorter, neatly trimmed), costumes (frequently "Muslim" of an especially exotic Middle Eastern type), and message (more didactic)" (Frederick 1982, 115). These efforts culminated in the film *Perjuangan dan Doa* (Struggle and Prayer) described by Frederick as "the world's first Islamic rock musical motion picture" (1982, 119).

After returning from the *hajj*, Rhoma Irama strengthened his resolve to use music to inform, instruct, and lead his listeners. He felt that music should be used for virtuous purposes rather than simply for entertainment and pleasure. For him, dangdut represented "the holy war we wage through playing music" (Piper 1995, 47). Figure 4.1 shows the large stone sculpture that sits at the entrance to one of the Soneta studios in Jakarta. It reads "Music is a responsibility to God and humanity."

FIGURE 4.1 Rhoma Irama's motto written in stone: "Music is a Responsibility to God and Humanity." Entrance to one of the Soneta studios, 14 July 2005 [photo: Andrew Weintraub].

For Rhoma Irama, dangdut had an important role to play in shaping a society's sense of morality, and could help to fight against various social ills: corruption in government; gambling; the use of narcotics; as well as sex outside marriage (pers. comm., Rhoma Irama, 14 July 2005).

Songs in this category often present an explicit message designed to instruct listeners in very strong and unambiguous language. For example, the word *jangan* ("don't") appears frequently in song texts. Songs include texts in Arabic, including Qur'anic phrases. There are two types of messages in this category:

> God is all-powerful, but you determine your fate: rich and poor are the same in the eyes of God ("Taqwa"), struggles in life should always be accompanied by prayer ("Perjuangan dan Doa"), the road to Heaven is simple, but many choose not to follow it ("Terserah Kita");
> Practice the tenets of Islam: don't sin, don't judge ("Kabar dan Dosa"), spread the word of Allah ("Musafir"), and avoid drugs and gambling ("Haram").

MORAL BEHAVIOR, NO MENTION OF RELIGION. Although religious terminology may not be explicit, a large group of songs pertains to moral behavior, as illustrated by the following three types of messages:

Exercise self-control: don't look at women as prey ("Lelaki"), don't make the same mistake twice ("Kehilangan Tongkat"), and watch what you say ("Lidah");

Be kind to others: don't seek revenge ("Dendam"), love your mother ("Mama"), and value friendship, because a good friend is hard to find ("Sahabat");

Don't give up, life is a struggle: after darkness, the light will shine ("Habis Gelap Terbitlah Terang"), nothing comes easy in this life ("Menggapai Matahari"), and there are many ways to achieve your goals ("Banyak Jalan Ke Roma").

MALE-FEMALE RELATIONSHIPS AND LOVE. As discussed in chapter 2, song lyrics in the *orkes Melayu* repertoire focused on male-female love and relationships. Rhoma Irama continued the tradition of writing love songs, and many of his songs are playful and light-hearted. But he also injected a strong moral and religious component into songs about love. Songs advising listeners on matters of love include the following two types:

1. Be careful in matters of love: control your sexual urges ("Birahi"), it's what's inside that counts ("Dasi dan Gincu"), love is a mystery ("Aneh Tapi Nyata");
2. Work through difficulties in a relationship: in love, there are always sacrifices ("Pengorbanan"), couples must work together ("Rambate"), and don't give up ("Sifana").

SOCIETY AND POLITICS. From 1977–1982, Rhoma Irama campaigned for the United Development Party (Partai Persatuan Pembangunan, PPP), a coalition party of Islamic religious groups. He localized Islam by addressing specific social and political concerns in his compositions as well as in performance. For example, at a concert to promote the Ka'bah Party (another name for the PPP), Rhoma Irama and his band played his hit song "Begadang" ("Stay Up All Night"), but instead of singing "Stay up all night, don't stay up all night" (*Begadang, jangan begadang*), he sang "It's all right to penetrate (the ballot for the Islamic party)," playing on the double meaning of "penetrate" for his largely male audience ("Dan Oma Serta Upit" 1977, 54) (see figure 4.2).

During the early 1980s, the Suharto regime enforced the public separation of religion and state. During the time that Rhoma Irama aligned himself with the PPP, he was banned from performing on the state-run television (TVRI) and radio (RRI) networks (Sen and Hill 2000, 175). Certain songs were banned by the government, and cassettes were removed from stores. In November

Begadang, jangan begadang, Kalau tiada artinya, Begadang boleh saja, Kalau ada perlunya.	Stay up all night, don't stay up all night, If there is not a reason, It's alright to stay up all night, If you have a reason.

Menusuk boleh menusuk, Asal yang ada artinya, Menusuk boleh menusuk, Asal Ka'bah yang ditusuk.	It's alright to penetrate, As long as it has meaning, It's alright to penetrate, As long as you vote for the Islamic Party.

FIGURE 4.2 Original and altered lyrics for "Begadang" (Stay Up All Night).

1977, videos of the songs "Human Rights" (Hak Azasi), "Rupiah" (Indonesian currency), and "A Shrimp Hiding Behind a Rock" (Udang di Balik Batu) were banned from television because they threatened to expose social problems, which, according to the Department of Information, would subsequently ignite audiences and destabilize the government (which, of course, only fueled Rhoma Irama's popularity and sales of recordings). As a result, dangdut became a symbol of resistance against the New Order military regime.[7]

By the mid-1980s, as Islam began to liberalize and state restrictions against Islam loosened, politicians began endorsing dangdut and building alliances with dangdut performers to gather popular support. In 1988, Rhoma Irama returned to television after an 11-year absence. In the 1990s, a period when Islam was publicly embraced by Suharto, Rhoma Irama moved closer to the New Order. Reconstructed and appropriated, dangdut was subsequently courted by government officials as the music of the New Order, the music that Secretary of State Moerdiono called "very Indonesian" (see chapter 6).

There are two types of messages in this category:

Social political problems: corruption ("Indonesia"), censorship ("Dilarang Melarang"), and unemployment ("Pengangguran");
Social political reform: political reforms ("Reformasi"), patriotism ("135 Juta"), and voting ("Pemilu").

EVERYDAY LIFE. In this category, messages are not explicitly religious or social-political. For example, in the song "Nose Blemishes," Rhoma Irama urges women to stay away from men labeled *hidung belang,* a term for a philanderer. "Bachelor-hood" ("Bujangan") seems to extol the virtues of being a bachelor, until it advises that it is better to be married. The two categories in this section are as follows:

Finding one's way in life: youth ("Darah Muda"), fate ("Nasibku"), and freedom ("Bebas");

Show compassion for others: a blind man ("Buta"), the poor ("Tangan-tangan Hitam"), and a child ("Permata Bunda").

The songs described above illustrate the topics that Rhoma Irama used to instruct or advise his audience in matters of moral behavior, male-female relationships and love, society and politics, and everyday life. Rhoma Irama viewed dangdut as a tool for molding audiences, but as we shall see later, people responded to his music in a variety of ways. In the following section, I will describe his musical and performance style.

Musical style of Rhoma Irama

Rhoma Irama has referred to himself using the English term "amphibian," someone who has absorbed and adopted many diverse musical streams in his musical evolution. In the following section, I will discuss these streams in terms of his major musical influences: rock 'n' roll; *orkes Melayu* and *pop Indonesia*; Indian film music; and hard rock.

ROCK 'N' ROLL. In the early 1960s Rhoma Irama formed the bands Tornado and Gayhand, which covered the music of Paul Anka, Andy Williams, and the Beatles. He imitated the vocal qualities of Elvis Presley and Tom Jones, especially Elvis's rapid vibrato and Tom Jones's powerful vocal production (Rhoma Irama, pers. comm., 14 July 2005). Elvis's quivering vocal technique ("Kiss Me Quick") can be heard in Rhoma Irama's "Darah Muda" (Young Blood). Tom Jones's vocal technique of breaking off a phrase by shifting quickly into falsetto ("Delilah") is especially evident in songs including "Kelana" (Wandering) and "Cuma Kamu" (Only You).[8] He later composed his own songs based on formal harmonic structures of early rock 'n' roll, including "Joget" (Dance), "Darah Muda" (Young Blood), "Begadang" (Stay Up All Night), and "Bujangan" (Bachelorhood). In the first section of "Bujangan," shown in figure 4.3, he transforms a 12-bar blues pattern (each line corresponds to one measure) into an original composition. Additional rock elements include stop time, call and response, an electric guitar solo, and a lyrical theme reflecting a youthful attitude of freedom from responsibility. [◐]

The harmonic progression in the first verse (song A) is similar to a 12-bar blues, the form used extensively in early rock 'n' roll songs (for example, in well-known recordings of "Johnny B. Goode" [Chuck Berry, 1958], "Rock Around the Clock" [Bill Haley and His Comets, 1954], "Hound Dog" [Elvis Presley, 1956], and "Blue Suede Shoes" [Carl Perkins, 1955]). However, notable differences between the first verse in "Bujangan" and verses in the 12-bar blues-based

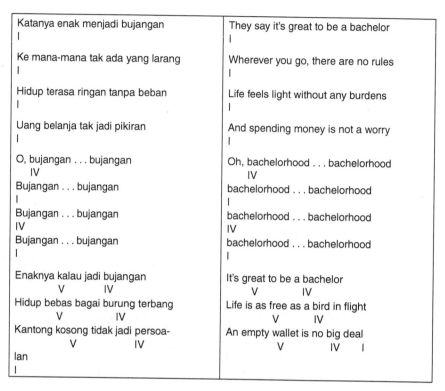

Katanya enak menjadi bujangan I	They say it's great to be a bachelor I
Ke mana-mana tak ada yang larang I	Wherever you go, there are no rules I
Hidup terasa ringan tanpa beban I	Life feels light without any burdens I
Uang belanja tak jadi pikiran I	And spending money is not a worry I

O, bujangan . . . bujangan
  IV
	Oh, bachelorhood . . . bachelorhood
	  IV

Bujangan . . . bujangan I	bachelorhood . . . bachelorhood I
Bujangan . . . bujangan IV	bachelorhood . . . bachelorhood IV
Bujangan . . . bujangan I	bachelorhood . . . bachelorhood I

Enaknya kalau jadi bujangan
    V   IV
	It's great to be a bachelor
	    V IV

Hidup bebas bagai burung terbang
    V   IV
	Life is as free as a bird in flight
	     V IV

Kantong kosong tidak jadi persoa-
     V   IV
	An empty wallet is no big deal
	     V IV I

lan I	

FIGURE 4.3 Lyrics and chords in "Bujangan" [courtesy of Rhoma Irama].

rock songs mentioned above include the harmony in bars 6 and 7 and an increase in the harmonic density in bars 9–12. The tempo is also much slower, as shown in a comparison with those tunes in figure 4.4.

Futher harmonic and temporal transformations of the blues form follow the first verse in "Bujangan." The harmonic progression accompanying the guitar solo in "Bujangan" approximates a 12-bar blues structure in cut time; its duration is half as long as the verse (indicated in figure 4.5). However, the progression does not return to the tonic in bar 12. The following 8-bar *suling* solo is also in cut time, and extends the subdominant harmony. The second verse (song B), however, returns to the temporal structure of the beginning verse, followed by a repeat of the *suling* solo. A transitional verse (song C) leads back to song A. These harmonic and temporal shifts extended and reshaped the blues-based rock form in unique ways.

ORKES MELAYU AND POP INDONESIA. Rhoma Irama sang *pop Melayu* and *pop Indonesia* songs in several bands during the late 1960s. He recorded "In the Motorized Pedicab" (Di Dalam Bemo), a duet with *pop Indonesia* singer Titing

Measures	1	2	3	4	5	6	7	8	9	10	11	12	Duration
Bujangan	I	I	I	I	IV	I	IV	I	V (IV)	V (IV)	V (IV)	I (V)	30"
Johnny B. Goode	I	I	I	I	IV	IV	I	I	V	V	I	I	20"
Rock around the Clock	I	I	I	I	IV	IV	I	I	V	V	I	I	15"
Hound Dog	I	I	I	I	IV	IV	I	I	V	IV	I	I	18"
Blue Suede Shoes	I	I	I	I	IV	IV	I	I	V	V	I	I	20"

FIGURE 4.4 Harmonic progressions in "Bujangan" and four early rock 'n' roll songs.

Yeni, accompanied by Zakaria's *pop Melayu* group Pancaran Muda (see chapter 3). He also recorded a few *pop Indonesia* songs, accompanied by the bands Zaenal Combo (directed by Zaenal Arifin) and Galaksi.

In 1968, Rhoma Irama joined Orkes Melayu Purnama, directed by Awab Haris and Abdullah (known collectively as Awab Abdullah). Awab and Abdullah introduced several key innovations to the *orkes Melayu* of the period. As stated in the previous chapter, they changed the drum from the single *gendang kapsul* to the double drum *gendang* (*gendang tamtam*). The band expanded the role of lead electric guitar (*gitar melodi*) within *orkes Melayu*. In an effort to approximate the sound of Indian film music, their *suling* player S. Shahab created the dynamic bamboo-flute style that would become characteristic of dangdut.

In O. M. Purnama, Rhoma Irama began singing duets with Elvy Sukaesih, who would eventually go on to a successful solo career as the "Queen of Dangdut" ("Ratu Dangdut"). He also recorded an album called "Ingkar Janji" (Broken Promise) in 1969 with Orkes Melayu Chandraleka, directed by Umar Alatas.

Rhoma Irama formed the band Soneta Group in 1970, and added the moniker "The Sound of Moslem's" [sic] on October 13, 1973. He named the band

measures	1	2	3	4	5	6	7	8	9	10	11	12	duration
guitar solo	I	I	I	I	IV	IV	IV	I	V	V	IV	IV	15"

measures	1	2	3	4	5	6	7	8	duration
suling solo	I	I	IV	I	I	I	IV	I	9"

measures	1	2	3	4	5	6	7	duration
verse B ("Wo!")	I	I	I	I	IV	V	I	18"

FIGURE 4.5 Three sections following the first verse in "Bujangan."

after the poetic form of the English sonnet, because he liked its formal qualities. The transnational flavor and innovative style of presentation of this new band introduced several important innovations to popular music.

In 1975, recording company Yukawi Indo Music released "Begadang" (Stay Up All Night), O.M. Soneta, volume 1, the first of 15 Soneta albums. It was actually half of an album; side A contained ten songs by O. M. Soneta, and side B contained ten songs by O.M. Sagita, featuring singers Megi [Meggy] Z. and Anna B.

The album "Begadang" featured songs with a strong Indian flavor, accompanied by electric guitar, mandolin, bass, *suling,* accordion, electric piano (Fender Rhodes), *gendang,* and tambourine. Rhoma Irama sang four songs, Elvy Sukaesih sang three songs, and they sang three playful and romantic songs together. The songs have a sexual undertone. "Until the Morning Hours" ("Sampai Pagi") is about a man and a woman dancing intensely and vigorously all night. It also presents a message that would become common in dangdut: "rather than dwelling on our huge debts piling up, it's better that we just enjoy ourselves" (*daripada mikirkan utang numpuk segudang/lebih baik kita senang-senang*). The emphasis on dancing bodies and material realities would become canonical in dangdut.

Although the sound of O.M. Soneta did not stray far from O.M. Purnama, the marketing and image of "Begadang" was different. The cassette cover suggests that this is something new. In figure 4.6, Oma Irama appears in a rock star pose: shirtless, adorned with jewelry, wearing tight pants, and holding a Fender Stratocaster electric guitar upright.

The song "Begadang" picked up on a popular saying of the time. The song actually urges listeners not to stay up all night, unless they absolutely need to (as workers), for they will become sick and useless to society. The workers could be young unemployed males who while away the evenings hanging out on the side of the road. According to Rhoma Irama, they could also be prostitutes who need money (*ada perlunya*) and whose bodies could become sick from the night breeze (*kena angin malam*) (pers. comm., 14 July 2005). Contradictions are a key feature of dangdut songs; for example, the first line of "Begadang" states "stay up all night, don't stay up all night" (*begadang, jangan begadang*). "Begadang" became an anthem for young males, who would stay up all night singing the humorous line "stay up all night, don't stay up all night!" [◉]

INDIAN FILM SONGS. Rhoma Irama perpetuated the strong link between Indian film songs and Indonesian popular music. These songs were credited to the original Indian composers on cassette covers of the period, as shown in figure 4.7.

FIGURE 4.6 Cassette cover, Rh(oma) Irama, "Begadang" v.1 (Yukawi Indo Music) [courtesy of Rhoma Irama].

Rhoma Irama departed from previous singers of Indian-inspired songs in three ways. First, he collaborated with singers on recordings. In these recordings, he sang in Hindi, and his counterparts sang in Indonesian. Second, he credited Indian singers as authors or co-authors. Third, he performed in India.

Indian film song	Rhoma Irama
Bol Radha Bol Film: Sangam (1964) Music: Shankar-Jaikishan Lyrics: Shailendra Singer: Mukesh	Kata Pujangga
Neele Gagan Ki Tale Film: Hamraaz (1967) Music: Ravi Lyrics: Saahir Ludhianvi Singer: Mahendra Kapoor	Purnama
Aane Se Uske Aaye Bahar Film: Jeene Ki Raah (1969) Music: Laxmikant Pyarelal Lyrics: Anand Bakshi Singer: Mohammad Rafi	Gulali
Mere Mitwa Mere Meet Re Film: Geet (1970) Music: Kalyanji-Anandji Lyrics: Sameer Singers: Mohammad Rafi, Lata Mangeshkar	Puja
Mere Mitwa Mere Meet Re Film: Geet (1970) Music: Kalyanji-Anandji Lyrics: Sameer Singers: Mohammad Rafi, Lata Mangeshkar	Wahai Pesona Singers: Rhoma Irama, Lata Mangeshkar
Main Tulsi Tere Aangan Ki Film: Main Tulsi Tere Aangan Ki (1978) Music: Laxmikant Pyarelal Lyrics: Anand Bakshi Singer: Lata Mangeshkar	Tak'kan Lagi
Do Naina Aur Ek Kahani Film: Masoom (1983) Music: R.D. Burman Lyrics: Gulzar Singer: Aarti Mukherjee	Dunia
Tujhse Naraz Nahin Zindagi Film: Masoom (1983) Music: R.D. Burman Lyrics: Gulzar Singer: Lata Mangeshkar	Hubungan
Saagar Kinare Film: Saagar (1985) Music: R.D. Burman Lyrics: Javed Akhtar Singer: Kishore Kumar, Lata Mangeshkar	Di Tepi Pantai Singers: Rhoma Irama, Lata Mangeshkar
Jeeye To Jeeye Kaise Film: Saajan (1991) Music: Nadeem-Shravan Lyrics: Sameer Singers: Kumar Sanu, Anuradha Paudwal, S.P.Balasubramaniam	Sifana
Bahut Pyaar Karta Hain Film: Saajan (1991) Music: Nadeem Shravan Lyrics: Sameer Singer: Lata Mangeshkar	Mardhatilla

FIGURE 4.7 Rhoma Irama compositions inspired by Hindi film songs.

While advocating for the Melayu basis of dangdut, his work acknowledged and publicized the links to Indian film music and singers.

HARD ROCK. Rhoma realized that the *orkes Melayu* framework could not compete with the rising popularity of rock: "They used outdated instruments, their lyrics were shabby and cheaply made. Their lyrics didn't instruct." (Rhoma Irama, pers. comm., 14 July 2005). Interestingly, the music that stimulated his most creative compositional activity was not Melayu but what he called "crazy music," or hard rock, specifically the music of English rock bands Deep Purple, Rolling Stones, and Led Zeppelin:

> Our music at that time was melodious [soft]. But hard rock was something foreign and noisy, and it could make people crazy. That was "crazy music."...At that time, our music was very polite. I was afraid our music orkes Melayu would be overtaken. So, I changed everything. Before, our instruments were acoustic: guitar, drum, accordion. But I had to compete with rock!" (Rhoma Irama, pers. comm., 14 July 2005)

INSTRUMENTS. In order to capture the sound of hard rock and maintain the elements of *orkes Melayu,* Rhoma had to have a much larger ensemble, and one that included electric instruments: electric guitar (two); mandolin; electric bass; trap drum set; timpani; tambourine and other percussion; backing vocals; winds (trumpet and saxophone); and electronic keyboard and organ (*farfisa*). In addition, the band featured *suling* and *gendang.*

SOUND. The high quality and loud volume of Rhoma Irama's sound system was designed to compete with those used by rock bands. It was reported that at a show in the Senayan stadium in Jakarta on New Year's Eve, 1977, Rhoma Irama's Soneta Group was backed by a 6,000-watt sound system, which was more powerful than the 4,000-watt system used by contemporary rock band God Bless ("Dua Orang Raja" 1978, 41).

Rhoma Irama was not the only musician to use the electric guitar, but he popularized the instrument to play fills and solo parts in the interlude sections of his songs. He modeled his sound on Richie Blackmore, the guitarist for Deep Purple: "If you look at my songs, you'll see the colors of Deep Purple. The color of my guitar playing is like the color of Richie [Blackmore's] melodious hard rock sound" (pers. comm., 21 August 2006). Rhoma Irama emulated Blackmore's distinctive string bending and vibrato (which Blackmore produced on a guitar with a scalloped fretboard). The screaming and melodious sound modeled after Blackmore's guitar timbre can be heard in the introduction and interlude of "Buta" (Blind). Rhoma Irama also modeled his solos on Blackmore's bluesy licks and phrasing.

He experimented with sound by using new electronic sound technologies and a wide variety of percussion. He stated that "our arrangements rumbled like distant thunder, like waves" (Surawijaya 1991, 57). His music picked up on trends in progressive rock of the 1970s. The Rick Wakeman–like synthesizer sound comes through in "Malapetaka (Catastrophe)," where the synthesizer imitates the rumbling sound of God's wrath as He wreaks havoc on earth. Other synthesizer effects used to create an "epic" sound include the lush washes of sound in "Pedih" (Pain), and the majestic lines in "Pengorbanan" (Sacrifice).

Sound qualities associated with progressive rock expanded Rhoma Irama's compositional palette. Hammond organ solos feature prominently in "Ghibah" and "Renungkan" (To Daydream). A vibraphone accompanies Rhoma Irama reciting a letter in "Surat Terakhir" (The Last Letter). A powerful driving flute solo, resembling the work of Jethro Tull's Ian Anderson, can be heard in "Sahabat" (Friend). And high-pitched backing vocals, another Deep Purple trademark, are heard in several songs including "Buta" (Blind), "Judi" (Gambling), and "Haram" (Forbidden).

EXTENDED FORMAL STRUCTURES. "Stop" appears in the film *Kemilau Cinta Dilangit Jingga* (Radiant Love in an Orange Sky; 1985, dir. Muchlis Raya). "Stop" evokes the type of music played by progressive rock bands of the late 1970s and early to mid-1980s: (a) extended formal structure developed into suites with multiple sections; (b) uneven phrase lengths; (c) irregular meters; and (d) arrangements that feature different instruments in each section. The English-language title of the song ("Stop") signifies Western influence. However, the song shows the highly adaptable amphibian-like nature of Rhoma Irama's compositions, skillfully blending genres of Indian, Melayu, Middle Eastern, and American/English rock music. The rhythmic framework for the piece is a 6/8 meter characterized by metrical contrast or hemiola (*kuraca*).[9] Phrase lengths in several sections are uneven, and include phrases of 7, 5, and 4½ measures. The formal structure of "Stop" is shown in figure 4.8. [◐]

The piece has three song sections: A, B, and A´ (a variation of A). Each section has roughly the same number of measures (28, 26, and 24 measures, respectively). The piece begins with a long 33-measure segment made up of three phrases (4 + 16 + 13 measures). This segment returns in a 32-measure variation, made up of two phrases (12 + 20 measures), and sets up song section B. The return of the A section (A') follows immediately after the B section, without the intervening material.

section	Intro	Bols 1	Interlude 1	A	Bols 2
measures	4	16	13	28	12
phrase lengths (measures)		4+4+4+4	8+5	8+12+8	3+3+3+3
vocal phrases and instrumental sections		abab	suling/keyboard + sax/trpt	cdc	efef
time (video)	0.25	0.34	1.10	1.40	2.45

section	Interlude 2	B	A'
measures	20	26	24
phrase lengths (measures)	8+7+5	4½+5+4½+12	8+12+4
vocal phrases and instrumental sections	suling/keyboard +guitar+sax/trpt	gh-[sax/trp]-gh-it	cd'c'
time (video)	3.12	3.58	4.58

FIGURE 4.8 Formal structure of "Stop."

The piece incorporates two sections of Indian drum syllables, which I have labeled "Bols 1" and "Bols 2" after the Indian music term for drum syllables. In both of these sections, an instrumental phrase precedes the chanting of "bols." However, the two "bols" sections have different internal structures, syllables, and rhythmic emphases. The "Bols 1" section ("sa-da-pak") is made up of 16 measures, divided into four phrases of 4 measures each (abab). The "Bols 2" section ("trang-dang-dung-dang") is made up of 12 measures, divided into four phrases of three measures each (efef).

The piece has two interludes, Interlude 1 and Interlude 2. In Interlude 1, there are two phrases of eight and five measures, respectively. Interlude 2 includes these two phrases, as well as a middle phrase of seven measures. The seven-measure middle phrase alludes to the rich instrumental texture of Middle Eastern orchestral ensembles.

The musical composition paints the text. Musical phrases seem to clash abruptly against one another, representing the force of the command "Stop." The song combines didactic lyrics ("Stop!"), jarring musical rhythms, a commanding performance style, bright lighting, and loud amplification to express the message to "stop" fighting.

COSTUMES AND SETS. In the early 1970s, Rhoma Irama appropriated an image associated with American and British hard rock musicians: long hair, facial hair, tight pants, open shirt collar, and platform shoes. The band Soneta wore matching costumes in concert. After taking the pilgrimage to Mecca, Rhoma Irama and his band began to wear white Islamic robes, headdresses, and sandals on stage. Rhoma Irama's stage outfits reflected his strong commitment to Islam.

Performance sets were equally spectacular, as shown in the film performance of "Stop." The stage was illuminated by bright, flashing, multicolored lights. Elaborate sculptures appeared at the back of the stage. Smoke billowed out of smoke machines and fireworks exploded onstage. Messages were written in flashing lights. In the film performance of "Stop," stage hands released white birds onstage to symbolize the theme of peace in the song.

PERFORMANCE STYLE—ENERGY. Rhoma Irama's performance style in the 1970s was designed to compete with Indonesian rock groups of the period:

> Rock was identical with movement. Rockers would cut rabbits and drink their blood [referring to Mickey Bentoel from the band Bentoel Malang]. That was the rock style. They would hang from the stage [referring to Ucok Harahap from the band AKA Band Surabaya]. Crazy! (pers. comm., 14 July 2005)

He performed choreographies with members of Soneta, as seen in the film performance of "Stop." In communicating his message, Rhoma Irama often mimed the song lyrics; for example, in "Stop," he raised his hand to emphasize the word "Stop."

PERFORMANCE SPACE. As Rhoma Irama's popularity grew, he performed live concerts in stadiums and open-air town squares. At these concerts, the mostly male audience members milled around, hung out with friends, and danced themselves into "a state where they [were] unaware of their surroundings, free of self-consciousness and inhibition" (Yampolsky 1991, 1). A description of a concert in 1976 illustrates the scene at a public concert:

> On July 2 and 3 [1976], at the large public fairgrounds in Tegallega Bandung, Oma Irama and his band Soneta performed. As it turned out, Oma's fans in Bandung were explosive. In fact, Oma himself said that these fans were the most energetic he had ever seen. I witnessed firsthand the masses of people jam-packed into the fairgrounds to the point that the fences surrounding the grounds were torn down. The road around the field was so congested that cars could not pass. From babies to grandmothers, they crowded in to get a look at Oma. A small pool, originally slated to serve as a barrier between the stage and the audience, was invaded by people and transformed into a dance arena. According to reports, many fainted and broke their arms. When some fans got out of control, Oma reminded them that his goal was to spread the word of Islam. If they didn't want to listen, they were being anti-Islam. That shut them up.

This is Oma's skill: in addition to being able to gather together
thousands of people, he can also control them." (Navis 1976, 16–17)

Like his song texts, Rhoma Irama's music and performance style did not simply
articulate the people's preexisting desires and aspirations. He combined various musical genres to create something new, exciting, and "crazy." The loud
music, fantastic sets, and elaborate costumes used in stadium concerts were
entirely new. Rhoma Irama's celebrity image, mediated through film, radio,
television, and popular print media, was constructed "for the *rakyat*," as
described in the next section.

Rhoma Irama's Fans

Historian William Frederick writes that "Indonesia's first true entertainment
superstars" were produced in the late 1970s in dangdut (1982, 103). Frederick
makes the point that capital (to produce music recordings as well as film), new
technology, and mass distribution networks contributed to the development of
dangdut superstars.[10] I will use the term "celebrity" (rather than its counterpart
"superstar") to refer to the confluence of economics, technology, and mass
circulation networks in the social construction of fame. A celebrity as a text
refers to the celebrity's visual image as well as "all elements of the complex con-
stellation of visual, verbal, and aural signs that circulate in society and constitute the celebrity's recognition value" (Coombe 1992, 1280 n5).

In Indonesia, the intimate yet highly mediated relationships between
celebrities and audience were constructed through tabloid stories and interviews that conflated the public and private lives of celebrities. Dangdut celebrities were referred to not simply as musicians or performers, but as *artis*
("entertainment personalities"). A dangdut celebrity's visual image and personality were just as important as his or her musical product, talent, or
performance style.

Film and television were central to the construction of celebrity in dangdut. The relationship between dangdut and film was important, as films were
marketed together with popular music recordings. A subgenre of "dangdut
films" (*filem dangdut*) was created in the late 1970s (Mousli 1980c; Des 1977).
Through the lens of the camera, viewers entered into an intimate (yet ultimately
distant) relationship with dangdut stars. Commercial media institutions of
music recording, radio, television, and popular print media helped to construct
"an illusion of intimacy" between the celebrity and an anonymous audience
(Newbury 2000). For example, in films and television, the dangdut star often
played himself or herself; audiences reacted to dangdut stars as people, and not
simply as actors or characters.

Rhoma Irama's dangdut films from the late 1970s to the early 1990s (more than 20) exemplify these processes of identification. The films narrate his personal relationships with lovers, family, band members, and ruthless music executives. He is shown composing music, being interviewed at press conferences, and performing in concerts. He is always depicted as the hero. Onstage, baring his chest in tight-fitting outfits, he emerges heroically from the haze of smoke machines and flashing lights. Crowd scenes and applause are edited into concert footage to emphasize his heroic stature.

By watching films, according to Rhoma Irama, his fans could have a more direct personal experience with him, as compared to his concerts, where they were separated by barriers and elevated stages. Rhoma Irama's dangdut films depict a "cross-class success story in which the underdog wins against all odds" (Frederick 1982, 115). In many of his films, Rhoma Irama plays a poor struggling musician who is misunderstood by society at large. His films presented a fantasy of an individual triumphing over adversity through hard work and perseverance. For example, the film *Oma Irama Penasaran* (Curious, 1976, dir. A. Harris) paints a picture of an underclass boy who falls in love with a girl whose family is rich. But what is more important, as stated in one review of the film, is the way in which Rhoma Irama tells his own story, as someone from the *rakyat* himself (*kelompok jelata*). The critic writes: "Through the narrative of this film, [Rhoma Irama] represents a victory for the downtrodden" ("Satria berdakwah" 1984).

Yet, he was clearly not like the mass audiences that he addressed in films and music. Unlike most dangdut musicians, he came from a relatively well-to-do family. Onstage, he dressed in clean and sparkling white outfits, including Muslim robes. He wore larger-than-life costumes in promotional materials. He lived in an expensive home and drove expensive cars. He was not simply another dangdut singer; he was a celebrity. And his celebrity increased the distance between him and his fans.

Not only in films did he triumph. Offstage, he wielded social and economic power. Gossip columns linked him to numerous romantic affairs, which most men admired but could never carry out on their own. He spoke out against government censors of the Suharto regime, and seemed to actually benefit from bans against broadcasts of his songs on television and radio. He spoke with religious authority and became involved in political campaigns.

Given that Rhoma Irama's sound was so unusual, foreign, and "crazy," why did fans respond so positively? In fact, male fans had mixed reactions to Rhoma Irama's work. Some felt empowered through their identification with the heroic figure represented by Rhoma on stage and in films. Some desired to see him do things in the fantasy world of film that they could not; for example, to have romantic affairs with multiple women, and to speak out against government corruption. Others were critical of the notion that his music and films represented the masses. His songs and films presented clear, unambiguous narratives of right and wrong, but life for people in socially and economically marginalized positions did not operate in the same way. The triumph of good over evil through hard work did not represent the reality of the majority of his fans.

Rhoma Irama represented an image that people could admire, but they had no desire to be like him. Composer Endang Kurnia, one of his musical disciples, stated:

> His male fans did not identify with him, as in "He's just like me. I can be like that." He was not the common man. He was an extraordinarily uncommon man. But we identified with him as "wow, that's amazing that someone can do such extraordinary things. I want to be part of him." (Endang Kurnia, pers. comm., 15 November 2006)

Although fans desired to participate in his image and behavior, they discerned the reality behind the image and adopted a more cynical attitude by separating the life and work of the celebrity. Female fans that I interviewed were able to separate Rhoma Irama's personal views about women from his love songs. They appreciated his clever melodies and his poetic lyrics, but they described his religious views as rigid (*fanatik*).

From Rhoma Irama's point of view, people did not desire to see social reality reflected in their music or in their films. Happy endings were largely a fantasy, as he himself stated, in a discussion about French film:

> Unhappy endings in film, to tell you the truth, for Indonesians, there is something unsettling about them. Our audiences cannot tolerate an unhappy ending for the main character. It's like [French actor] Alain Delon, who dies at the end of a film. For our audiences, no matter how great the film, if the hero dies, it's not satisfying. They're disappointed. (quoted in Yudhistira and Pudyastuti 1987, 105)

Rhoma Irama used dangdut as the medium to create happy endings for people. He perceived *orkes Melayu* songs as pessimistic, full of suffering and sorrow. He countered these types of narratives with optimistic messages. In concerts, he depicted himself as a leader, calming the people down, inserting religious messages, and expressing commands. In films, he portrayed a character who worked hard to achieve and always obtained successful results. He stood up to power, whether it was a village bully or a sleazy music producer. The lifestyle he portrayed on film and in the popular print media was a fantasy.

These images and meanings contrasted sharply with the highly specific ways in which his audience was constructed in popular print media, as described in the next section. These stories help to explain how Indonesian middle and upper classes inferred that the culture of the underclass (exemplified by dangdut and the popular music of the streets) was aesthetically worthless. The writing of these stories in the mid-1970s coincides with the formation of middle classes in Indonesia. These images and meanings helped to distinguish class boundaries, especially between the emergent middle classes and the underclass.

Dangdut *as* the *Rakyat*

In newspaper and magazine articles of the 1970s, which most dangdut fans would never read, sandwiched between advertisements for products that most dangdut fans would never consume—expensive alcohol, luxury hotels, air-conditioned cars, golf, and hi-fidelity electronic equipment—were stories about dangdut singers, concerts, recordings, and fans themselves (Weintraub 2006). The consumers of these magazine and newspaper articles were not the fans of the music; rather, dangdut stood for the masses "out there." In these stories, middle-class and elite readers of newspapers and magazines positioned themselves in relation to dangdut's underclass audience. The masses that constituted dangdut's audience were generally imagined in a negative light as uneducated, ignorant, and irrational. They were viewed as incapable of acting together in an organized way; rather than acting, they were acted upon as objects that could be read about in popular print media. When they did become active, at concerts for example, they were accused of being unruly and violent.

In the 1970s, the music magazine *Aktuil* featured articles on dangdut as part of its broader reportage on Indonesian popular music. *Aktuil*, as described on the magazine's credits page, was a "magazine for youth as well as those who are young at heart." Published from 1967 to 1981, the magazine featured stories about bands, interviews with musicians, concert reviews, and advertisements for jeans, sunglasses, and other accessories of a modern lifestyle. Each issue included a full-color foldout poster of Western bands, including Led Zeppelin and Deep Purple, as well as Indonesian bands, including God Bless and Giant Step.

Aktuil had a love-hate relationship with dangdut in its depiction of singers and audiences. The rock contingent, most of them teenagers (*remaja*) from middle-class and elite families, identified symbolically with dangdut's disruption of proper social behavior. For example, dangdut fans were depicted as explosive, raging, and wild (*membludag*), and fans were portrayed as belonging to "dangdut gangs" (*komplotan dangdut*).[11] But the rock audience could not quite accept the Indian-inflected vocal ornamentation of dangdut's singers, the garishness of dangdut's fashions, or its concert etiquette. Female dangdut singers were ridiculed for wearing short skirts and high boots that stretched up to the knees. Singers "screamed" songs (*meneriakkan lagu*) rather than sang them. For rock audiences of the period, music was something that should be listened to and appreciated for its sound. Describing the audience at one dangdut concert, the author wrote: "The scene was truly wild...it was such a shame that the audience couldn't just sit and enjoy the show and appeared so unruly" (Miloer 1978, 53). Unfortunately, the author missed the point that dangdut audiences moved their bodies during a show rather than listening intently to the music and applauding after each song.

During the 1970s, dangdut was broadcast on television, but it was portrayed as a subcategory of *pop Indonesia* and not seriously considered in its own right (Soemardi 1979, 40). The first television programs specifically geared to dangdut did not feature popular dangdut artists, but rather university-based dangdut groups from the prestigious University of Indonesia and Gadjah Mada University. Although dangdut exerted a notable presence in middle-class and elite media, the voices of dangdut artists and audiences were absent. On television, they were replaced by university students performing humorous parodies of dangdut lyrics and dangdut presentational styles (Simatupang 1996, 35, 80–81).[12] These university versions of dangdut, although humorous and irreverent, were made by an elite class of performers which had access to televisual representation.

Dangdut was placed in relation to other competing genres of popular music in order to make distinctions among different classes of people. During the early 1970s, dangdut was often represented in the pages of *Aktuil* and other popular print media of the period as backward and unsophisticated (*kampungan*).[13] In contrast to its *kampungan* associations, rock and pop music were progressive (*gedongan*, based on the word for "building"). Dangdut was the music of the streets, roadside food stalls, neighborhoods, and open spaces, as opposed to rock and pop (played in buildings: nightclubs, hotels, and bars) (Ramedhan 1977). These spatial differences are reflected in the socioeconomic terms *kampungan* and *gedongan*. The *gedongan* group, including members of the highly successful rock bands Panbers and God Bless, was made up of middle- and upper-class youth. They could afford to buy the latest musical instruments and recordings from the United States and England. They were connected.

Popular press articles helped to define notions of *kampungan*—"backward," represented by people who listen to dangdut—and *gedongan*—"progressive," as in those who listen to other kinds of music, namely, *pop Indonesia* and rock. In the pages of popular print media, dangdut became a social text for assigning all sorts of meanings upon which elites could register their own class position. Despite the fact that elites were not the target audience of the music, dangdut became both a sign and a target of essentialist elite constructions of Indonesian identity.

Dangdut's relationship with *pop Indonesia* was similarly class-inflected. News magazine *Tempo* labeled 1979 "the year of dangdut" and published the first historical account of the genre in a cover story entitled "The Day of the Dang Duts" (5 May 1979). The feature article focused on the rising popularity of dangdut, which had begun to challenge the dominance of *pop Indonesia*, a genre of music largely oriented toward "the middle class and above" (*kelas menengah ke atas*). As a result, a few pop singers began crossing over to dangdut to capitalize on its market success. Popular print media emphasized the schism between *pop Indonesia* and dangdut, whose audience was "the middle class and below" (*kelas menengah ke bawah*). Pop singers distinguished themselves by their inability to sing dangdut, as if it were a foreign style.[14]

Some producers believed that the popularity of dangdut was rising because the popularity of *pop Indonesia* was falling. But pop stars had different opinions on the matter. Titiek Puspa asserted that pop singers only sang dangdut because producers wanted them to. She noted that it would be much more difficult for a dangdut singer to sing pop, than for a pop singer to sing dangdut. For Titiek Puspa, dangdut required a different kind of feeling (*penjiwaan*). Chrisye loved dangdut, but did not feel he could sing it. Franky of Franky and Jane was also not interested and remained loyal to *lagu country* (American-inspired folk songs). Bob Tutupoly and Grace Simon (who sang a dangdut song in 1973 that did not become popular) thought that dangdut was fine, but was just having its day (like they had their day). For Melky Goeslaw, being a Christian made it hard to sing dangdut because its melodies came from India and its rhythms and vocal style were close to Arabic-influenced forms like *gambus* and *qasidah*, especially the ornaments in the vocal part. Jazz artist Jack Lesmana felt that pop singers could not possibly be successful in the dangdut style, so it was solely a matter of a desire to be commercially successful that drove their participation in dangdut. Lesmana is quoted as saying that dangdut did not compare favorably to jazz: "Why eat *gado-gado* [Indonesian mixed vegetables] when you can have steak?" (Harsono 1988, 2).

At this juncture, dangdut was stylistically different from *pop Indonesia*. In contrast to *pop Indonesia* songs, which were generally composed in the 32-bar American song form (AABA), dangdut songs had variable lengths. Dangdut songs generally had an instrumental intro, two different verses (song A and song B), an interlude, and an outro. Refrains could be added. Dangdut song forms were often 48–52 bars, including intro, verses, interludes, fills, and outro. As shown earlier in this chapter, Rhoma Irama's song forms were even longer.

In general, however, commentary by pop stars tended to focus on dangdut as a commodity form, and they downplayed its aesthetic and social value. For pop singers, dangdut was even more foreign to them than American music. Further, dangdut did not signify prestige or progress. As musician Remy Sylado observed, "Dangdut always looks to the past. With pop, its orientation is to America."[15]

Dangdut as a named genre has been a commercial music since its inception in the 1970s, part of an industry that involved "big bosses" (*tauke*), tastemakers, and commercial media tie-ins (Frederick 1982, 125). Clearly, dangdut was a middle-class and elite concern, demonstrated by the number of articles in popular print media, as early as the 1970s. The middle and upper classes were missing in these articles as the objects of representation, but they were in fact the ones producing and consuming these commentaries.

Conclusion

Dangdut invigorated the body of stories about the *rakyat*. In popular print media and artist's discourses of self-promotion, dangdut "is" the blood, soul, and voice of the *rakyat*. In a different vein, dangdut "as" the *rakyat* helped middle classses and elites establish and solidify their own social class positions. Rhoma Irama created music "for" the *rakyat*. In the transition from *orkes Melayu* to dangdut, Rhoma Irama relied on foreign or "crazy" music, a fantastic performance style, elaborate costumes, and changing forms of media and technology to address the *rakyat*. Drawing on *orkes Melayu*, rock 'n' roll, Indian film music, and hard rock, he used dangdut as an instrument for change:

> An artist is the leader of society. If the leader fails, the people will fail too. We have to be responsible with music because music can make people good, and it can make people bad. Out of 100 people, if one of them changes his ways, then that's more than enough (Rhoma Irama, pers. comm., 14 July 2005).

In 1980, Rhoma Irama was the most powerful individual artist in the Indonesian music industry. He had created his own band to play only his music (and band members were not allowed to play with other bands). He bought the struggling recording company Yukawi and created his own label and distribution company (Soneta Records) in order to exert greater control over the production and distribution of his products. Films designed around his music gave him the opportunity to expand his business laterally. Rhoma Irama's success in the entertainment industry stimulated the development of new musical forms and meanings in dangdut, the emergence of new stars, and the expansion of the dangdut industry, as we will see in chapter 5.

NOTES

1. In a classic formulation, Raymond Williams writes that there are no masses, only ways of seeing people as masses (1961, 289).

2. Around 1970, the governor of Jakarta, Ali Sadikin, carried out a campaign to transform Planet Senen into an economically vibrant area, a plan that displaced many urban dwellers.

3. Managing editor Remy Sylado claimed that the word "dangdut" first appeared in print in *Aktuil* in 1972 (Pioquinto 1998, 77). But, after reviewing all of the issues for that year, I was not able to find the citation. The first published reference that I have found is in *Tempo* in 1972: "Melayu songs, which often blend Middle Eastern songs with 'Dang-Ding-Dut' India, have an important role to play in Indonesian popular music" ("Dunia Ellya Khadam" 1972, 36).

4. Rhoma Irama quoted in "Berjuang dalam Goyang" 1989, 17. Other derogatory names used to describe the music (and based on the sounds produced on the *gendang*) include *madun,* and *bangdun* (Elvy Sukaesih, pers. comm., 20 July 2005).

5. Rhoma Irama has reportedly composed over 500 dangdut songs (Deddy Irama, pers. comm., 12 October 2006).

6. Most of the songs in the sample were sung by Rhoma Irama, except for those composed for female voices or as male-female duets. Female singers include Indonesian singers Elvy Sukaesih, Rita Sugiarto, Nur Halimah, Riza Umami, and the legendary Indian film song playback singer Lata Mangeshkar. I have not included songs by other composers that Rhoma Irama recorded. Compositions include jointly authored songs credited to Rhoma Irama and Indian film composers.

7. Ariel Heryanto, interviewed in Barraud 2003. News magazine *Tempo* reported that Rhoma Irama was banned from TVRI in 1977 because of a contractual dispute with recording company Remaco, which had strong ties to TVRI's dangdut program "Mana Suka" ("Hak Asasi Dilarang" 1977, 17). Rhoma Irama was told that the reason for the banning was due to the use of the *gendang,* but he was not told why ("Dua Orang Raja" 1978, 42).

8. This technique, called a "cry break" among working-class "country" music singers in Texas, is "iconic of the ravaged voice of a character textually narrated explicitly or implicitly as 'crying'" (Feld et al. 2008, 74).

9. I have not been able to trace the origin of the term *kuraca;* initially, I assumed this was from the Spanish dance *guaracha,* or the song "La Kukaracha," but the Indonesian rhythm bears no resemblence to these forms. It could be a Spanish-sounding name that Indonesian musicians applied to a 6/8 rhythm; similarly, perhaps musicians chose the Indian-sounding term *chalte* for the Indian-sounding rhythm described in chapter 3.

10. "By 'superstar' I mean not only an important and recognized figure, but one who is clearly significant beyond a relatively small economic or intellectual elite, to a genuinely mass audience. There have been entertainment 'stars' for many years in Indonesia, but it is only relatively recently that superstars have become a possibility from the point of view of economics and technology" (Frederick 1982, 103 n3).

11. The descriptions cited in this paragraph are all from Miloer 1978, 53.

12. Humor can be seen in the names of bands, which included "The Morality Orchestra of the Petromak Lantern Emission Ray" ("Orkes Moral Pancaran Sinar Petromak," based at the University of Indonesia); "The Rocking Horse" ("Jaran Goyang," based at the Fakultas Teknik, Gadjah Mada University); and "The Ugly but Stylish Student Band" ("Orkes Mahasiswa *Jelek tapi Setil*" [or "OM Jetset"], based at the Psychology Department, Gadjah Mada University), "Dangdut, Setelah Halal di TV-RI" 1979, 51; see also Simatupang 1996, 35–36.

13. A *kampung* is a neighborhood that can be located in a village, town, or city. However, *kampungan* does not simply describe a person's living space, but it connotes inferiority, backwardness, nonrefinement, lack of formal education, and a low position in a hierarchical ordering of social classes.

14. The following data are from "Dangdut, Setelah Halal di TV-RI" 1979.

15. Surawijaya 1991, 53 (see also Mousli 1980a, 37 on this point).

Chapter 5

"Suffering" and "Surrender": Dangdut and the Spectacle of Excess

> There is a woman, and she lives in a small house in a neighborhood with lots of big expensive houses. She is a divorced mother, and life is hard. Why don't others see her? Is this some kind of punishment for something she did in the past? Or is this God's plan to put her here, as an example, to inspire rich people to give alms to the poor? That's the topic of a dangdut song. (Elvy Sukaesih, pers. comm., 20 July 2005)

In the mid- to late 1970s, following the commercial success of Rhoma Irama's music recordings, live concerts, and films, a cultural industry around dangdut began to take shape. Catapulted by the portable, inexpensive, and easily pirated medium of the audiocassette, the sound of dangdut traveled far beyond its point of production in Jakarta and Surakarta recording studios.[1] A genre of "dangdut films" created a visual culture around dangdut and made stars out of singers Rhoma Irama, Elvy Sukaesih, and A. Rafiq. Dangdut grabbed a large market share of music sales in relation to other popular genres (including *pop Indonesia, langgam, kroncong,* and Western popular music). The genre's popularity grew, as did the number of singers and spin-off styles.

Song lyrics in this era of production centered on male-female relationships and everyday social issues, but, unlike Rhoma Irama's songs, they rarely expressed didactic or religious messages. Rather, a large number of texts portrayed emotional pain and suffering, usually a result of failed relationships, as well as economic hardship, social injustice, and dashed hopes. Instead of offering advice about how to fix one's problems, or countering difficulties with a higher moral power (as in songs by Rhoma Irama), the lyrics reflected fatalism, acceptance, and idealism.

In conjunction with these emotionally gut-wrenching texts, dangdut became the music of dance and pleasure in nightclubs, bars, and discos. The combination of emotionally powerful lyrics, upbeat dancing, and a camp performance style captivated audiences and baffled critics. It seemed contradictory to commentators that the songs of this period would memorialize people's emotional and material suffering, while consumers simultaneously tried to "forget themselves" (*melupakan diri*) within the contexts of dance and pleasure. This apparent contradiction was viewed as a kind of "pressure-valve" mechanism in which people released the stiffness of a hard day's work through a night of pleasure. For example, a magazine report describes members of the audience at a dangdut event wearing "t-shirts and thong sandals looking to release some steam from their stiff muscles" (Mandayun 1991, 65). As I will show, this binary relationship of pain released by pleasure does not adequately explain popular music production and consumption. The texts were not simply melancholy, nor was dance simply a space for pleasure.[2]

Further, according to government cultural officials, dangdut texts of this period were vulgar or "pornographic" (*porno*) and "weepy" (*cengeng*). Vulgar lyrics allegedly led to sexual excess, while weepy lyrics led to indolence. These critical positions did not allow space for the multiplicity of meanings embedded in dangdut's texts that exceeded these simple definitions. Audiences were much more creative in their interpretations, as I will show in this chapter.

I will argue that dangdut represents a linguistic and visual "spectacle of excess," a phrase originally used by Roland Barthes to describe the public display and meaning of "Suffering, Defeat, and Justice" in wrestling (Barthes 1972 [1957]). Wrestling, like dangdut, portrays for its audiences "emotion without reserve." Its "excessive gestures [are] exploited to the limit of their meaning." Signified to its furthest capabilities, nothing is left but "a light without shadow." Similarly, dangdut tests the boundaries of what can be expressed and what stories can be told in the public sphere. Performers use a heightened sense of theatricality, costumes, and movements to express emotions. Like the spectacle of wrestling, dangdut contains images "filled to the brim" and juxtaposes seemingly contradictory elements, notably texts about emotional pain and contexts of bodily pleasure. In wrestling, "there is no symbol, no allusion, [and] everything is presented exhaustively." However, rather than following meaning to a logical conclusion, dangdut exposes possibilities and poses questions, as indicated by the quote that begins this chapter. In contrast to Barthes's "light without shadows," dangdut songs are full of shadows, grey areas, and multiple interpretations.

In the analysis that follows, I situate dangdut's highly unstable meanings in commercial practices of production and consumption. During the 1980s, producers, musicians, arrangers, and singers pushed the limits of commercial accessibility, constantly stretching out and innovating to find new audiences. Yet the consumption of those products was highly unpredictable. Audiences produced a variety of meanings based on inside jokes, in-group references, and intertextual relationships among songs. The explosion of new styles, seemingly contradictory texts and music, and polysemy generated the pleasure and commercial popularity of dangdut.

Commercial Music and the Expansion of Dangdut Styles

Only by placing music sound, text, and performance in its commercial context, can we understand the symbolic meaning of dangdut in this period. Dangdut fulfilled a niche as the main form of mass-mediated popular dance music of the late 1970s and early to mid-1980s. As the market for dangdut grew, production teams created spinoff genres including "sweet dangdut," "pop dangdut," "rock dangdut," and "Mandarin dangdut," among others. Pop singers crossed over, including "pure rock" performer Achmad Albar, who had been a member of the band God Bless, and pop singer Titi Qadarsih, who had previously been "anti-dangdut" ("Dangdut, Setelah Halal" 1979, 52).

In the following section, I will discuss the most dominant groups and artists of this period: two prominent production teams (Tarantula and Radesa) and three celebrated singers (Camelia Malik, Mansyur S., and Elvy Sukaesih).

Pop Dangdut: Tarantula

> We tried to measure and fit people's tastes, and that's not easy. To make one song that people will remember and enjoy, that's tough. Even though people might think that song is cheap, like a peanut."
> (Camelia Malik, pers. comm., 18 July 2005)[3]

In the mid-1970s, Reynold Panggabean and his wife Camelia Malik formed a band called Tarantula. Composer Reynold Panggabean was a rock musician and studio wizard who had honed his skills in the rock band The Mercy's. Camelia Malik, the daughter of film director Jamaludin Malik, was an emerging actress who had already appeared in several films. As the former wife of drummer Fuad Hassan of God Bless, she had also been involved in the rock scene several years earlier. Tarantula was originally conceived as a playful experiment to merge the instrumentation of pop and rock (guitar, bass, drums, and keyboard) with dangdut (*gendang, suling,* mandolin, tambourine) (Camelia Malik, pers. comm., 18 July 2005). The music they produced was unabashedly

commercial. Camelia Malik discussed the band's first hit "Colak-colek"
(Touching Lightly) (1977):

> Of course, a composer is inspired to write a good song. But for a
> recording to sell, we have to find its commercial value. We knew that
> "Colak-colek" would be a hit because the previous [dangdut] hit was
> [the similarly titled] "Cubit-cubitan" [Pinching Each Other]. After that
> we made "Raba-raba" [Groping] (Camelia Malik, pers. comm., 18 July
> 2005).

The band continued in this commercial vein, releasing a string of hits based on
the same linguistic formula: "Ceplas-ceplos" (Speaking Frankly), "Kecup-kecup"
(Kissing), "Kasak-kusuk" (Whispering), "Asyik-asyik" (Exciting), "Sayang-sayang"
(Loving), "Kedap-kedip" (Winking), and "Manis-manis" (Sweetness). As demonstrated by these song titles, Tarantula song lyrics reflected a playful, teasing, and
flirtatious quality.

The band aimed to produce commercial music for a growing youth market
of consumers. In the song lyrics for "Colak-colek," sex is treated as a "hobby"
(hobi). Sexual freedom was something new ("that's what kids are doing nowa-
days"), and not something that could be put off until marriage (they desired to
"have everything" at once). Sex, like money, was something that could be pos-
sessed. The last line was based on a popular phrase of the era: "if you don't have
money, you won't get love." This phrase can be interpreted as the exchange of
money for sex, as in "no money, no honey" (Murray 1991). However, the song
text refers not only to the commodification of sex, but also love and affection
(sayang). The lyrics comment on the changing social conditions of urban youth
during the era of the late 1970s, in which social relationships were becoming
increasingly dependent on money (see figure 5.1).

Colak-colek colak-colek, Hobi anak sekarang, Colak-colek colak-colek, Usil bukan kepalang.	Colak-colek colak-colek, that's what kids are doing nowadays, Colak-colek colak-colek, they just can't stop touching each other.
Kalau ada maunya, Kalau ada maunya, Semua harus ada, Tak bisa ditunda.	If you have the desire, If you have the desire, You have to have everything, Can't put it off 'til later.
[repeat verse]	[repeat verse]
Memang aneh dunia jaman sekarang, Banyak orang bilang, Tak ada uang tak sayang.	This is a strange time, Lots of people say, No money, no love.

FIGURE 5.1 "Colak-colek" (Touching Lightly) [courtesy of Reynold Panggabean].

The song "Colak-colek" heralded a new era of pop dangdut that merged short catchy melodic phrases, salsa, rock, and disco, with dangdut rhythms (based on Indian and Middle Eastern patterns) and instruments (*suling* and *gendang*). In addition, the group added the Indian sitar, an instrument that connoted both Indian film music and English rock of the 1960s. []

By taking advantage of new technology within the recording studio, Tarantula introduced a new studio practice in which the arrangement for each verse is different for each section. Previous songs had not used this additive technique, and it became a trademark of the Tarantula style.[4] In the following song guide (see figure 5.2), an instrument is added (bold) or subtracted (italics) for each repetition of song A and song C.

Several elements in this arrangement signified the sound of *pop Indonesia* and appealed to a youth audience, especially among the rising middle and

section (measures)	Intro (8+3)	
melody (measures)	acoustic guitar solo (8)	break (3)
lyric	--	--
arrangement	keyboard (electric piano-blok) acoustic guitar, bass, tabla, bongo, tambourine	acoustic guitar and drums
time	0.00	0.31

section (measures)	A (8+2)	
melody (measures)	vocal (8)	fill (2)
lyric	Colak-Colek	--
arrangement	keyboard (electric piano-blok), **organ**, acoustic guitar, **electric guitar**, bass, tabla, bongo, tambourine	**synth**
time	0.18	0.32

section (measures)	Interlude I (8+8)	
melody (measures)	electric guitar solo (8)	suling solo (8)
lyric	--	--
arrangement	keyboard (electric piano-blok), organ, *acoustic guitar*, electric guitar, bass, tabla, bongo, tambourine, synth	**suling**, *synth*
time	0.35	0.48

FIGURE 5.2 Song guide "Colak-colek."

section (measures)	B (8+2)	
melody (measures)	vocal (8)	suling (2)
lyric	Kalau ada maunya	--
arrangement	keyboard (electric piano-blok), organ, electric guitar, bass, tabla, bongo, tambourine	**suling**
time	1.01	1.14

section (measures)	A' (8+2+4))		
melody (measures)	vocal (8)	suling (2)	mandolin (4)
lyric	Colak-colek	--	--
arrangement	keyboard (electric piano-blok), organ, electric guitar, bass, tabla, bongo, tambourine	**suling**	**mandolin**
time	1.18	1.31	1.34

section (measures)	C (8)	C (8)
melody (measures)	vocal (8)	vocal (8)
lyric	Memang aneh	Memang aneh
arrangement	keyboard (electric piano-blok), organ, electric guitar, mandolin, **sitar**, bass, tabla, bongo, tambourine	keyboard (electric piano-blok), organ, **acoustic guitar**, electric guitar, mandolin, *sitar*, bass, tabla, bongo, tambourine
time	1.41	1.54

section (measures)	A" (8+2)	
melody (measures)	vocal (8)	suling (2)
lyric	Colak-colek	--
arrangement	keyboard (electric piano-blok), organ, *acoustic guitar*, electric guitar, *mandolin*, bass, tabla, bongo, tambourine	**suling**
time	2.07	2.21

section (measures)	Interlude II (8 + 8)	
melody (measures)	electric guitar solo (8)	suling solo (8)
lyric	--	--
arrangement	keyboard (electric piano-blok), organ, electric guitar, bass, tabla, bongo, tambourine, **synth**	**suling**, *synth*
time	2.24	2.38

FIGURE 5.2 *Continued*

section (measures)	B' (8+2+4)			
melody (measures)	vocal (8)		suling (2)	mandolin (4)
lyric	Kalau ada maunya		--	--
arrangement	keyboard (electric piano-blok), organ, electric guitar, bass, tabla, bongo, tambourine		**suling**	**mandolin**
time	2.51		3.04	3.08

section (measures)	C (8)	C (8)
melody (measures)	vocal (8)	vocal (8)
lyric	Memang aneh	Memang aneh
arrangement	keyboard (electric piano-blok), organ, **acoustic guitar**, electric guitar, mandolin, bass, tabla, bongo, tambourine	keyboard (electric piano-blok), organ, *acoustic guitar*, electric guitar, mandolin, bass, tabla, bongo, tambourine, **synth**
time	3.14	3.28

section (measures)	C (8)	C (8)	C (4)
melody (measures)	vocal (8)	vocal (8)	fadeout (4)
lyric	La la la la	La la la la	La la la la
arrangement	keyboard (electric piano-blok), organ, electric guitar, mandolin, tabla, bongo, tambourine, *synth*, **suling**	keyboard (electric piano-blok), organ, electric guitar, bass, tabla, bongo, tambourine, *suling*	keyboard (electric piano-blok), organ, electric guitar, bass, tabla, bongo, tambourine
time	3.41	3.55	4.08

FIGURE 5.2 *Continued*

upper classes. In contrast to the highly ornamented vocal part in *orkes Melayu* (described in chapter 2), Camelia Malik's vocal part was barely ornamented. Her vocal timbre had a smooth quality, different from the thin vocal quality of Ellya Khadam (chapter 3), or the rich texture of Elvy Sukaesih's vocal timbre, described later in this chapter. Parallel harmonies (in the mandolin part and in the vocal arrangement) were characteristic of *pop Indonesia* and not Melayu-based music.

Camelia Malik brought a new kind of visuality to dangdut. In live performances during the late 1970s, she performed movements from a new modernized Sundanese dance style called *jaipongan*. Unlike the freestyle dance movements used in dangdut, *jaipongan*, as well as other styles, required formal study, thus distinguishing her from other performers. These "learned" forms of dance also signified "class": "Anyone can shake her hips back and forth.

I danced choreographed movements that I had studied formally: jaipongan, modern dance, and ballet" (Camelia Malik, pers. comm., 18 July 2005).

In its promotional literature, Tarantula broadened dangdut's audience by bridging pop and dangdut, and by targeting middle- and upper-class consumers. For example, an advertisement in music magazine *Aktuil* described the band's 1980 album "Raba-Raba" as "a musical work of elite dangdut, featuring sweet arrangements, played by *qualified* musicians, unlike traditional dangdut" (italics mine; Advertisement, PT Virgo Ramayana Record 1980, 32). The "sweet" style of dangdut would be extended by Mansyur S. and his band Radesa.

Sweet dangdut: Mansyur S. and Radesa

Mansyur S. (b. 1948) grew up on Radesa Street in Central Jakarta. As a young boy, Mansyur was a talented Qur'anic chanter (*qari*). He could memorize songs easily, which made it easy to remember Indian songs that he heard in films. He would use these songs as the inspiration for his own compositions. His production team of musicians and arrangers grew up in the same neighborhood, and would come to be known as Radesa. (see figure 5.3)

Beginning with the hit song "Khana" in 1978, Mansyur S. and Radesa created a trademark sound that he called "Dangdut Sweet." As in many of Mansyur S.' songs, the lyrics for "Khana" express the male subject's desire for an exotic woman (other song titles in this vein include "Jamilah," "Salome," "Shanti," and "Zubaedah"). In "Khana," a maiden (virgin) from India draws the singer's attention (see figure 5.4).

"Khana" has elements that are similar to many Indian film songs of this era. [◉] For example, the song begins with a long melismatic unmetered vocal prelude accompanied by rolling arpeggio patterns (*blok,* or *bloking*) played on a piano, and an intervening melody played on the sitar. The prelude sets the mood for the following story. The song form [intro—A-{:interlude-B:}] includes two verses, song A and song B, in which song B centers around a higher pitch. "Khana" is built around a 6-measure refrain ("Khana...Khana... you are a beautiful maiden from India") that appears twice in both the A and B sections. Mansyur S.' Indian-inspired songs emphasized long and highly ornamented phrases. Further, he often used the Indian sitar in his arrangements.

Chalte, described in chapter 3, is the main rhythm played on the *gendang* in "Khana." In the "sweet" dangdut style, the *gendang* part is often played on a tabla (North Indian 2-drum set), and emphasizes a long "du-ut" and a high-pitched "tak." The drummer does not simply play the same *chalte* pattern

FIGURE 5.3 Mansyur S. in concert [courtesy of Mansyur S.].

throughout a composition. In my lessons with percussion virtuoso Husein Khan (whose father, Hanif Radin, was a Radesa musician), he stressed that the drummer must know the form of the song, and must follow the contours of the melody. The drummer plays different patterns for verses, transitions (breaks), fills, and interludes, following the formal structure of the tune.

"Khana" alternates between two main patterns, chalte 1 (Ch 1) and chalte 2 (Ch 2), as shown in figures 5.5 and 5.6.

Oh . . . oh . . . oh . . . Khana.	Oh . . . oh . . . oh . . . Khana,
Khana . . . Khana . . . engkaulah gadis India.	Khana . . . Khana . . . you are a beautiful maiden from India.
Khana . . . Khana . . . engkaulah gadis pujaan,	Khana . . . Khana . . . it is you that I worship,
Senyum serta gayamu sungguh mempesona,	Your smile and style are truly enchanting,
Khana . . . Khana . . . engkaulah gadis India.	Khana . . . Khana . . . you are a beautiful maiden from India.
Pandang matamu penuh cahaya,	Look at your eyes full of light,
Mengundang rasa ingin bercinta,	Inviting me to fall in love,
Aduhai Khana engkau bagaikan,	Oh Khana you are like,
Sekuntum bunga mawar berseri.	A red rose in bloom.
Khana . . . Khana . . . membuat hati tergoda,	Khana . . . Khana . . . you torment me,
Khana . . . khana . . . engkaulah gadis India.	Khana . . . Khana . . . you are a beautiful maiden from India.

FIGURE 5.4 "Khana" [courtesy of Mansyur S.].

section	Intro		
melody	vocal		
lyric	Oh Khana	--	Khana
# measures	Unmetered (accomp. piano)	-- (accomp. sitar, organ, and piano)-	-- (accomp. piano)
gendang	--	--	--
time	0.00	0.24	0.42

section	A		
melody	vocal		
lyric	Khana	senyum	Khana
# measures	8 (2+6)	4	6 (2+4)
gendang	Ch1		
time	0.54	1.06	1.14

section	Interlude	
melody	sitar	suling, sitar
lyric	--	--
# measures	4	8 (4+4)
gendang	Ch1	Ch2
time	1.23	1.30

section	B				
melody	vocal				
lyric	pandang	mengundang	aduhai	Khana	Khana
# measures	4 (2+2)	4	10 (4+4+2)	6 (2+4)	6 (2+4)
gendang	Ch1		Ch2	Ch1	
time	1.44	1.51	1.57	2.13	2.23

section	Interlude	
melody	sitar	suling, sitar
lyric	--	--
# measures	4	8 (4+4)
gendang	Ch1	Ch2
time	2.32	2.39

section	B				
melody	vocal				
lyric	pandang	mengundang	aduhai	Khana	Khana
# measures	4 (2+2)	4	10 (4+4+2)	6 (2+4)	6 (2+4)
gendang	Ch1		Ch2	Ch1	
time	2.53	3.00	3.06	3.22	3.32

FIGURE 5.5 Song guide "Khana."

FIGURE 5.6 *Chalte* 1 and *Chalte* 2 in "Khana."

The "sweet" sound of Mansyur S. and Radesa relied on rich sound textures and trademark instrumental and vocal timbres. Mansyur S. sang with a relaxed vocal quality, in a high register, utilizing falsetto extensively. The electronic keyboard played a prominent role, and included both arpeggiated chords that support the harmonic structure, as well as lush string textures (*strings*). The sitar had a ringing resonant quality, produced by doubling in the recording, or, in later years, by using various mechanical filters. The bass was very active and often played in a high register. As dangdut's consumer base grew, new spinoff genres of "pop dangdut" (Tarantula) and "sweet dangdut" (Radesa) satisfied developing market niches. However, the most powerful female voice in the dangdut recording industry belonged to Elvy Sukaesih.

Elvy Sukaesih: The Queen of Dangdut

Elvy Sukaesih was born in 1951 in Jakarta. Like Mansyur S., she was a talented chanter of the Qur'an (*qariah*), a skill that gave her the ability to sing highly ornamented melodies. As a young girl, she listened to Indian film music, American pop music, and a wide variety of Indonesian folk and popular music at home:

> I sang school songs like "Lenggang-lenggang Kangkung" (Swaying-walking). I loved to listen to the radio. I listened to Connie Francis, Nurseha, Oslan Husein, and Sundanese songs. I sang those songs at parties as a young girl. And I sang Melayu songs like "Butet" and "Onde-onde" as well as Padang songs like "Sing sing song," which was popular at the time, and songs with Calypso rhythms. (Elvy Sukaesih, pers.comm., 20 July 2005)

In 1964, 13-year-old Elvy Sukaesih recorded the Indian-derived hits "Curahan Hati" (Sharing Feelings) (composed by M. Harris) and "Rahasia Sukma"

(Secrets of the Soul) (composed by Ilin Sumantri), accompanied by Zakaria's band Pancaran Muda. Her outstanding vocal quality, versatility, and attractive presentation made her one of the most sought-after female vocalists of the 1970s (see figure 5.7). Her many hit records during the 1970s and 1980s earned her the moniker "Queen of Dangdut" (figure 5.8). Her recording career has been documented in eight stages, although precise dates are difficult to determine (figure 5.9) (Tanaka 2005).

The life story of Elvy Sukaesih "reads exactly like a story from a melodramatic stage play (sandiwara)" (Jafisham and Soemardi 1979, 20). Tabloids described her pain and suffering as a daughter, wife, and mother of five children. As a child performer with her father's group, she often sang late into the night. Upon returning to school the next morning, her schoolmates called her derogatory names like "chicken" (another word for prostitute) (Elvy Sukaesih, pers.comm., 20 July 2005). After her father died, all the money she earned from singing went to support the household (Ensiklopedia Tokoh Indonesia, "Elvy Sukaesih"). In 1965, she married Zeth Zaidun, who initially forbade her from singing in public, but eventually relented, after her constant protests. He eventually became her manager and the producer of several of her albums. Juggling career and family was a difficult task, memorialized in films in which she played herself (for example, the films *Irama Cinta* and *Mandi Madu*).

FIGURE 5.7 Elvy Sukaesih with fans c. 1970 [courtesy of A. Kadir].

FIGURE 5.8 Elvy Sukaesih dressed as the "Queen of Dangdut" [courtesy of Elvy Sukaesih].

In interviews, she contributed to this image of female suffering. For example, in 1980, an interviewer asked her: "Why don't you become a producer like Rhoma Irama?" She answered:

I'm a woman. Our steps have to be small. Rhoma can compose songs, play musical instruments, compose film scores, act, and produce. If I am too ambitious in my career, my home life will fall apart! (Hoetabarat 1980, 50).

Recording Company	Year(s)	Activities
Remaco (first period)	1964-late 1960s	Solo voice accompanied by several O.M. bands including O.M. Pancaran Muda; O.M. Chandralela; O.M. Purnama
Irama, Dimita, and other labels	around 1970–1975	Recordings under her own name; recordings with Rhoma Irama
Yukawi	1975–1976	Duets with Rhoma Irama
Remaco (second period)	mid-1970s	Solo recordings
Pernama (first period)	mid-1970s–1984	Peak performances as a soloist
Insan	1984–85	Two albums; decrease in number of recordings
Wave	1991–92	Two albums on Japanese label
Pernama (second period)	1994-present	Self-produced albums distributed by the Dian label

FIGURE 5.9 Recording career of Elvy Sukaesih (Tanaka 2005).

Elvy Sukaesih attributes her success to her ability to relate to the suffering of her mainly female fans. In performance, she was one of them, if only briefly (Elvy Sukaesih, pers. comm., 20 July 2005). She embodied the pain of women in relationships in songs that she made famous, including "Kejam" (Harsh); "Ijinkanlah" (Give [me] Permission!); and "Menangis" (Crying). Elvy Sukaesih's songs express emotional excess, whether the soaring heights of everlasting love, or the desperate lows of a breakup. In most of her songs, it is usually the man who has transgressed, and the woman who suffers. Her skill lay in fully capturing the message of a song and communicating that feeling to listeners, as if the story elaborated within the song had really happened to her:

> Fans love to hear me sing sentimental songs because I sing them with feeling. Sometimes they cry, especially if they have a story that relates to that song…I have a good imagination, and it comes through in all my songs. Like the song "Sudah kubilang," [I Told You] where I plead "Don't gamble," as if I'm terribly upset. One time I was singing with Rhoma Irama and after the duet, he asked me why I was so upset with him! It's because I embody the character of every song. (Elvy Sukaesih, pers. comm., 20 July 2005)

Elvy Sukaesih's early recordings from the 1960s and 1970s reflect a sweet, lilting, melodious vocal quality. Indeed, Elvy Sukaesih was considered the heir to Ellya Khadam's Indian-inflected style of singing. But as she developed her own style in the late 1970s, and especially during the 1980s, her vocal quality became richly textured, breathy, and characterized by a wide range of vocal techniques. Her song lyrics and performance style became more overtly sexualized, as described in the following section.

"Mandi Madu" (Honey Shower) is one of Elvy Sukaesih's signature songs of the 1980s. The lyrics create an image of bodies bathed in honey, drenched in sweat, and filled with passion. Not only is her body overcome ("throughout my whole body" / *seluruh tubuh*), but her heart is consumed by the depth of the relationship ("this heart is wet" / *basah hati ini*), as shown in figure 5.10.

In "Mandi Madu," Elvy's voice is brash, energetic, and confident. [◉] In the introduction and interlude, she interjects pleasurable coos and joyful screams. She stretches the "ah" syllable in "sya*hdu*" ("calmness in love") and the "a" in "cinta" ("love") and she sighs at the end of each phrase. Her sensuous delivery comes through in the beginning of each line ("ah, ah, ah") as in song A:

Line 1: "bas*ah*, bas*ah*, bas*ah*"
Line 2: "*ah, ah, ah*"
Line 3: "*manis, manis, manis*"
Line 4: "*ah, ah, ah*"

Her breathy delivery, intricate vocal ornaments, sighing descending portamenti, and steamy vocal interjections fill the musical space, as if it is one continuous melody. The impression of filling the musical space signifies passion and excitement. It is an assertion of female appetite and agency.

A: Basah basah basah seluruh tubuh, Ah, ah, ah, menyentuh kalbu, Manis manis manis semanis madu, Ah, ah, ah, menyentuh syahdu.	Wet, wet, wet all through(out) my body, Ah, ah, ah makes me feel love, Sweet, sweet, sweet, as sweet as honey, Ah, ah, ah I'm so satisfied.
Basah diri ini basah hati ini, Kasih dan sayangmu, Menyirami hidupuku, Bagaikan mandi madu.	My body is wet, my heart is wet, With your passion and your love, Washing over my being, Like a honey shower.
Ah, ah, ah mandi madu.	Ah, ah, ah, like a honey shower.
[interlude]	[interlude]
B: Kau taburkan sejuta pesona, Dirimu tak dapat kulupakan, Kau sirami bersemilah cinta, Bungapun kini mekarlah sudah.	B: You spread a thousand spells, I can't get you out of my mind, You bathe me with your growing love, Even the flowers are blossoming.
Manis manis cintamu, Manis manis kasihmu, Diri ini bagai mandi madu.	Your love is so sweet, Your love is so sweet, My body is showered in honey.

FIGURE 5.10 "Mandi Madu" (Bathed in Honey) [courtesy of Toto Ario].

The song form [intro—{:A-interlude-B:}—outro] is typical of dangdut. Half-measures and rhythmic accents create rhythmic kicks that propel the song forward and create rhythmic interest for dancers. *Chalte* variations and transitional motives are pinned to individual sections, as in "Khana." The prolongation of the dominant chord in both song A (*kasih dan sayangmu* / "love and affection") and song B (*manis manis cintamu* / "sweet sweet your love") sustains the narrative of longing developed in the song text (see figure 5.11).

Elvy's appeal to fans was also based on the lavish physical quality of her performance. Stories about her revealing outfits and the busty shape of her body proliferated in popular print media. For example, at a concert in Ujung Pandang (Sulawesi):

> Elvy's fans were worried about the news that reported her buttocks was not real, but rather padded to make it look sexy and voluptuous. On the other hand, some believed the news that Elvy's buttocks was real. ("Elvi Sukaesih" 1979, 35)

section	Intro		
# measures	4	4	3 1/2
lyric	--	--	--
vocal interjections	Male: ya ! Female: Oh, ah	Female: ah	
time	0.00	0.11	0.22

section	A		
# measures	8	6	2
lyric	Basah, basah, basah	Basah diri ini	Ah, ah, ah mandi madu
vocal interjections			
gendang	Ch1	Ch2	Ch1
time	0.32	0.54	1.10

section	Interlude		
# measures	4	2	2
lyric	--	--	--
vocal interjections	Ooh!		
gendang	Ch1		
time	1.16	1.26	1.31

section	B			
# measures	4	1/2	4	4
lyric	Kau taburkan		Kau sirami	Manis manis cintamu
vocal interjections				
gendang	Ch1			Ch2
time	1.37	1.46	1.49	2.00

FIGURE 5.11 Song guide "Mandi Madu": Intro—A-interlude-B.

Described in gossip columns, she wore "tight black pants, and a red blouse wide open at the chest" ("Pokok & Tokoh" 1979a, 38); and "sparkling costumes" ("Elvi Sukaesih" 1979, 34). Her eroticized dancing emphasized her hips and buttocks (*goyang pinggul*) and her quick flirtatious glances to the audience (*lirikan mata*) ("Pokok & Tokoh" 1984, 23). She adopted dance movements from Indian film, especially shoulder movements, which were accentuated by drum sounds in performance. Dressed in tight-fitting, flashy, and seductive stage outfits, her body "fit" the aesthetic of excess communicated in her songs.

The narrative of excess extended to the magical effect she had on fans. Her voice, individualized vocal ornaments, and stage show could "hypnotize" (*menyihir*) audiences (Ensiklopedia Tokoh Indonesia, "Elvy Sukaesih"). Audiences sometimes got out of control, and sometimes shows had to be cancelled. At a concert in Aceh, for example, people reportedly threw shoes and even rocks onstage and many were injured ("Pokok & Tokoh" 1979, 38).

The "bewitching" quality of Elvy Sukaesih's voice and the eroticized movements of her body, along with the unruly audience behavior she reportedly caused, contributed to the portrayal of female singers in dangdut as dangerous and in need of control. However, her songs and performance style became even more sexualized and excessive during the late 1980s.

The excessive visual quality of Elvy Sukaesih's performance style can be seen in the video "Gula-gula" (Mistress). [◐] The title itself suggests multiple meanings. *Gula* means "sugar," whereas *gula-gula* is defined as (1) "bonbon, candy, sweets"; (2) "anything that gives pleasure," and (3) "mistress, concubine" (Stevens and Schmidgal-Tellings 2004). The song lyrics and story depicted in the video "Gula-gula" exploit all three meanings.

The scene takes place in an imaginary past in a palace inhabited by throngs of colorfully clad dancers and musicians. A harem scene opens the video. Perhaps it is India, perhaps Egypt. This is clearly not a real-life situation. The place is not even in Indonesia. The male characters in the story belong to an invented historical past full of royal male characters who have mistresses, as well as additional wives.

Women in the harem serve food, drink, and sex. Elvy's husband in the scene is lured by a woman into one of the tents (0.19). Meanwhile, in another tent, the voluptuous Elvy, wearing a crown and heavy makeup, is having henna applied to her hands (0.36). Informed that her husband is with another woman, she brushes aside her retinue and begins to sing: "How could my husband possibly go home with *you*?" (0.40) Elvy points at the woman ruefully and sings: "How could my husband possibly fall in love with *you*?" (0.50).

A fire breather appears, as women dancers enter a court scene in yet another part of the palace (1.06). Elvy sings: "A bird that flies away won't come back. But a man who is let go, can always be lured back" (1.18). Standing in an aggressive posture, Elvy points at her husband's lover: "How could he go away with you, when you can't give him the sweet honey!" (1.44). The woman exits. A song interlude follows with shots of musicians playing the Indian sitar and *suling* (actually, composer Fazal Dath) (2.08).

In the next scene, Elvy is shown tenderly offering her husband drinks, as a midget massages his legs (2.22). The dancers perform Indian–style movements mixed with American disco choreographies. She sings: "How could he be tempted? Maybe he entered your house temporarily for a bath or a meal, but that was all" (2.50). Elvy performs her trademark shoulder movements, and sings "A clever man at love will always lie, but he'll throw away the candy" (3.10). The bird reappears. "A stray man can always be loved again. How could my husband go with you?" (3.47). The dancers and musicians dance to the chanting of "Candy, candy, candy" (or "Mistress, mistress, mistress") (4.32).

In "Gula-gula" excess is represented by a postmodern pastiche of images, characters, music, and dance styles. The video is saturated with Orientalist Arabian Nights visual and aural signifiers. The over-the-top style of presentation has an exaggerated camp quality. Elvy's mocking attitude toward the mistress is expressed by a physically tough quality as she points her finger directly at the mistress as if beckoning her to battle.

Humorous tongue-in-cheek elements abound. It is difficult not to laugh at the stylized Indianesque dance movements, and one senses that Elvy and the dancers are laughing, too. The bird in the video pecks at Elvy's beaded tiara (1.21) and bites the hand of her attendant (he feigns pain, then laughs) (3.53). The mistress first appears in a headdress with her hair pulled back, looking proud and dignified (1.41). But she appears at the end as a discarded lover, her hair unkempt (4.12). And the man does come back to his wife, like a child who has been scolded (4.00).

The song text and video narrative simultaneously create male and female fantasies. In the male fantasy, two women fight for one man's affection. Further, men are allowed to have extramarital affairs while their wives wait for their husbands to come home. For women, the fantasy begins with the impossibility that a man will not have extramarital affairs: "How could my husband possibly go home with you?" A woman's love is enough to satisfy her husband. The "sugar" in the story represents the love that a wife gives to her husband. Elvy's character is bursting with confidence that her husband will not need anything sweeter than her. However, even if a husband strays, a wife can be reassured because he will always return to the roost.

But it is the counternarrative that gives the song its interest and pleasure. The narrative does not flow in a continuous manner. For example, the text in the middle of the song is a moralistic message that urges women to avoid men who are "clever in matters of love" and will lie to get what they want (3.19). This text disrupts the story, alerting the viewer/listener to step back and reflect on the story (and the sexual behavior of men).

The song and video create a humorous fantasy around the phrase *gula-gula*, which can simply mean sweets, but has the connotation of sexual pleasure. Elvy's theatrical presentation seems to reverse the underlying seriousness of a song about a man having extramarital affairs. She redirects the male gaze from the mistress to her own sexualized body. Her frequent winks, smirks, and raised eyebrows carefully captured by the camera suggest a tongue-in-cheek quality. The joke is on the men, who will always come back. Even when she offers advice to a brooding woman ("men will be men"), she feigns pathos, but cannot help but smile and wink. Rather than despair, her presentation is overwhelmingly joyful. These visual and sonic elements suggest an interpretation that changes the meaning of a song about infidelity to a song that celebrates female agency and sexuality.

Mournful Lyrics and Upbeat Dance Tunes

Many of the lyrics in hit songs of the 1980s expressed sentiments of suffering (*derita; sengsara; rana*). In these songs, suffering came in many forms: failed relationships, economic hardship, social injustice, and cruel social conditions of everyday modern life. For some commentators it seemed untenable that audiences would want to be reminded about social problems and their own suffering as they enjoyed themselves and danced at concerts, nightclubs, and parties. According to these sources, lyrics about suffering and social problems conflicted with the idea of dangdut as a form of escape. Lyrical narratives of suffering, and the perception that they do not match up with social contexts of pleasure, are common in dangdut. For example, in the 1990s song "Menari Diatas Luka" (Dancing on Top of an Open Wound), Imam S. Arifin sings "You danced on top of my open wound/when I needed your love/As if I were a smelly piece of garbage /how easily you threw away my love" (*Kau menari diatas lukaku ini / di saat aku membutuhkan cintamu / Seakan diriku bagai sampah yang berbau / begitu mudah kau campakkan cintaku*).

This perceived disjunction between lyrics and music has been explained in two ways. First, there is the notion that song lyrics are not important to dangdut—people are not listening. Second, there is the idea that melancholy lyrics combined with dance music prove that composers produce bad music for people who cannot tell the difference—people are listening, but they just have bad taste.

In the following section, I argue that people are listening, but in specific ways. Numerous factors are at play in understanding the relationship between texts and music of this period. In order to explain this relationship, I emphasize the commercial nature of the music and the multiplicity of meanings that the music made possible. I will examine the song texts themselves, as well as what people actually do with them in social contexts of listening and performance.

"Lyrics Are Not Important": People Are Not Listening

In my interview with dangdut singer Mansyur S., I was surprised at his comment that "lyrics are not important." In response to my question about the meanings of lyrics in his songs, Mansyur S. asserted:

> Dangdut audiences do not generally pay much attention to the lyrics; maybe there are some examples, like 'Bang Kodir, why haven't you come home for three days?' But that's not what they're looking for. Dangdut audiences want something that's tasty, enjoyable, and good for dancing. That's dangdut! (Mansyur S., pers. comm., 12 July 2005)

If people do not pay attention to lyrics, then how do people know the lyrics to songs, and why do people sing them at all? I believe that Mansyur S.' response was based on the critical opposition to his songs within the official discourse of the New Order. Many of his songs had been labeled *porno* (pornographic) or *cengeng* (mournful) by New Order cultural officials and were subject to banning on the government-run radio and television network. Therefore, he had become accustomed to telling people (especially in interviews) that people do not pay attention to *his* lyrics. Further, Mansyur S.' song melodies are among the most difficult to sing by the average fan (unlike Rhoma Irama's melodies, which tend to be more "singable").

Second, if lyrics are unimportant, why are many songs carefully constructed and considered to be poetic in style? For example, the song "Senyum Membawa Luka" (A Smile Brings Pain) is full of metaphors (love and red wine; love and a beautiful tapestry; "the rope of love is tied around my neck"), the sensuality of spoken sounds through alliteration and assonance (*anggur* and *kuanggap; aku* and *kalut*), and materialization of emotional suffering and loss ("the cure for love is expensive"), as shown in figure 5.12.

Third, the literal meaning of certain lyrics may not articulate a sociopolitical message, as in Rhoma Irama's songs, but they nevertheless have a communicative function. For example, "Colak-colek," described earlier in this chapter, may not have a narrative form or a didactic message, but it uses playful language ("Colak-colek" [Touching Lightly]) to communicate the fun, pleasure, and humor of youth.

Fourth, successful lyrics gave rise to humorous plays on language. People would often make up new lyrics based on words or phrases from songs they had heard. For example the song "Jablai," described in chapter 9, was formed by combining the syllables from the phrase *jarang dibelai* ("rarely caressed"). However, by changing the first word to *janda,* which has the same initial syllable, a different meaning emerged: *janda dibelai* ("a divorcee caressed").

Fifth, dangdut lyrics existed on their own, outside the realm of dance music. As the music circulated widely on recordings, radio, and television, dangdut was not limited to clubs, bars, and discos. People did not *only* dance while they

Anggur merah yang selalu memabukkan diriku, Kuanggap belum seberapa . . .dahsyatnya, Bila dibandingkan dengan senyumanmu, Membuat aku jatuh bangun.	Red wine, which always makes me drunk, Is nothing in its effect . . . awesome, Compared to your smile, That can make me dizzy in love [rise and fall].
Anggur merah yang selalu memabukkan diriku Kuanggap belum seberapa . . .dahsyatnya, Bila dibandingkan dengan senyumanmu, Membuat aku lesu darah.	Red wine, which always makes me drunk, Is nothing in its effect . . . awesome, Compared to your smile, That makes my blood weak.
Untuk apa kau berikan aku benang yang kusut? Sementara diriku harus membuat kain, Kain yang halus.	Why did you give me a knotty thread? When I am trying to weave a beautiful tapestry? A beautiful tapestry.
Untuk apa kau hidangkan aku cinta yang kalut? Sementara tanganmu telah engkau berikan pada yang lain, Sungguh teganya dirimu, teganya, teganya, teganya... oh pada diriku.	Why did you offer me such a messy love? While you gave your hand to someone else? Oh how you were able to do that to me.
Aku masih belum mau mati karena cintamu lalu menderita, Walaupun tali cinta masih mengikat-ngikat di leherku.	I do not want to die because of you although I suffer, Even though the rope of love is still tied around my neck.
Lebih baik kukecewa daripada kumerana hingga terluka, Karena pengobat cinta sungguh sangat mahal-mahal harganya.	I'd rather be disappointed than suffer the pain of my wounds, Because the cure for love is very "expensive."

FIGURE 5.12 "Senyum Membawa Luka" (A Smile Brings Pain) [courtesy of Fazal Dath].

listened to dangdut. People listened to and sang lyrics as they traveled, relaxed at home, hung out on the streets, and engaged in myriad other activities.

Sixth, dangdut gave people the words to express difficult sentiments. For example, in the song "Anak Haji" (Child of an Islamic Pilgrim), a girl and boy from different backgrounds fall in love and plan to marry, but they face opposition from the girl's parents. The girl's parents have made the pilgrimage to Mecca, whereas the boy's parents are gamblers. How does one present this image in language? The boy sings: "It's not because I don't love you, that I'm pushing you away; but your parents say it would be sinful to have a son-in-law like me."

Finally, dangdut songs not only gave people the language to say things, but a style or inflection with which to express them. When I asked fans about certain songs, they frequently made reference to a lyrical phrase that was accented in a certain way. For example, the way Latif Khan sings a simple line like "moistened are her lips when she greets me, a wink of her eyes as she giggles" ("Dibasah basah bibir"); or the flirtatious way that Elvy Sukaesih expressed the third "ah" in the second line of "Mandi Madu" (three tones connected by portamenti, in which the second tone descends and the third tone rises above the first).

"Lyrics matter": People are listening

Having shown the importance of lyrics, I will now focus on different ways that songs could be interpreted, and point out why this was so. As Yampolsky (1989) and Williams (1989) have shown for *pop Indonesia* and *pop Sunda*, respectively, publicly voicing everyday problems in popular music was not good for Indonesia, according to the New Order discourse about culture, especially if the songs were thought to be *cengeng, porno,* or related to getting intoxicated. Yampolsky defines *cengeng* as a characteristic of songs that "are usually sung by girls and deal with broken promises, hopeless love, faithless boys, sweethearts separated by fate or by their parents' plans for arranged marriages" (1989, 2). Yampolsky writes that "if popular songs start taking about abusive husbands and infidelity and divorce, who knows what they might talk about next?" (1989, 9). Dangdut was especially vulnerable to these charges, as its topics and themes emerged out of people's everyday lives.

However, despite critical condemnation, composers maintained that the meanings of dangdut texts were more complicated. Mournful texts gained currency as commercial products, but singers and fans did not agree with the characterization of dangdut lyrics as *cengeng*. Composer Muchtar B. argued that "cengeng songs or laments are about killing oneself or giving up hope" (Kusumah 1991, 63). Dangdut lyrics acknowledged the difficulties of poverty, but that was not the same as giving up hope. For example, in reference to his song "Gubuk Derita" (Hut of Suffering), released in 1986, Muchtar B. stated:

> I come from a family of have-nots. Because of that, I always had to help out. There's a Betawi saying: 'whether we eat or not, we'll stick together.' Although we're poor, as long as we stick together, we can be happy. That's the message of 'Gubuk Derita.' (Theo 1986)

Giving up is different from acknowledging one's fate. Song lyrics expressed a narrative of surrender to something beyond an individual's control. This sentiment was echoed in Allison Murray's study of street traders and prostitutes in Jakarta during the 1980s:

> Past or impending disasters are shrugged off with, 'what's done is done' *(apa yang terjadi terjadilah)* or, 'it's just [my] fate' *(nasibnya saya)*, and the women can usually find something to laugh about in any situation, although they also occasionally sink into exhaustion and despondency. Religious conviction helps them to accept their 'fate.' (Murray 1991)

Dangdut songs articulated people's acknowledgment of powerlessness, as illustrated by three popular songs of the 1980s. In "Pasrah" (Surrender), for example, it would be less painful to be murdered by a sword than to die from heartache. In this song, physical pain symbolizes material existence (*lahir*), whereas emotional pain symbolizes one's inner spirit (*batin*). Emotional pain would be much more difficult to bear than physical pain. The subject surrenders to being a second lover, rather than having to endure the pain of a breakup. Even if the subject cannot make sense of it, he accepts it (see figure 5.13).

Lebih baik kau bunuh, Aku dengan pedangmu. Asal jangan kau bunuh, Aku dengan cintamu.	It's better if you kill, me with your sword. Just don't kill, me with your love.
Lebih baik aku mati di tanganmu, Daripada aku mati bunuh diri. Lebih baik aku mati di tanganmu, Daripada aku mati bunuh diri.	It's better that I die by your hands, rather than killing myself. It's better that I die by your hands, rather than killing myself.
Ku tak menyesali kalau diri ini, Engkau jadikan diriku, Cinta kedua darimu. Biarlah aku terima.	I won't regret it if, you make me, your second love. It's ok, I accept it.

FIGURE 5.13 "Pasrah" (Surrender) [courtesy of Leo Waldy].

In "Mandul" (Infertility), a husband accepts the fact that his wife will never bear children. They have surrendered to God, and they have not given up on each other (see figure 5.14).

In "Termiskin di Dunia," (The Poorest in the World), a woman accepts a male lover, despite his impoverished condition (see figure 5.15).

All three songs represent real-life situations, but the responses are idealized and open to interpretation. In "Surrender," would someone accept becoming a second lover? In "Infertility," would a man remain in a relationship with a woman who cannot bear children? And in "The Poorest in the World," can love truly conquer material circumstances? Perhaps not, but they do expose possibilities and pose questions. These three songs are based on real-life problems, and they present hopeful responses rather than desperate ones. They change the terms of discourse from melancholy songs about desperate circumstances to songs about the relationship between body and soul ("Pasrah"), fate and faith ("Mandul"), and material conditions and love ("Termiskin di Dunia"). They do not provide answers, but they do offer hope rather than despair.

Melancholy lyrics and dance music

Commentators cited what they perceived as the incommensurability of lyrics about social problems and suffering with a performance context of pleasure, humor, and fun. From this perspective, the melancholy lyrics conflicted with the upbeat rhythm of dangdut music. For example, one writer lamented the fact that lyrics such as "it's better to kill me with your sword, just don't kill me with your love" ("Pasrah"), and melancholy-sounding melodies (*nadanya*

F: Sepuluh tahun sudah kita berumah tangga, Tetapi belum juga mendaptkan putra.	F: Ten years we've been married, But we haven't been able to have children.
M: Jangan kau sedih, jangan berduka, Mohon padaNya dalam berdoa.	M: Don't be sad, don't be distressed, Confide in God, and pray.
F: Sebagai seorang istri, kumerasa sedih, Ku takut dirimu kecewa padaku.	F: As a wife, I feel sad, I'm afraid you will be disappointed with me.
M: Cintaku padamu tak akan pudar, Walau seumur hidupmu dalam kemandulan. (2x)	M: My love for you will never fade, Even if we never have children. (2x)
F: Kurasa tiada sempurna kebahagiaan kita, Tanpa adanya seorang putra belahan jiwa.	F: I feel we will never be completely happy, Without a child to share our souls.

FIGURE 5.14 "Mandul" (Infertility); F = female, M = male [courtesy of Rhoma Irama].

Spoken (female): "Yang, walaupun engkau orang termiskin di dunia, aku akan tetap mencintai."	Spoken (female): "Darling, although you are the poorest man on earth, I still love you."
Sung (male): Bukan ku menolakmu untuk mencintaiku, Tetapi lihat dulu siapakah diriku.	Sung (male): It's not that I am rejecting your love, But first look at who I am.
Kau orang kaya aku orang tak punya, Sebelum terlanjur pikir pikirlah dulu, Sebelum engkau menyesal kemudian.	You are rich and I am poor, Before anything happens, think about it first, Before you regret it later.
Jangankan gedung, gubuk pun aku tak punya, Jangankan permata, uang pun aku tiada, Aku merasa orang termiskin di dunia, Yang penuh derita bermandikan air mata.	A building, much less a hut, I do not own, Jewelry, much less money, I do not own, I feel like the poorest man on earth, Full of suffering, bathing in my own tears.
Itulah diriku ku katakan padamu, Agar engkau tahu siapa aku, Sebelum terlanjur pikir pikirlah dulu, Sebelum engkau menyesal kemudian.	This is who I am. I'm telling you, So that you will know who I really am, Before anything happens, think about it first, Before you regret it later.

FIGURE 5.15 "Termiskin di Dunia" (The Poorest in the World).

mendayu-dayu) would most likely discourage people from wanting to dance: "who would dance when they're sad?" (Kusumah 1991, 62). A television program director at TPI thought it was ridiculous that people would dance to songs with lyrics such as "I lost everything to gambling" (*Aku melarat karena judi*) (Nala Rinaldo, pers. comm., 11 July 2005). For these commentators, dangdut expressed contradictory meanings that should have been resolved in the songs themselves.

We should not assume that lyrics expressing a particular lyrical sentiment should be homologous with the sonic nature of the music, no matter how those sentiments or sonorities are defined. For example, we should not assume that a "sad" lyrical sentiment must be accompanied by a slow wailing melody in the minor mode. It is not unusual in many kinds of music that melancholic sentiments are placed together with upbeat fast tempos. The notion that lyrics tell the same story as the music closes off the possibility of irony, for example, that can possibly occur between text and music. It disallows the possibility of counternarratives.

But this does not explain why the juxtaposition of these seemingly contradictory elements formed such a powerful and persistent characteristic in dangdut. I argue that dangdut, as a commercial music, often privileged market concerns over formal aesthetic conventions. Production teams brought together ideas, sounds, and images that they thought would sell. For example, when I asked dangdut composer and singer Meggy Z. what made a good dangdut song, he answered: "one that sells" (Meggy Z., pers. comm., 12 July 2005).

Most of his songs happened to be based on male-female relationships, which are often full of suffering, and many became hits. So he continued writing them. From a commercial perspective, lyrics based on male-female relationships gained a privileged place in the repertoire.

The creation of hit songs relied on production teams assembled by the recording company producer. Munif Bahasuan contrasts ideas of production in American/European popular music and dangdut:

> In the U.S. or Europe the producer is an individual with a specific function. But here, a producer IS the recording company. The producer chooses the singer, the composer, and the arranger and organizes the recording session. The producer owns the master, and sells the product. (Munif Bahasuan, pers. comm., 16 July 2005)

Munif Bahasuan explained that the Indonesian producer took on some of the roles conventionally carried out by the executive producer in the American and European music industries. For example, the Indonesian producer also provided the initial capital to make the recording and oversaw the recording and mixing process. When the product was ready, the producer took the record to distributors. Payments to the composers, arrangers, musicians, and recording engineers, as well as the financial arrangements with distributors, were taken care of by the producer. Separate tasks characterized production, and each person was paid for that task, usually per recording.

In some cases, the composition of the melody and text, as well as the musical arrangement, could be performed by one person. Poets (who were sometimes also the composer) wrote lyrics about real-life themes presented, for the most part, in direct everyday language. Arrangers (and not the composer of the tune) composed music for the introduction, interlude, fills and outro. Arrangers worked with musicians and sound engineers to create a trademark sound or a certain kind of texture. Some composers did not play musical instruments and were not capable of making their own arrangements. Arrangers had an important role in creating musical settings that had the potential to be commercially successful.

Composers created songs tailored to particular singers. Composer Fazal Dath, who created many commercially successful songs during the 1980s and 1990s, states:

> Making a song for a singer is like making a shirt. Will it be small, medium, large, or extra large? We have to measure the tones and the rests for the singer. If you're an extra large singer, I have to make extra large patterns. But it's up to me to accessorize: maybe there's a

button over here, maybe one over here, or something a little sexy over there. (Fazal Dath, pers. comm., 12 July 2005)

Composers imagined themselves as fans when they composed, as explained by composer Ukat S. (b. 1947):

> I don't write lyrics based on my own experience. I observe what's happening in life. I don't make songs to satisfy my own heart, but rather for consumers out there. What is the story of someone in love? I think about someone else. (Ukat S., pers. comm., 22 August 2006)

Composers inserted lyrics that would sell at the moment the products were released. Lyrics described situations that happened to people in everyday life, so that they would be easy to understand and remember. A hit song quickly became the topic of conversation. Asmin Cayder, whose songs were said to have negative *porno* connotations, noted that his songs "represent the hopes and aspirations of people at this moment in time": "Sudah Tahu Aku Miskin" (You Know I'm Poor); "Tembok Derita" (Walls of Suffering); "Anak Haji." (Child of a Pilgrim) ("Asmin Cayder" 1992). Songs were created for particular audiences in particular places at particular times. As one dangdut fan told me, "there is a dangdut song for every social situation."[5]

Hit songs were often generated from words and phrases in circulation at the time the song was written. When a word or phrase became "hot," composers followed up with songs that used that word. In these cases, the story or image of the song was built around the word or catch phrase that generated the song. Knowing the original source would demonstrate a certain kind of "hipness" or belonging. These in-group phrases were often created by breaking up existing words into syllables and using those syllables to form new terms, known as *istilah* ("term" or "catchphrase"). For example, the song "Salome" is about a woman named Salome who has many male lovers. The word "Salome" is pulled apart into three individual syllables, and these syllables are used to create additional words that form the crude catch phrase for the song: "SAtu LObang raME-rame" ("one busy hole"). In this example, the name gave rise to the phrase, and then became a song.[6] In a related practice, individual syllables of words from an invented phrase were extracted from the phrase and combined to form a new word. The meaning of the new word was related to the meaning of the invented phrase. For example, the word "Wakuncar" was formed by combining syllables of the phrase "WAktu KUNjung paCAR" ("time to visit your girlfriend/boyfriend"). This practice of building songs on textual hooks persists to the present day. Further, individual letters from a preexisting song title could be extracted to form an acronym. In this practice, the song title generated new acronyms that were only familiar to an in-group of people familiar with the song. For example, "B. B. T." is an acronym formed from the initial letters of each word in the song "Bisik-Bisik Tetangga" about gossipy chattering neighbors.

Songs were often composed with titles and lyrics that referred back to earlier songs. After Obbie Mesakh's song "Hati Yang Luka" (A Wounded Heart) was censored by Minister of Information Harmoko in 1988, Mesakh brought a similar song to singer Meggy Z. called "Lebih Baik Sakit Gigi Dari Pada Sakit Hati" (A Toothache Is Better Than a Broken Heart); it later became a hit, with the shortened title, "Sakit Gigi" (Toothache). The intertextuality of the lyrics and melodies was more important than whether the lyrics homologized with the music.

Rather, at the point of production, composers aimed to create songs featuring: a) "images filled to the brim"; b) the juxtaposition of seemingly disparate elements; and c) an abundance of signs. As composer Endang Kurnia stated, songs that made different meanings possible would have a better chance at becoming commercially successful (pers. comm., 15 November 2006). In the following section, I explore some of these possible interpretations and meanings in songs of the 1980s.

Songs and Their Multiple Interpretations

The hit song "Two Eat from One Plate" (Sepiring Berdua) can signify poverty, in the sense that a family cannot afford a plate of food for each person. While eating from the same plate is about not having enough to eat, it also presents a romantic image of a couple sharing what little they have. Eating from the same plate is a metaphor for lessening their suffering. The song works because of this narrative tension between poverty and comfort (see figure 5.16).

Songs could be interpreted as simultaneously melancholy, pornographic, or humorous. For example, the song "Angka Satu" (Number One) is seemingly a melancholy song about being alone (see figure 5.17).

'Pabila ku ingat dirimu, Disaat bersama hidup sengsara, Makan sepiring kita berdua, Tidurpun setikar bersama.	When I think about you, When we suffered together, Two eating from one plate, Sleeping together on one mat.
Diriku merasa bahagia, Mendampingi dirimu dalam suka duka, Walupun hujan basah berdua, Demi cinta akupun rela.	I feel happy inside, Being with you, through ups and downs, Even though the rain poured down on us, For love, I am willing.

FIGURE 5.16 "Sepiring Berdua" (Two Eat from One Plate).

Masak masak sendiri, makan makan sendiri, Cuci baju sendiri, tidur pun sendiri.	Cooking alone, eating alone, Doing laundry alone, even sleeping alone.

FIGURE 5.17 "Angka Satu" (Number One).

The song depicts the lonely life of a man who does everything alone. But it also elicits nervous laughter because sex ("sleeping alone") is not commonly discussed in public. Further, one dangdut fan suggested that the "number one" in the song title stood for a man's erect penis. He is like the number 1, stiff, standing alone, by himself. The sentiment was not sad, but it was taboo and humorous.

In "Minta Ajimat" (Asking for a Spell) a man dreams about meeting an angel who will satisfy all of his fantasies. The song turns on an axis of fantasy and reality, rather than loneliness and despair (see figure 5.18).

In the story, the man fantasizes about an imaginary partner. He sings alone in the bathroom, a euphemism for masturbation. He grimaces, and finally ejaculates (*keluar sendiri*). He asks a purveyor of spells (*Pak Dukun*) to give him a magical formula, which, while common, is somewhat humorous in modern Indonesia (see chapter 8).

Suffering could even have a lighter side, as in the song "Sakit Gigi" (Toothache; figure 5.19). In this song, the man compares his suffering in love to the pain of a toothache. Unlike a toothache, which can be cured by going to a dentist, a heartache has no cure. And even an ant, the smallest creature on earth, would be outraged and unwilling to accept this type of mistreatment. It is a romantic sentiment, but the image of an angry ant that has been mistreated by his lover is funny, not to mention the association of an ant with a toothache.

Bosan bosan begini, tanpa seorang istri. Tidurku sendiri, berkhayal, bermimpi. Ketemu bidadari,	I'm so bored without a woman, I sleep alone, imagine, and dream, Of meeting an angel.
Bosan bosan begini, nyanyi di kamar mandi. Meringis sendiri tertawa sendiri. Keluar sendiri.	It's boring to sing in the shower, Grimace alone, laugh alone, Come alone.
Pak Dukun, Pak Dukun Tolonglah, tolonglah, Buatkan ajimat istimewa, Supaya, supaya diriku diriku, Mendapat jodoh dengan segera.	Pak Dukun, Pak Dukun, Help me, help me, Give me a magical spell, So that I, Can get a wife immediately.
Tak perduli janda atau perawan, Yang penting tidak mata duitan.	I don't care if she's been married or a virgin, She just can't love me for money.

FIGURE 5.18 "Minta Ajimat" (Asking for a Spell) [courtesy of Fahmy Shahab].

Jangankan diriku,	Don't treat me like this,
Semut pun kan marah bila terlalu sakit begini,	Even an ant would be angry, if forced to
Dari pada sakit hati lebih baik sakit gigi ini,	experience such pain,
Biar tak mengapa,	Rather than heartache, a toothache would be better,
Rela, rela, rela aku relakan,	I would rather have a toothache,
Rela, rela, rela aku rela.	I can accept it, I can accept it.

FIGURE 5.19 "Sakit Gigi" (Toothache).

This song articulates acceptance within a religious context. Even in the most difficult times, God will take care of living creatures, even those as small as an ant.

And in "Cinta Sabun Mandi" (Bathsoap Love), humor emerges out of the expression of love (see figure 5.20). From one perspective, this is a very endearing romantic image of a man in love. On the other hand, the image of a man walking around without pants on, or serving as a coolie for his lover, is humorous and ridiculous.

These songs reveal tensions based on polarities of poverty/comfort; public/private; fantasy/reality; and anger/humor. They do not resolve. Rather, they leave open the possibilities of interpretation and their themes test the boundaries of what is pronounceable in public.

Popular Print Media and 1980s Dangdut

Despite these different ways of interpreting dangdut song texts, the meaning of dangdut described in popular print media took on a rather essentialized quality. Popular print media emphasized dangdut's sexual connotations, vulgar language, excessive emotionality, and overblown quality of performance. Popular print media stressed the connection between dangdut and "the glittery lifestyle" (*dugem,* or *dunia gemerlap*) characterized by alcohol, prostitution, and dancing in entertainment areas where dangdut was frequently played. In East Java, a corridor of nightclubs connecting Gresik, Lamongan, Tuban, and Bojonegoro

Kujual baju celana itu semua demi Nyai,	I would sell my pants for her,
Aku kerja jadi kuli demi Nyai,	I would work as a coolie for her,
Walaupun Madonna cantik Marilyn Monroe juga cantik,	Although Madonna and Marilyn Monroe are also pretty,
Tetapi bagiku lebih cantik Nyai,	To me, she is more beautiful,
Aku rela korban harta demi Nyai.	I would sacrifice everything for her.

FIGURE 5.20 "Cinta Sabun Mandi" (Bathsoap Love).

formed a trail for dangdut acts (Mandayun 1991, 66). In Surabaya, the entertainment complex "Dolly" could support 10 official groups, each group composed of 6–12 singers. These places were often pictured in films of the period to depict prostitution and vice. The relationship between dangdut and the sex industry was characterized in popular print media as follows:

> In the lower class prostitution quarters this music is king. And the characteristic of dangdut in these places is eroticized, the lyrics are pornographic [porno] and weepy [cengeng]. Female singers attract their [primarily male] audiences by dancing eroticized movements in miniskirts and tight vests. (Mandayun 1991, 60)

In a 1991 article published in the newsmagazine *Tempo*, the author states that "dangdut has a very loose musical framework. That's the reason why dangdut is like a nude woman who is willing to be dressed any which way."[7] Why does the author use the gendered image of a naked woman and her clothing in a story about the musical structure of dangdut? Perhaps the statement alludes to the widely acknowledged yet repressed desire of men to be attracted to entertainment clubs despite the discourse prohibiting such desires. Perhaps the statement refers to the ascendance of female vocalists, whose participation in dangdut made at least some of them economically independent and socially powerful. Or perhaps the statement alludes to the entertainment quarters of large cities, where dangdut was "king" and where clothed men paid to watch women "dressed any which way" on the dance floor. The statement indicates the market strength of dangdut, which could be understood as a formulaic style, a musical treatment that could "dress" different kinds of melodies; indeed, a variety of spin-off musical styles based loosely on a dangdut framework emerged in the 1980s to attract new audiences. The statement demonstrates a common perception expressed in popular print media that dangdut was loosely structured, and therefore cheap and unsophisticated.

Populist messages resonated with the majority of society, but they conflicted with the aims of the authoritarian Suharto regime. Through censorship, the hickish and unformed could be transformed into proper national subjects. This pattern of state censorship illustrates the construction of dangdut's audience as an object of a top-down New Order discourse about culture and the arts in the 1980s characterized by government regulation and monitoring (Zurbuchen 1990; Lindsay 1995; Yampolsky 1995). The top-down approach to culture was carried out within other media, notably the state television network TVRI (Kitley 2000). TVRI targeted those who watched television—middle classes and elites, not the majority of society—and programming followed its audience's desires. Dangdut's most influential artist, Rhoma Irama, was banned from performing on TVRI from 1977 to 1988. Other dangdut artists were featured regularly on the TVRI music television show called *Aneka Ria Safari,* but dangdut was not promoted on any other shows.[8]

Populist chic

Concommitant with the top-down approach to culture, it became trendy to use dangdut as part of a discourse about Indonesian national character in popular print media of the 1980s. William Frederick, describing Rhoma Irama's music, noted the fascination with dangdut as a kind of "populist chic":

> In the eyes of many observers, the music not only gets the majority of its fans from the majority of society—the lower classes—but evinces a sympathy with and understanding of them that is unique. Indeed, this last characteristic has been strong enough to breed a kind of "populist chic" (*kegenitan sosial*) among the elite and middle class. For these reasons some have concluded that the dangdut style, by virtue of what it reflects as well as what it imposes, matches more accurately than any other yet devised the much sought-after national character or "countenance" (*wajah Indonesia*). (1982, 124)

Yet, in popular print media, the emotionally excessive, overblown, and extreme nature of dangdut would have to be tempered in order for dangdut to be fully integrated as part of the Indonesian national character. In a 1987 issue of *Mutiara,* a glossy fashion magazine, dangdut music was described as "unsophisticated, weak, tacky, and whiney."[9] These characterizations resonated with middle class and elite opinions about dangdut, as described in chapter 4. But rather than simply denigrating the music as *kampungan* (backward), as had numerous other articles, the author found a redemptive quality in dangdut: "Dangdut is not just light entertainment to pass the time, but it can be considered a tool for expression, an instrument to express the culture of the people" ("Rhoma Irama…Sampai Titik" 1987, 21). The article cited interviews with university faculty experts from the arts and sciences, including Dr. Ryadi Gunawan, a member of the literature faculty at Gadjah Mada University, who called dangdut music a "social barometer" (ibid., 22). Dr. Hasan Basri from the Psychology Department at the same university depicted Rhoma Irama's music as a form of psychotherapy (ibid.). According to Dr. Lukman Sutrisno, whose affiliation was not cited, dangdut served a positive role in society, but only because of its ability to "repress" (*meredam*) feelings of frustration among its audiences (ibid.). And Dr. Kuntowijoyo, a historian and cultural expert, noted that Rhoma Irama's songs could "sublimate" (*mensublimasi*) social protest through culture and the arts (ibid., 23). Its musicians and fans could be valued only when their desires and behaviors were repressed, sublimated, or otherwise transformed.

Another article represented the populist chic attitude in a way that suggested a deeper understanding and appreciation of the music (Suyitno 1991, 33). In an article entitled "Dangdut Music and its Excesses," Dr. Ayid Suyitno wrote that "as people with our own culture, we should be proud of the strength of dangdut on our native soil" (ibid.). The author quite accurately summarized the lyrics of dangdut songs as follows:

> [T]here is an honesty and openness difficult to find in other forms of Indonesian popular music. Don't be alarmed by hearing about a "shot-gun wedding"; "a divorcee's heartache"; "a husband has another lover"; and "true love doesn't value material circumstances" (ibid.)

Dangdut's strength lay in its ability to express the emotional realities of ordinary people. But according to the article, its messages were being diverted (*diselewengkan*) by singers' inability to speak the language properly, and the vulgar quality of "overacting" by performers and audiences. Unless properly transformed, the style of its delivery would forever doom dangdut to reside among the lower classes in Jakarta's slums:

> I'm sorry, but the words are extremely vulgar, inaccurate, and not particularly intelligent. This may constitute one of the strongest arguments for proving that dangdut is only appropriate for the lower class, and moreover points to its vileness. (ibid.)

Despite the author's familiarity with dangdut's lyrical content and its high level of emotional expression, the article represents a contradiction that is impossible to resolve. Dangdut's ability to communicate honestly and openly with its audience was grounded in a particular style of language ("vulgar, inaccurate, and not particularly intelligent") and performance ("overacting"), yet these linguistic and performative qualities were marked as responsible for diverting its messages. Cleaning up the language of dangdut and transforming the way performers perform and people act (by "acting" but not "overacting") would somehow enable dangdut fans to improve the social and economic conditions of their lives. In this text, dangdut could be appreciated only when it was *not* dangdut, when its meanings were fixed.

Contradictions

Life in 1980s modern Indonesia was full of contradictions. The state ideology of *pancasila*, which emphasized democracy and social justice, was being redefined as loyalty to the president, above all others. *Pancasila* called for justice and civilized humanity, and yet the army engaged in violent clashes with citizens in Aceh, Lampung, and East Timor. In a society that was getting richer, the poor were getting poorer.

Under these circumstances, it is understandable that people would want to "avoid hassles" (*tidak mau ambil pusing*) or "look the other way." As narrated in the song "Sampai Pagi" (Until the Morning Hours), rather than "thinking about debts piling up, it's better to just have a good time" (*mikirin utang numpuk segudang, lebih baik kita senang-senang*). At least a night of pleasure would allow people to "throw problems far away" (*buang masalah jauh-jauh*). And yet, the mechanism of pleasure tempering people's pain does not adequately explain the types of meanings that emerged in the songs of this era. Dangdut opened up interpretive possibilities rather than neatly closing them off. Dangdut did not provide answers to problems. Rather, it pushed the limits of what was allowable in order to expose an excess of possibilities.

Beyond the invisible fictions about dangdut audiences constructed in texts inscribed by commercial, government, and critical institutions, however, lies the wild exuberance and pleasure of dangdut. In this temporal register, dangdut does not look forward (as in "mournful songs are not good for the nation" or "songs about drugs will not lead to the production of good ethical citizens," or "pornographic songs are not good for our children"). It does not look backward, as in "our lives are so wretched that we need some pleasure to make life worth living." Rather, dangdut exists in the present, as a "structure of feeling," in the unresolved contradictions of everyday life.[10] These contradictions are signified by mournful lyrics and joyous dancing; hyper-commercialism and strong identification with stars; and entertaining escapist fantasies vs. the banal existence of overcrowded living conditions, oppressively meager working wages, and lack of representation in the public sphere. Beyond the powerful apparatuses that regulate and monitor people's behavior lies an undomesticated space where people can do all sorts of things that would be considered unacceptable according to middle class and elite standards of behavior. In dangdut, this is the space of exaggeration and excess, whether it is the garishness of your outfit, the teasingly erotic way you swing your hips, the vulgar language you use, or the articulation of social issues that cannot be broached in the public sphere. Elites might describe these practices as *overakting* (from the English "overacting") because they cross over the boundaries of acceptable behavior. But for dangdut audiences, active participation—in a music and dance form that emphasizes openness, spontaneity, playfulness, and passion—represents the heart and soul of what dangdut is all about.

NOTES

1. The main recording studios in the 1970s were Remaco, Metropolitan (also called Musica), Yukawi, and Dimita (all located in Jakarta) and Lokananta (Surakarta).

2. Bettina David addresses a similar topic but comes to different conclusions (David, forthcoming).

3. A denigrating term for dangdut during this period was *musik kacang goreng*, or "fried peanuts music" (Takari 1997, 21).

4. Subsequent recordings of their songs produced by other artists did not follow this practice; for example, Elvy Sukaesih's version of "Colak-colek" on *Elvy Sukaesih: The Dangdut Queen*, 2005.

5. Ening Rumbini, pers. comm., 20 March 2006.

6. Two examples include "Cileduk," the name of a place 24 kilometers south of Cengkareng Airport in Jakarta, which became CInta LEwat DUKun ("Love Obtained through Magical Spells"); and "Romantis," an Anglicization of "romantic," became ROkok MAkan graTIS ("Cigarettes and Food Are Free"). Many of these "love terms" (*istilah cinta*) were immortalized in Obbie Messakh's humorous song "Istilah Cinta" (see Sastromuljono 2005).

7. *Musik dangdut punya satu pola yang sangat terbuka. Itu sebabnya musik dangdut bagaikan gadis telanjang yang siap dibajui apa saja.* (Surawijaya 1991, 57).

8. A famous dangdut composer, who refused to be identified, noted that "on television dangdut can only be promoted via Aneka Ria Safari, and not on other shows. [The program] Selekta Pop, which only plays pop, has been closed off to the possibility of dangdut entering there" ("Lebih jauh dengan Rhoma Irama," 1988).

9. "Rhoma Irama... Sampai Titik," 1987, 21. In another magazine, fans were described as "hysterical" (*histeris*) ("Berjuang dalam goyang" 1989, 13).

10. Raymond Williams used the term "structures of feeling" to describe how culture is lived and felt through cultural forms (Williams 1977, 128–135).

Chapter 6

Dangdut Nation: "We Bring the Happiness of Dangdut"

In the 1990s, at state-sponsored concerts, in popular print media, and televised speeches, dangdut was touted as the music of *all* Indonesians. Formerly associated with the disenfranchised underclass—the *rakyat*—it was reported that the music's audience now extended to middle-class and elite audiences as well. For example, a 1991 article in news magazine *Tempo* proclaimed that dangdut had quietly risen in social status due to its current popularity with "bureaucrats, from government ministers up to the vice governor—and quite likely many others" (Surawijaya 1991, 49). As a national election approached in 1992, top government and military officials pronounced dangdut as Indonesia's national music. In the 1990s, newspapers and tabloids reported on dangdut's wide appeal not only among people of different classes, but divergent ethnicities, as indicated in figure 6.1 which shows the all-female Java-based dangdut band Ken Dedes visiting a group of men in Irian Jaya (Sarsidi 1995a).

The notion that dangdut represented all Indonesians, together with its massive popularity, was a common story told in popular print media during the early 1990s. The story went something like this: sung in lyrics that nearly all Indonesians could understand, expressing feelings that everyone could relate to, and with a beat that everyone could dance to, it was natural that dangdut had become iconic with the nation. As a result, dangdut's representation and meaning changed from the music of ordinary people who occupy the bottom of the social and political system, to a genre celebrated as national music in the 1990s.[1]

Dangdut, which appealed to the majority of Indonesians, was a privileged field for creating identifications with the ideals and values of a national culture.

Group Ken Dedes ketika berkunjung ke Irian Jaya.

FIGURE 6.1 Ken Dedes group in Irian Jaya, *Dang Dut* 1 (6), July 1995, 7 [courtesy of Zakaria].

In conjunction with the stated recognition and approval of dangdut, the central government promoted particular singers, musical forms, and meanings about "nationalized" dangdut in the 1990s. Nationalized dangdut was (1) profitable (for some); (2) regulated through government censorship and official cultural organizations; (3) Jakarta-centric and yet international in scope; (4) glamorous in image; and (5) respectable and subdued according to middle-class and upper-class standards.

Yet, for the large base of dangdut fans, the value and meaning of dangdut had not changed. Fans already knew very well that dangdut was *their* music. The public approval of dangdut by high government officials, bureaucrats, middle classes, or elites made little difference to dangdut fans. As shown in the previous chapter, dangdut had developed an aesthetic around a spectacle of excess that challenged notions of containment. Unlike nationalized dangdut, its lyrics were open to multiple interpretations, its costumes were garish and flashy, its performance style was campy and eroticized, and its music was stylistically diverse.

In this chapter, I will ask: When and in what form did dangdut become a signifier for the nation? I will discuss contrasting meanings about dangdut: the upgraded contained kind that articulated with state-supported culture, and the downgraded excessive kind that did not belong. I will show how the discourse about inclusiveness, in which dangdut encompasses the whole nation, was actually very selective and exclusive in terms of its form, representation, and meaning.

Dangdut on TV

The popularity of televised dangdut produced by the new private commercial stations in the early 1990s was one of the main factors that led to dangdut's incorporation into a national discourse about culture. Prior to the first commercial television broadcast by RCTI in 1988, the state-run television network TVRI held a monopoly on television. The state television network instrumentalized television from above as a tool to create an "audience-as-nation" (Kitley 2000, 79).

Private commercial stations were licensed in the late 1980s, but ownership of the stations was still in the hands of Suharto family members or cronies, and subject to government constraints. Ratings drove all programming decisions. As television executive Ishadi S. K. told me, "Our motto was 'don't ever produce a program that can't be sold'" (Ishadi S. K., pers. comm., 7 November 2006). In contrast to the state television network, commercial television catered to popular taste. In 2006, entertainment constituted approximately 75 percent of programming (ibid.). Dangdut, a commercial form of popular entertainment, flourished under these cultural and economic conditions.

When private commercial stations emerged, dangdut became a valuable commodity that could be sold for commercial time. Government-funded TVRI did not compete against the private stations, and it continued to resist promoting dangdut in any significant way. TVRI's programming of dangdut was limited and its content was controlled. Although TVRI programmed five music shows at the national level, there were limits on the amount of dangdut programming allowed on these programs.[2] Discussing two programs, Hoediono Drajat, director of planning for music and entertainment at the central TVRI station in Jakarta, stated that "the percentage of dangdut on Aneka Ria Safari can be up to 50 percent, and on Album Minggu it can be up to 40 percent" (Surawijaya 1991, 50).[3] A year later, TVRI surpassed its limits, as dangdut's popularity grew:

> Dangdut shows are not allowed more than 30% [on music programs].
> As it turns out, dangdut dominates with almost 75% of music
> programs. "Dangdut is now the trend. We are satisfying the tastes of
> the people," said Hoediono. (Pudyastuti 1992, 108)

But it was not purely a matter of serving the people that led to an increase in dangdut programming. During the height of the Suharto regime, the very highest ranking political officers working under the banner of Golkar created these links between media, politics, and culture, as described by Ishadi S. K.:

> Aneka Ria Safari was a profitable program [for TVRI] because that is
> where new songs were promoted. It was coordinated by Eddy Sud,
> under the name of Golkar, to raise money. Producers had to pay for
> their songs to be played on television. That was the rule. And at that
> time, dangdut was booming, so to get a song on Aneka Ria Safari was
> expensive. (Ishadi S. K., pers. comm., 7 November 2006)

It is important to note that recording companies had to pay for their singers to
be promoted on television. The inclusion of singers, and subsequently, their
popularity, depended on who could pay. As one composer told me: "In
Indonesia, everything can be bought, even popularity" (Fazal Dath, pers.
comm., 12 July 2005). As long as the recording company could afford to buy
time on the show, creating a hit song was relatively easy since there was only
one television station. For example, during this period, TVRI promoted heavily
a video of the song "Tidak Semua Laki-laki" (Not All Men), sung by vice
governor of Jakarta and chair of Golkar Basofi Sudirman. Not only was programming a matter of payola, but also politics:

> TVRI was very politicized at that time and every program was under
> the banner of Golkar. Dangdut was the music of the people, and so it
> was always used as a tool to reach the masses in political campaigns.
> Eddy Sud used the popularity of dangdut to move closer to the
> leadership of Golkar. Then he used Golkar to get access to TVRI,
> which was under Harmoko's control as Minister of Information.
> TVRI was the only station at that time. So dangdut was a political tool
> as well. (Ishadi S. K., pers. comm., 7 November 2006)

The emergence of commercial television changed the face of popular music.
Deregulation of the television industry encouraged diversity of programming
and an emphasis on entertainment (Kitley 2000, 249). Airtime on the private
stations could be bought relatively cheaply, compared to TVRI. In the early
1990s, dangdut's established audience began watching more television, and
the private stations catered to a growing market of potential consumers of
products advertised during these programs. Taking the lead was the
"Indonesian Educational Television" station (Televisi Pendidikan Indonesia,
TPI).[4] RCTI, another private station which had previously refused to broadcast dangdut, soon followed suit. The fees paid to RCTI producers were the
highest among all stations (Pudyastuti 1992, 108). SCTV was the last station
to have a dangdut show because their target audience was the middle and
upper classes, and that demographic did not like dangdut: "If 90% of our
viewers *did* like dangdut, why not [broadcast it]? Television is a taste industry,"

said Idriena Basarah, operations director of SCTV (italics mine; "Gebyar dangdut" 1994, 3).

Since the early 1990s, and particularly since the fall of ex-president Suharto in 1998, commercial television has played a dominant role in boosting dangdut's national popularity. Dangdut programs, including music videos, quiz shows, comedy programs, and contests, proliferated during the 1990s. The market for dangdut expanded beyond live public performances (attended by mostly males) to televised performances watched by females at home. Dangdut extended its reach into middle-class living rooms, and the genre began to shed its previous image as "backward" (kampungan). This shift in social geography, signified by dangdut's popularity among males and females, among the masses and the middle classes, placed dangdut in a powerful social position. What changes in content accompanied these new media contexts? Did increased media exposure translate into new social meanings for dangdut? How did television "bring the happiness of dangdut"?[5]

The stated goal of the private television stations was to attract middle- and upper-class audiences to dangdut. Producers began cultivating a new crop of glamorous singers in the 1990s, including Evie Tamala, Iis Dahlia, Ikke Nurjanah, and Cici Paramida. These stars belonged to a national class of singers and represented an upgraded form of dangdut. With the exception of Iis Dahlia, their songs emphasized a pop Indonesia vocal style rather than a Melayu quality.

Private television stations worked closely with the central government to produce made-for-television dangdut shows. For the 1995 celebration of the country's fiftieth anniversary, TPI (with the help of former Tarantula singer Camelia Malik, the director of the entertainment committee) secured funds from the central government to sponsor a large concert (Pergelaran akbar Semarak Dangdut 50 Tahun Indonesia Emas). The concert took place on 5 August 1995 in Ancol, Jakarta in front of a live audience reportedly numbering over 250,000 people ("Lingkaran Berhadiah Penonton Semarak Dangdut" 1995, 29).

Television programs experimented with a variety of formats that revolved around dangdut. In addition to dangdut music videos, television producers developed dangdut television dramas (sinetron). These programs constructed themes from dangdut songs, an idea that came from Indian films ("Balada dangdut," 1997). The program Salam Dangdut, a product of MTV Asia that first aired in 1999, featured music videos, interviews with stars, and tips on how to shake one's hips (goyang) (Ema 1999, 5).

While dangdut's audience has certainly grown, I remain skeptical that dangdut has been thoroughly incorporated into the national culture of Indonesia, as claimed by government and military officials in popular print media. In the 1990s, however, televised dangdut became a privileged site for inserting images, sounds, and texts about national belonging, described in the next section.

Dangdut as National Music in the 1990s

The relationship between dangdut and the New Order state became particularly focused and concentrated during the 1990s, garnering close attention in popular print media.[6] Major New Order figures involved in dangdut included Basofi Sudirman (vice governor of Jakarta and chair of Golkar), who recorded the song "Tidak Semua Laki-laki" (Not All Men) in 1992; Siti Hardiyanti Rukmana (Suharto's eldest daughter), the main shareholder of television station TPI, which led the way in broadcasting dangdut; B. J. Habibie, minister of state for research and technology; and Moerdiono, secretary of state, among others. In the New Order newspaper *Pos Kota*, Habibie and Moerdiono were shown dancing at a rally in May 1992, urging the crowd to vote in an upcoming Golkar regional election in June ("Moerdiono dan Habibie" 1992).[7]

Quotes by high-ranking ministers assimilated dangdut to the slogan-laden language of New Order politics. Basofi Sudirman claimed that "with dangdut we will success-ify development" ("Basofi Sudirman" 1994, 2). Another 1994 article, entitled "Pesta Demokrasi Praktisi Dangdut Mencari Figur Pemimpin," compared the search for a new leader of a dangdut cultural organization with the New Order's quinquennial "festival of democracy" (*pesta demokrasi*) (Harahap 1994, 5). Moerdiono called dangdut a "commodity with potential for unlimited development...[and] a chance to go international" in the 1990s (quoted in Piper 1995, 44). In its reconstructed international commodity form, dangdut could now allegedly symbolically represent Indonesia among the nations of the world.

Based on governmental, commercial, and critical support for dangdut, and publications about dangdut's heightened presence on television and in elite entertainment venues, it is tempting to argue that dangdut had finally become accepted among all Indonesians as "national music." For example, the day after Secretary of State Moerdiono sang at a highly publicized concert featuring national dangdut stars, the newspaper *Suara Pembaruan* reported: "Dangdut is our music, the music of our people" ("Moerdiono Bergoyang Dangdut" 1994).

It is worth examining in more detail the ideological content and functioning of these media. Some of them, like the newspaper *Pos Kota*, emphasized the close links between the New Order and dangdut. *Pos Kota* was controlled by

Minister of Information Harmoko and was the first newspaper in Indonesia to focus on crime. Others, like newsmagazine *Tempo*, used dangdut as a way to express a position critical of the New Order state (Surawijaya 1991, 55). For example, *Tempo* reported that Secretary of State Moerdiono loved dangdut, which he listened to as he was being chauffeured to extravagant state functions in his expensive Volvo B-50. On the road, he listened to songs like "Sepiring Berdua" (Two Eat from One Plate) and "Gubuk Derita" (Hut of Suffering). Based on an interview with the secretary of state, the article highlights the incongruity of dangdut representing a high government official.

> "The words to those kinds of songs can make us more empathetic toward each other," he said to TEMPO female reporter Linda Djalil. "I feel represented by those words," said Moerdiono. He did not elaborate on what he meant by "represent." Let's not forget that he is certainly not someone who "eats from a shared plate." What is clear is that his driver put his tape collection together. "He is the one I order to buy cassettes." (Surawijaya 1991, 55)

Moerdiono's remarks suggest that dangdut songs about suffering and not having enough to eat could make people feel more empathetic and compassionate toward the majority of Indonesians. This was a very humanizing gesture by an individual who may have had a genuine love of the music. But the article addresses him as secretary of state of a government that funneled the wealth of the nation-state to Suharto and his cronies and had little empathy for the majority of its people, many of whom were living below the poverty line. Moerdiono does not explain what he means by "represent," suggesting a statement that he cannot support. The author immediately highlights the odd notion that Moerdiono could possibly be represented in a song about not having enough to eat. Further, if he has to "order" someone to choose the music that he reportedly loves, then how much can he actually know about dangdut? *Tempo* editor Goenawan Mohamad explained:

> Moerdiono's love for dangdut has to be viewed within the context of the relationship between Moerdiono and [Minister of Information] Harmoko, who had banned dangdut from being shown on TVRI. They were political rivals, although both belonged to the Suharto regime, and they did things behind the scenes. (pers. comm., 2 July 2006)

Tempo was famous for inserting hidden messages into their reports, especially when quoting high-ranking government officials (Steele 2005, 87–113). By affirming that he liked dangdut, Moerdiono sent a signal of his dislike of

Harmoko, the Minister of Information who sanctioned the banning of Rhoma Irama on TVRI (1977–1988). Moerdiono expressed a position against Harmoko on practically every political issue, mostly in a covert way. The relationship between Moerdiono and Harmoko characterized the inner-party conflicts within the New Order regime, which was not a monolithic entity. *Tempo* used Moerdiono's dislike of Harmoko, which was veiled in Moerdiono's support for dangdut, to promote its own critique of the New Order regime. In the hands of *Tempo*'s editors, Moerdiono's identification with dangdut became a tool to expand the wedge between two of the New Order's top political strategists. The New Order regime recognized *Tempo*'s strategy to pit these power brokers against one another, and this may have been one of the reasons for the government taking strong action against *Tempo*. *Tempo*'s publishing license would be revoked three years later under an order from the Department of Information, and Harmoko was suspected of being the mastermind behind the banning of *Tempo* (Steele 2005, 235).

National development and cultural organization

The relationship between dangdut and the state was established in the late 1970s. In 1978, the central government encouraged the formation of a musician's organization, the Indonesian Organization of Entertainers and Melayu Music (Yayasan Artis dan Musik Melayu Indonesia, YAMMI). The first director was a former general and vice governor of Jakarta, Eddie Nalapraya, whose stated platform was to elevate the status of dangdut by organizing regional festivals and singing competitions in Jakarta and surrounding areas (Bogor, Tangerang, and Bekasi) ("Pokok & Tokoh," 1979b, 19). YAMMI received funding from the regional cultural office of Jakarta (Dinas Kebudayaan Jakarta). In 1980, it changed its name to the Indonesian Institute of Melayu Musical Entertainers (Lembaga Artis Musik Melayu Indonesia, LAMMI), and in 1985, its status was officially recognized and documented by the regional Jakarta government (Soeprapto 1985).

In 1989, LAMMI changed its name to the Indonesian Union of Melayu Musical Entertainers (Persatuan Artis Musik Melayu Indonesia, PAMMI). PAMMI created a bridge between dangdut and the central government. The goal of PAMMI was to support and develop Melayu music (dangdut) and to coordinate the activities of singers and musicians in the region of DKI Jakarta (Atmodarminto 1989). The governor of Jakarta stated in New Orderese that "in addition to entertaining people, it is hoped that the music will stimulate fans to raise the level of their work and spirit to develop. Further, musical compositions should contain messages that emphasize the spirit of development" (Atmodarminto 1990).

Another one of its stated aims, articulated by officer Rhoma Irama, was to regulate the activities of its members (Surawijaya 1991, 60). Rhoma Irama was especially concerned with the kinds of costumes and movements that women displayed in public performance, a topic that will be discussed in chapter 7.

PAMMI supported efforts to write the history of dangdut during the mid-1990s. In addition to stories about the lives of singers, the tabloid *Citra* produced a special issue on dangdut that included an interview with former band leader, composer, and PAMMI official Zakaria about the history of dangdut (*Citra* no. 209, IV, 28 March–3 April 1994). The first article in the issue stressed that "dangdut is our music, representing Indonesian culture, and [therefore] we have to protect it" (Nizar 1994, 7). The emphasis on protection characterized the discourse about culture in the New Order, even though the politics and policies of protection often led to state-led development and change (Acciaioli 1985).

In Zakaria's view, the history of dangdut mirrors the history of the independent Republic of Indonesia. Zakaria characterizes the development of dangdut as a banyan tree, a symbol of the Golkar regime (see figure 6.2). The genre took root during the 1940s, when the independent nation was officially established. For the period 1950 to 1975, Zakaria describes the most noteworthy groups, their musical directors, and their singers, corresponding to five-year blocks. These five-year blocks suggest parallels to the New Order's five-year economic development plans (*rencana pembangunan lima tahun*, or *repelita*).

1940–1960: (1950–1955; 1955–1960): *akar* (roots)
1960–1975: (1960–1965; 1965–1970; 1970–1975): *batang* (trunk)
1975–1990: *cabang dan ranting* (branches and twigs)
1990–2000: *dedaunan* (leaves)

This timeline contrasts with other stories about the history of dangdut, for example those described in chapter 2, that place the development of dangdut in 1930s *orkes gambus,* or in 1950s *orkes Melayu* (or earlier, in Melayu Deli).

Going International

In the April 1991 issue of the tabloid *Nova,* "Kopi Dangdut" (Dangdut Coffee) was celebrated as the fourth most popular album in Japan, demonstrating dangdut's global market strength, and promoting national pride in the music at home (Jubing et al 1991, 10).[8] Dangdut's appearance on concert stages in Malaysia and Japan reportedly led to its heightened reception at home ("Perjalanan Musik Dangdut" 1992). An instructor in the Psychology Department at the University of Indonesia stated that "dangdut can become the main music

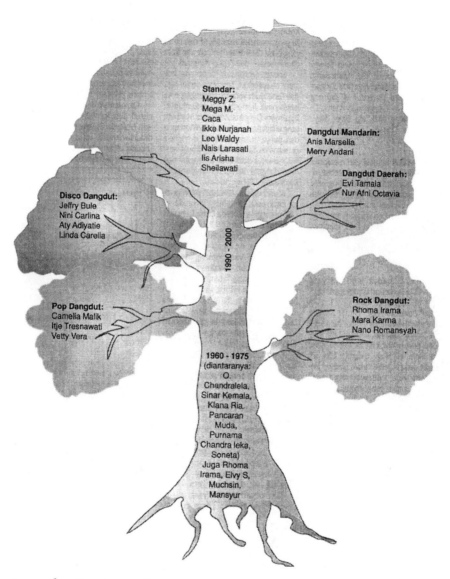

Standar:
Meggy Z.
Mega M.
Caca
Ikke Nurjanah
Leo Waldy
Nais Larasati
Iis Arisha
Sheilawati

Dangdut Mandarin:
Anis Marsella
Merry Andani

Dangdut Daerah:
Evi Tamala
Nur Afni Octavia

Disco Dangdut:
Jeffry Bule
Nini Carlina
Aty Adiyatie
Linda Carella

1990 - 2000

Rock Dangdut:
Rhoma Irama
Mara Karma
Nano Romansyah

Pop Dangdut:
Camelia Malik
Itje Tresnawati
Vetty Vera

1960 - 1975
(diantaranya:
O.
Chandralela,
Sinar Kemala,
Klana Ria,
Pancaran
Muda,
Purnama
Chandra Ieka,
Soneta)
Juga Rhoma
Irama, Elvy S,
Muchsin,
Mansyur

FIGURE 6.2 Dangdut tree diagram, (Nizar and Suherman 1994, 2).

of Indonesian culture. Even foreigners are interested in it, right?" (Surawijaya 1991, 55–56). Its commodity value outside Indonesia, rather than its popularity and value among a huge population of Indonesians, helped to convince middle and upper classes that dangdut had social value. On the contrary, dangdut fans felt that dangdut was just fine as it was. For them, "going international" did not make a difference.

What is the cultural logic of "going international"? This discourse emerged from the "middle classes and up," which had long been involved in shaping the discourse about dangdut for particular material and ideological purposes (see chapter 4). As a commodity, it could be marketed abroad and used in tourist campaigns and advertising slogans. And as a symbol of the nation, it could be used to integrate dangdut audiences into the national formation. But in order for dangdut to fulfill those goals, the music and its associations would have to be transformed.

First, dangdut had to dispel its image as backward (*kampungan*): "It cannot be considered 'kampungan' anymore because it has already gone international" (Ema 1999, 5). No longer content to stay where it was, these sources reported, dangdut was on the move. The headlines declared that "dangdut had climbed up to the summit" in the late 1990s (Yurnaldi and Rakaryan 1997, 20). Dangdut was for everyone, from those at the bottom of the political system, to those at the top. Better yet, dangdut could even function as "aspirin" (*obat pusing*) to cure the country's social ills, which were considerable after the Asian economic crisis in 1997, when the following article was published:

> Dangdut has become the glue that holds together our nation's social classes. As 'aspirin,' it can be enjoyed by shoe polishers, newspaper sellers, hard laborers, chauffeurs, housewives, and up to governors and government ministers. ("Generasi baru Dangdut dut..." 1997)

Yet, what ideas, images, and meanings about ordinary people—via dangdut—actually appeared in popular print media and on television in the 1990s? Images and stories related to dangdut became even further removed from most people's everyday lives. Pictures and stories about the glamorous lives of dangdut celebrities flooded the tabloid market. Stars were shown performing in sparkling television studios or on spectacular concert stages; dressed in jeans and sportswear at home enjoying their vast leisure time with family; or driving expensive cars, dressed in brand-name clothes, and sitting in cafes with fellow celebrities.[9] Sponsorship flowed in from cigarette and drug companies (for example, aspirin).

As Suharto's New Order regime gasped for breath in mid-1997, the television station TPI sponsored an awards show entitled *Anugerah Dangdut 97*. The award for "Dangdut Figure of the Year" was not given to a singer, musician, composer, arranger, or producer, but to Secretary of State Moerdiono. Attended by high-ranking government ministers and army generals, among other elites, it was "proof that dangdut had achieved a position of respect: sparkling, well-groomed, and, yes, even prestigious" ("Generasi Baru, Dangdut Dut..." 1997). Touted as the new generation of dangdut, celebrities walked down the red carpet in evening gowns and designer suits. The values of the "new generation" contrasted with the unglamorous, ordinary, and increasingly disordered lives of the majority of its fans.

But what did this "success" mean, as it was reported in popular print media? It meant that producers were busy manufacturing dangdut sound recordings, television broadcasts, and popular print media that they imagined would appeal to middle classes and above. Television station RCTI brought in singer Meggy Z. and composer Toto Ario to help attract the "A-B audience," whose monthly household income was around US$ 1,000 or more per month, or about four times the average salary of a government employee ("Asyiknya Digoyang Dangdut" 2001). These dangdut musicians were hired to help create arrangements and themes, especially for middle-class and elite audiences. Dangdut singer and film star Camelia Malik noted that dangdut had to be purified of its earlier associations:

> For the pop audience, dangdut was hickish, erotic, not poetic, and too explicit. So we had to purify (mengharamkan) dangdut of its earlier associations. (Camelia Malik, pers. comm., 18 July 2005)

The campaign that "dangdut was for everyone" was largely a matter of packaging. Camelia Malik stated:

> I don't want to tell people what to like. I just want to show that dangdut can be wrapped in banana leaves (daun pisang) and it can also be wrapped in aluminum foil (aluminium). It can be put in a box...Dangdut has been relegated to the lower class. But it turns out that the middle class and above want it too. They said, "help us out, our tastes need to be satisfied too." As performers, we have to be able to serve anyone and everyone. (quoted in Purwanto and Purwadi 2000, 6)

If dangdut was for everyone, then why did popular print media concentrate so heavily on representing the wealthy and powerful, the minority of society? As dangdut allegedly began to stand for everyone, the majority of society receded even further from representation. This new rhetoric of incorporation contradicted the messages presented in these social texts. As a result, the majority of society, who could not identify with the lifestyles represented in these texts, were forced to occupy a position outside these representations.

Dangdut Gets Rich?

As the dangdut industry grew in the 1990s, dangdut signified profitability for the private television shareholders, music industry executives, cassette producers, and some artists. Ties between government and mass media allowed certain popular forms to flourish, namely those produced in industries with strong government connections (television, for example).

One indicator of dangdut's increasing popularity was reportage about sales of recordings in popular print media. In 1991, *Tempo* published an extensive feature article about the wealth and status of dangdut stars (Surawijaya 1991, 55). Whereas they used to earn only enough for "two to eat from one plate" (after the song "Sepiring Berdua") now they each have enough to own "two cars per person" (*dua mobil seorang*). The article stated that "dangdut—that kampungan form—not only sounds like a drum, but it also sounds like the ringing of a cash register" (ibid., 60).

Sales figures printed in *Tempo* in 1992 demonstrated dangdut's commercial potential in relation to *pop Indonesia*.[10] The economics of the cassette industry made dangdut more profitable than *pop Indonesia* because the cost of producing a pop album was more expensive than a dangdut album, and dangdut cassettes were also cheaper to buy (Pudyastuti 1992, 108). As a result, pop singers continued to cross over to dangdut (e.g., Chrisye, Trio Libels, Ruth Sahayana). Recordings by pop singers who had not crossed over were put on hold (e.g., Jamal Mirdad, Denny Malik, Hetty Koes Endang) (ibid.). This period marks a difference from the late 1970s, when dangdut was regarded as difficult to sing and too close to "the people" (see chapter 4). As the demand for dangdut increased, and the profits increased, pop singers were more willing to cross over.

However, reports about the number of albums sold made it sound like artists were sharing in the profits. One article states:

> ...from one song "Lebih Baik Sakit Gigi" (A Toothache Is Better), which sold 300,000 copies, Meggy Z was given a new model Mazda 323 car. From one song "Duh Engkang" (Oh, My Dear), which sold 800,000 copies, Itje built a mosque in her town of birth, Tasikmalaya. (Surawijaya 1991, 49)

These articles highlight the tremendous popularity of dangdut, but they present a skewed image of the economics of the recording industry. Even those stars who had recorded national hits received a flat fee ("flat pay") as opposed to royalties. They received the same amount regardless of the number of units sold. Therefore, a large number of sales did not correspond to a high income for these singers. National recording star Meggy Z. noted:

> I agreed to receive flat pay because I didn't want to know how many units were sold. If I had chosen to receive royalties I would start to think about it and it would make me suspicious. And I would get

tired asking "Boss, how many were sold?" What's the use when they won't let us see the sales figure reports? (pers. comm., 12 July 2005)

Further, the sales figures quoted in these sources did not seem accurate to musicians, who were not privy to the number of units sold. For Meggy Z., 300,000 units seemed like a low number, considering the number of dangdut fans and the population of Indonesia:

We [musicians] don't know how producers determine "flat pay." That's a secret in the recording industry. Producers are not open about their management operations. Take, for example, the matter of sales. They say that a hit record sells 300,000 cassettes. The majority of Indonesians like dangdut. At that time [early 1990s] the population of Indonesia was about 180 million. Let's say that 1,000 people from each village [kelurahan] bought a cassette. How many villages are there in each region? And they say that only 300,000 units were sold? That's nonsense! (pers. comm., 12 July 2005)

Even among those singers who recorded hit songs, only very few of them made very much money from recordings. The top national stars with hit songs made up the smallest category. The mid-level regional stars, who comprised the middle category, had recorded albums but had not delivered a national hit. And those who had not recorded made up the largest category. For most singers, even those in the middle category, dangdut was not profitable, as shown by the following example.

Euis Cahya

Euis Cahya (b. 1965) was a rock singer in Bandung who crossed over to singing popular music, and to dangdut when it became popular in the 1980s.[11] Her look was hot and sexy. She performed frequently in Bandung and throughout West Java, and she became one of a handful of very well-known Sundanese female dangdut singers.

Despite recording 11 albums between 1980 and 1994, she never achieved national fame. She signed a contract with the recording company Billboard Indonesia in the early 1980s while still a teenager, but the duration of the contract was not specified. Therefore, she was in fact contracted for life, which excluded her from recording with another company. Further, the company owned all the rights to her recordings, so they could re-release a song at any time without renegotiating her contract.

In 1989, one of her albums, *Isabella,* sold very well, with estimated sales of over 400,000 cassettes. The company wanted to reward her with a car, but it was not simply to be given to her. Rather, she had to pay the car off with profits from her next album. Even if they had given her the car, the profits far outweighed the cost of buying it.

Euis Cahya worked on a royalty system and frequently wondered how many of her albums Billboard had actually sold. She often asked to see the figures listing albums sold, but the company kept different sets of sales figures, depending on who wanted to see them. For the tax office, for example, they kept a book showing losses. It was only after the urging of the warehouse manager who handled the shipments of *Isabella* that she was able to find out that it had sold much better than she was being told. In 1990 she forced Billboard Indonesia to pay her royalties in cash, which they did. Subsequently, she refused to honor the remaining terms of her contract and moved to a smaller production company with a correspondingly smaller budget for promotion. From then on her recording career nose-dived.

Euis Cahya's story illustrates that cassettes were thought to be a privilege for singers that could be used to advertise live concerts. The explanation she was given in 1990 by the owners of Billboard Indonesia was that artists should regard their recording opportunities not as profitable activities but as good publicity for improving their profile. She was told that singers could not expect to make good money from record sales, but would only ever prosper from live performances, which she had to arrange independently, separately from any recording activities. Indeed, she always made far more from live performances (especially since Billboard underpaid her for records sold).

Television worked similarly. Television performances were funded by payments made directly by a Billboard representative to the TVRI producers or directors (presumably some of which were distributed upward to TVRI senior management). Entertainment journalists were also given money by Billboard to publicize her.

An implicit subtext was that Euis should consider herself lucky to even have a recording contract, and that Billboard was doing her a favor, not vice-versa; that she must do exactly as Billboard instructed to receive any attention from them; and that there were plenty of young singers who would be obedient and could easily take Euis's position as one of the Billboard artists.

Toward the end of her career, her main backer and patron was Tetty Kadi, a famous Bandung singer from the 1970s who had become a music industry entrepreneur and Golkar politician. In 1993 Tetty Kadi recommended Euis to Colonel Prabowo Subianto, President Suharto's son-in-law, who was looking for a bilingual singer to entertain the many foreign and English-speaking guests

Prabowo received as the commanding officer of the Special Commando Force (Komando Pasukan Khusus, Kopassus) in Bandung. Euis had lived in Australia and was a well-known name in Bandung. From then on, she lived at the beck and call of Prabowo and Kopassus. Armed military personnel would come to her home to pick her up for gigs, making sure she arrived on time. She would have to stay until the wee hours of the morning and was only released when Kopassus was ready to let her go home. But the money was great, and her career took off.

The discourse of dangdut stars getting rich from the success of a booming cultural industry does not match the experiences of artists themselves. Euis Cahya was a mid-level star who did not earn much income from recordings and live performances, but rather from her involvement with New Order sponsorship. So, while dangdut was profitable for the cassette and television industries, the money did not trickle down to the artists. However, commercial producers maintained their control over singers by withholding access to royalty figures and by making them feel that they were lucky because there were plenty of artists ready to replace them. These techniques strengthened their hold on singers and perpetuated a system where "that was just how things were done."

Censorship, Women, and Nation

What kinds of images, values, and meanings about the nation were made available to people in dangdut during this period? The Department of Information, through its national television station TVRI, exerted strict controls over what could be shown on television. Songs were banned for allegedly creating a bad image of Indonesia, including "Gadis atau Janda?" (Are You a Virgin or Not?), and "Jagung Bakar" (Grilled Corn), which were both banned from being shown on TVRI in early 1992 (Persda 1992; Tobing 1992; "Asmin Cayder" 1992). Censorship of dangdut songs was based on lyrics and visual images that were considered immoral or critical of the Suharto regime.[12] However, the guidelines for controlling content were not clearly stated. Dangdut fans reportedly complained about being offended by the lyrics and erotic movements that they had viewed on television (Tobing 1992). But these reports have to be questioned, given that the government did not have a mechanism to identify people's opinions on these matters.

In the following section, I will discuss two songs that were released around the same time, "Duh Engkang" (Oh My Dear; first released in 1988, followed by several more versions and a television drama sinetron of the same name) and "Gadis atau Janda" (Are you a Virgin or not?) (1992). These two songs signify differently within the national discourse about culture, as shown by their different relationships to TVRI. "Duh Engkang" was heavily promoted on TVRI, both in music programming as well as in a *sinetron* of the same name. The video for "Gadis atau Janda" was banned from being played on TVRI. These two songs present very different images of women, particularly the ways in which women articulate symbolically with the nation. By using representations of women as symbolic markers of the nation, I aim to understand why certain narratives of the nation were deemed acceptable, and others unacceptable, during this period.

"Duh Engkang" was a hit song that producers developed into a *sinetron* in 1996. [◐] The song is part of a larger story about a family that has left its rural village in West Java for a better life in the capital city of Jakarta. After migrating to the city, the husband has forgotten his experience of poverty, which has caused him to lose his soul. His wife urges him to return to the simple and traditional lifestyle of the village.

Itje Tresnawati, the wife of TVRI producer Eddy Sud, recorded the song and performed it many times for various national television broadcasts. Itje Tresnawati's presentation style reflected a pop orientation. She appeared on television with salon-styled hairdos in glamorous evening dresses and expensive shoes. Her movements, although modeled on the dynamic and eroticized style of Sundanese *jaipongan,* were extremely slow, fluid, and reserved. Her vocal quality was thin and breathy, similar to an entire class of female singers in the 1990s. In contrast to Elvy Sukaesih, for example, there was little ornamentation of the vocal line.

The primarily Indonesian-language song incorporates Sundanese words and phrases to give the song a regional connotation. *Engkang* (or its abbreviated form, *kang*) is a Sundanese form of address for a male of equal or higher status, and it is often used by a woman to address her husband. Other regional Sundanese signifiers include the sound of Sundanese instruments *angklung* (shaken bamboo rattle) and *suling* (bamboo flute). These sonic signifiers index regionality, a topic I will discuss more fully in chapter 8. However, "Duh Engkang" was very much a national song in terms of its musical style, production, circulation, and meaning. Composed by Muchtar B., the song is the woman's plea to her husband to return home, as shown in figure 6.3.

Similar to standard *sinetron*, "Duh Engkang" (1996) featured an attractive star, complicated family situations, a love story, and a rags-to-riches narrative structure. Majid and his wife Dedeh live a happy, simple, and pious traditional life in a village in West Java. She dutifully and happily takes care of the household and the children. He is a farmer, while she sells snacks to earn extra income. He studies hard to earn his degree in business in order to pursue his dreams of material success.

After receiving his degree, Majid takes a company job in Jakarta, and moves his family there. Their lives change immediately. They live in a luxurious house with servants. Majid works at an office, plays golf, enjoys buying cars, and has

A: Duh engkang, naha teungteuingan? Duh engkang, sok ka bina bina, Engkang mulai lupa di kala hidup susah, Tinggal di rumah tua, Waktu kita di desa.	A: Oh engkang, how could you do this? Oh engkang, it's too much to bear, Engkang has forgotten when life was hard, Living in an old house, When we lived in the village.
A': Duh engkang, naha teungteuingan? Euh engkang, sok ka bina bina, Engkang sudah lupa waktu hidup sengsara, Makan dari mertua, Waktu kita di desa.	A': Oh engkang, how could you do this? Oh engkang, it's too much to bear, Engkang has forgotten how we suffered, Eating food from our parents, When we lived in the village.
[interlude]	[interlude]
B: Baru saja lumayan hidup di Jakarta, Engkang rek suka-suka engkang rek ngadua, Dari pada sengsara biar jadi randa, Biar banda teu boga asal bahagia, Euh engkang, sok ka bina bina.	B: Our lives have only just gotten started in Jakarta, You just want to have fun and share your heart, Rather than suffering, I'd rather be divorced, I'd rather not have things as long as we're happy, Oh, engkang it's too much.
[repeat verse A']	[repeat verse A']
[interlude]	[interlude]
B": Coba engkang renungkan niat hidup kita, Membangun rumah tangga kekal bahagia, Kita harus berkorban demi masa depan, Harta hanya titipan itu milik Tuhan, Duh engkang sadarlah kembali.	B": Try to remember engkang the goals that we shared, To build a home together and to be happy, We have to sacrifice for the future, Property is only temporary, it belongs to God, Oh engkang wake up and come home.
A": Duh engkang syukur pada Tuhan, Duh engkang terhindar cobaan, Hidup sederhana asalkan bahagia, Itu tujuan kita untuk selama-lamanya.	A": Oh engkang, pray to God, Oh engkang stay away from temptation, A simple life as long as we're happy, That's our goal for as long as we live.
[spoken] "Kang, ayo kita pulang ke desa saja biar hidup sederhana tapi bahagia Kang."	[spoken] "C'mon kang, let's go home to our village to live a simple and happy life."

FIGURE 6.3 "Duh Engkang" (Oh My Dear) [courtesy of Muchtar B.].

a mistress. Dedeh, however, yearns to return to the simple life of the village. Modern clothes feel foreign to her. The couple quarrels often. Dedeh manages to suppress her desire for change until the day she finds a photo of her husband and his mistress in his coat pocket. She returns to the village alone, while Majid stays in Jakarta and continues to advance in his company. Suddenly, he has a stroke, and has to stay in the hospital for three months. He is forced to quit his job at the company and loses everything. He returns to the village to be nearer to his mother and father. Meanwhile, Dedeh refuses to see him. But his parents arrange a meeting and she agrees to take him back home.

The figure of Dedeh offers a symbolic representation of nation in the New Order. The New Order regime defined roles of women as wives and mothers, with the family at the core of the state "family" (Sullivan 1991; Suryakusuma 1996).[13] Counterrepresentations of the feminine would threaten the construction of the state as a family, referred to as the "family principle" (*azas kekeluargaan*) in the language of the New Order (Suryakusuma 1996).

The story presents a nostalgic view of traditional life in which the village—the rural homeland represented by Dedeh—is safe and comfortable, and the city—the site of modernity represented by Majid—is full of temptation and potential danger. Dedeh embodies the preservation of the nation's culture and traditions, whereas Majid represents development, agency, and change.

"Duh Engkang" valorizes family values. Dedeh represents the ideal of a "good" Indonesian wife and mother. She works to support the goals of the collective community (the family) by sacrificing herself for Majid's education, following him to Jakarta, and then forgiving him when things do not work out. She suffers in silence, putting duty and family above her own interests. She contains her own desire for the sake of the family. She holds everything together while he goes out and destroys everything they have.

Without Dedeh, Majid has nothing. When he eventually comes home, broken and needy and seeking forgiveness, Dedeh is there for him. She nurses him back to health and to life. When he finally returns home, she gives him security and helps him regain his confidence.

The program is a morality tale that uses stock characters to demonstrate its point; the couple does not work through their problems. Majid would probably have remained in the city if he had not been stricken by disease. Instead, by the grace of God, circumstances force them back together. It is her fate to suffer and to sacrifice for him for the benefit of the family. And at the conclusion of the tale, after order has been restored, the family is reunited and stronger.

A very different image is depicted in the images, sound, text, and discourse of "Gadis atau Janda" (Are You a Virgin or not?). [●] Composed by Awab Haris in the 1960s, the arrangement and performance of "Gadis atau Janda" is a throwback to an earlier pre–New Order era of 1960s *orkes Melayu*. The prelude begins with a *gambus*-like melodic line accompanied by a *chalte* rhythmic framework (and variations) played on the Indian tabla (not the *gendang* commonly used in dangdut). The interlude features a keyboard set to an accordion timbre and a Middle Eastern drum pattern. These elements give the song a dated feel. Further, the two singers were in their forties by the time of the song's release.

"Gadis atau Janda" portrays a woman—a mother who has "many children"—who is sexually active, possibly with more than one man. The mood around male-female sexual relations as depicted in "Gadis atau Janda" is playful and fun (figure 6.4). It plays on the meaning of *kawin*, which can mean "marriage" but can also mean "sexual intercourse" (especially at the end of the song, when it is done with urgency, as in "let's just get married right now!"). By twisting the meaning of "marriage," the song disrupts notions of proper family relations.

F: Sudah berulang kali aku bermain cinta	F: So many times I've played the game of love
M: Jadi baru abang yang adik cinta	M: But never with me, sweetheart
F: Pemuda yang gangguku semuanya buaya	F: The young men that come to me are all creeps
M: Abang jadi ragu pada dirimu	M: But I'm uncertain about your feelings
F: Masa sih, bang?!	F: Really??
M: Kau masih gadis atau sudah janda?	M: Are you a virgin or not?
M: Baik katakan saja jangan malu	M: It's ok to tell me, don't be ashamed
F: Memangnya mengapa aku harus malu?	F: Why would I be ashamed?
F: Abang tentu dapat 'tuk membedakannya	F: You can certainly tell the difference
M: Kau katakan saja yang sesungguhnya	M: But I want you to tell me
F: Sesungguhnya diriku ah memang sudah janda	F: I'm definitely a divorcee
M: Walaupun kau janda tetap ku cinta	M: I don't care, I still love you
M: Kau masih gadis atau sudah janda?	M: Are you a virgin or not?
M: Baik katakan saja jangan malu	M: It's ok to tell me, don't be ashamed
F: Memangnya mengapa aku harus malu?	F: Why would I be ashamed?
F: Abang tentu dapat 'tuk membedakannya	F: You can certainly tell the difference
M: Kau katakan saja yang sesungguhnya	M: But I want you to tell me
[spoken]	[spoken]
F: Malu, ah!	F: I'm embarrassed
M: Malu ama siapa?	M: Embarassed by whom?
F: Tapi didengar orang	F: They can hear us
M: Mana? nggak ada orang	M: Where? There's no one else here
F: Itu	F: Over there
M: mana?	M: Where?
F: Itu!	F: Over there!
F: Kalau janda, masih mau kan?	F: If I'm a divorcee, would you still want me?
M: Tentu dong	M: Of course!
F: Anaknya banyak!	F: I have lots of kids!
M: Ngaak apa-apa. Yang penting kalau saya cinta?	M: That's ok. What's important is that I love you?
[sung]	[sung]
F: Sesungguhnya diriku ah memang sudah janda	F: I'm definitely a divorcee
M: Walaupun kau janda tetap ku cinta	M: I don't care, I still love you
M&F: Marilah segera kita kawin saja	M & F: Let's just get "married" right now!

FIGURE 6.4 "Gadis atau Janda" (Are You a Virgin or Not?) (F = female, M = male) [courtesy of Nilma Awab H.].

In the interlude, singers Elvy Sukaesih and Mansyur S. can be heard cooing, gasping, and laughing as they dance with each other. They create a dialogue about their ensuing love affair. Elvy is worried that they are being watched, while Mansyur S. assures her that no one is around. But, of course, we are all watching. The song brazenly exposes a very public demonstration of this very private moment. It tests the limits of what is socially acceptable, and confuses notions of public and private space. In live performances of the song, the ending dialogue section is improvisatory and open-ended. For example, I watched a performance of this song in 2008, in which two singers, an older man and a younger woman, stretched out the dialogue with the help of two emcees. The questions—"Are you a virgin or not?" and "Will you love me if I'm a divorcee?"—hung in the air as the emcees directed jokes toward the man and the woman, about their real and alleged romantic liaisons (some with members of the audience). This improvisatory section works against the grain of a set text with one fixed meaning.

The video cathects their erotic longing with sensual commodities including expensive cars, motorcycles, and clothing styles. It is set at a resort in the Puncak area of Bogor, a place for relaxation and leisure. Erotic desire articulates with the desire for commodities (Mankekar 2004). The pleasure of watching this erotic display of desire is similar to the longing for the expensive cars and lifestyles of the rich and famous.

The song and the video focus on the female singer, who represents erotic pleasure and desire. She is active and assertive. If Elvy's middle-aged body is not enough to hold the attention of viewers, cutaway shots of twenty-year-old dancing virgins (*gadis* and not *janda*) in tight black dresses will.

In this song text and performance, the woman's agency and interest in sex threatens the ideal family structure. The modern lifestyle depicted in the video is antithetical to tradition (nation). Therefore, it was not surprising that the song's video was banned from being shown on the national television network TVRI by the Indonesian State Censorship Board in the early 1990s. Singer Mansyur S. attributes the banning of "Gadis atau Janda" to the work of the Family Welfare Guidance Agency (Pendidikan Kesejahteraan Keluarga, PKK), a Suharto government program that served as a conduit for state ideology to travel between the state and women throughout the country: "They said that if people just go around having kids out of wedlock, they'll increase the population and that will multiply our social problems. The lyrics of the songs did not educate people, they said." (Mansyur S., pers. comm., 12 July 2005.) However, Mansyur S. resisted the notion that songs must have an educative function: "This is just a song! People aren't stupid; a song cannot make them have sex. Besides, regarding personal issues, if a guy wants to be with a divorcee, that's his business!" (ibid.).

Indeed, one of the main problems signaled by this song is a man's neglect of family. The problem was not the fact that men and women were having sex outside of marriage, but rather, that men were not responsible financially for the children that resulted from their sexual union. But the song raises other issues about women, especially the depiction of a woman who was in control of her own body, whether in marriage or not. In the following section, I will focus on these seldom articulated issues, voiced in the song.

The song depicts a woman in sexual terms, as either unavailable (*gadis*) or available (*janda*) for sex with men. *Janda* are central to numerous dangdut songs: "Janda Kembang" (A Childless Janda); "Jandaku" (My Janda); "Jandamu" (Your Janda); "Nasib Janda" (A Janda's Fate); "Mabok Janda" (Crazy about Janda); Digilir Cinta (Changing Love Partners); "Jablai" (Rarely Caressed). In

Hai serba salah jikalau menjadi janda,	If you're a janda, you can't do anything right,
Ke manapun saja orang curiga,	Wherever you go, people are suspicious,
Keluar rumah mau mencari rezeki,	You leave the house to make a living,
Disangka maunya cari lelaki.	And they think you've gone out to find a man.
Nasib, ya nasib,	That's fate, yes fate,
Begini nasibnya seorang janda.	That's the fate of a janda.

FIGURE 6.5 "Nasib Janda" (A Janda's Fate).

the popular imagination, *janda*—female widows and divorcees—are automatically presumed to be promiscuous because there is not a man in their lives regulating their activities. Marriage releases them from the authority of their fathers and other male members of their immediate family. If a woman does not have a husband, whether through the death of her husband or divorce, it is often assumed that she will have sex with anyone, and that she will tempt the husbands of others, as illustrated by the song "Nasib Janda" (figure 6.5).

The social stigma attached to *janda* status has very real effects, as described by dangdut singer Iis Dahlia. When asked by an interviewer, "Did being a *janda* have any psychological effects on you," Iis Dahlia answered:

> Because of the label "janda" there was a lot of gossip about me having many lovers. Because of that gossip, and that label, I decided to stay at home and limit my activities. But after limiting myself to such an extent, I felt somehow different, not like myself. I told myself to be careful of my actions. When I was married, I was very outgoing, but after getting divorced, I became very introverted so that people would not think negatively about me. (Ensiklopedi Tokoh Indonesia, "Iis Dahlia")

Janda were viewed as a problem for Indonesia because they did not adhere to the "family principle" that circumscribes a woman's role as wife and mother. As a result, single mothers were not supported by national policies, but only within local communities. Their marginal status challenged the model image underwritten by the nation-state (Sullivan 1991; Suryakusuma 1996). Alternative representations of women as anything besides "dependent, irrational, emotional, passive, and obedient" were rarely portrayed on television in the 1980s and into the 1990s (Aripurnami 1996), a situation that would change in the early 2000s (see chapter 7).

Summary

In this chapter, I have analyzed the discourse and practice of incorporating dangdut into the national cultural formation. Dangdut was mobilized by political and cultural institutions to create specific meanings about political unity. High government officials strategically placed dangdut within the discourse of national politics by appearing with dangdut stars on television, singing and dancing to dangdut in public, and promoting the music in popular print media. Cultural organizations helped to create the links between artists (musicians, composers, and arrangers) and the Indonesian state.

I emphasized the role of television as a medium for nationalizing dangdut. The central government actively promoted particular singers, forms, and meanings about dangdut in the 1990s. In contrast to dangdut described in chapter 5, nationalized dangdut was glamorous and subdued. Although it was intended to be more inclusive, as dangdut became more national, its established audience receded from the sphere of media representation.

Although national and mid-level stars did not profit from the sales of their commercial products, economic stakes in dangdut were high. Government officials promoted dangdut as the "music for everyone" not only in upcoming political campaigns, but as a way to increase their own salaries. Links between the central government and government-controlled mass media facilitated these links.

Symbolic representations of dangdut *as* nation appeared frequently in 1990s political and cultural discourse. Cultural organizations publicized a particular New Order version of dangdut history. And representations of women and the valorization of family values in "Duh Engkang" corresponded to the ideals promoted by the state. However, "Gadis atau Janda" challenged these dominant images. The independent, individualistic, and agential woman in "Gadis atau Janda" presented a counternarrative to the dominant image of the New Order woman in "Duh Engkang" as submissive, long-suffering, and "burdened" with representing collectivity and tradition.

After the fall of the New Order in 1998, dangdut was again embroiled in debates about women, national culture, and politics, as I will describe in the following chapter.

NOTES

1. Dangdut's popularity among the underclass made it particularly ripe for constructing a discourse about music and Indonesian national identity because the underclass constitutes the majority of society. This was noted in the early 1980s (Frederick 1982; Aribowo 1983, 16; "Satria berdakwah" 1984, 28). From an aesthetic point of view, it was ironic that dangdut could be deemed Indonesia's national music, because it was considered "light and not serious" (*tak berbodot*) (Aribowo 1983, 16).

2. The five programs were: *Aneka Ria Safari, Aneka Ria Safari Nusantara, Irama Masa Kini, Kamera Ria, Album Minggu,* and *Panggung Hiburan Anak-Anak.*

3. Programming at the local level followed the national trends; for example, on TVRI Medan (North Sumatra), a show called *Arena Ria,* modeled on *Aneka Ria Safari,* featured dangdut in half of its music programming (ibid.).

4. TPI broadcast *Nuansa Musik* and *Musik Musik* in 1992; *In Dangdut* in 1993; *Kuis Dangdut* in 1994, and *Aneka Musik Dangdut* and *Semarak Dangdut* in 1995.

5. pers. comm., Nala Rinaldo, production division head of Dangdut programming for TPI, 11 July 2005.

6. Dangdut had played a role in elections since at least 1977, when artists were involved in government campaigning. I would like to thank Philip Kitley for alerting me to a newspaper photo with the caption "Artists from the Kampung" showing media personalities H. Oma Irama [Rhoma Irama], Harry Roesli, Benyamin S., Iskak, Kris Biantoro, and Ateng ("Artists from the Kampung" 1977). Both Golkar and the PPP (the Muslim-based United Development Party) used dangdut to mobilize the populace in various election campaigns in 1982 (Frederick 1982, 129).

7. These practices parallel the "culturalization of the new rich" exemplified in public poetry readings by businesspeople, top state officials, Islamic leaders, and military elites (Heryanto 1999, 166).

8. In an ironic twist, this example could not have been "less" authentically Indonesian. Produced by Japanese producer Makoto Kubota, "Kopi Dangdut" is a translated version of the widely recorded song "Moliendo Café" composed by Venezuelan composer Hugo Blanco in 1958. The song has been translated into many languages, including Japanese ("Coffee Rumba"). The style of singing in "Kopi Dangdut" is closer to *pop Indonesia* than dangdut.

9. One exception was the1995 TPI program *Dangdut Siang Bolong* (Dangdut in the Daytime), shot on location in "dirty housing developments bordering the marketplace and motorcycle stands and crowded living conditions" of Jakarta ("Dangdut Siang Bolong" 1995).

10. "Duh Engkang" (Oh My Dear), sung by Itje Tresnawati, sold 800,000 units and "Lebih Baik Sakit Gigi" (A Toothache Is Better), sung by Meggi Z., sold 300,000 units (Surawijaya 1991, 50); "Di Mana Ada Kamu Di Situ Ada Aku" (Wherever You Are, I Will Be) sold about 800,000 copies; and "Mabuk dan Judi" (Drunkenness and Gambling), released in 1991 and sung by relative unknown Cucu Cahyati, sold an estimated 300,000 copies (Pudyastuti 1992, 108; Zar 1992, 23).

11. The following section is based on interviews with Euis Cahya and her husband Raden Dunbar (2006–2007).

12. Songs described as "porno" include "Judul-Judulan" (Fake Titles) and "Minta Ajimat" (Asking for a Magic Spell) (Kusumah 1991, 64).

13. The Indonesian case mirrors symbolic representations of women in other parts of the world, where the female body carries the "burden of representation" for the collectivity's identity and future (Yuval-Davis 1997, 45). As central actors responsible for cultural reproduction, women served as symbolic "border guards" for the nation (ibid., 23).

Chapter 7

"Dance Drills, Faith Spills": Islam, Body Politics, and Dangdut in Post-Suharto Indonesia

In February 2003, a woman's body became the focal point for public debates about religious authority, freedom of expression, women's rights, and the future of Indonesia's political leadership. At the center of these debates was Inul Daratista, a 24-year-old popular music singer/dancer from East Java, whose dancing was described as "pornographic" and therefore *haram,* forbidden by Islam. Inul's stage shows and performative discourse emphasize a style of dancing she calls *goyang ngebor* (the "drilling dance"), "gyration of the hips at break-neck speed that some people have likened to a tornado" (Asmarani 2003).[1] IslamOnline.Net, an internet site for education about Islam, described "a video clip...[that] depicts Inul scantily dressed and dancing in a suggestive and erotic fashion in front of an eager audience of Indonesian men" (Mahmood 2003).

The Indonesian Council of Ulamas (Majelis Ulama Indonesia, MUI) declared that her dancing and costume were circumscribed by its *fatwa* (edict) against pornography (Walsh 2003), and the local MUI chapter in Surakarta urged local police to block performances by Inul in their town (Rosyid 2003). MUI leader Amidhan stated that "a report of a man raping a girl after watching Inul dance is evidence that the way she dances is not fit for public viewing" (Nurbianto 2003).[2]

In March 2003, Majelis Mujahidin, a coalition of Islamic groups centered in Yogyakarta, protested a television show called *Duet Maut* (Deadly Duet) in which Inul appeared, stating that the show excited men to commit immoral acts and encouraged pre-marital sex (Ant/Ati 2003).[3] In May 2003, dangdut superstar and Muslim prosleytizer Rhoma Irama called a virtual, but not enforceable, ban on her, stating that she was degrading Islam (Effendi 2003).[4]

At a protest rally in Jakarta, demonstrators shouted "Dance drills, faith spills," a slogan that reflected a causal relationship between the rise of Inul and the drop in religious faith ("SCTV dan Trans..." 2003).[5]

Public statements by MUI clerics, Islamic groups, and Rhoma Irama ignited a huge debate in the popular print media among politicians, religious leaders, feminists, intellectuals, celebrities, fans, and even doctors, who warned female fans not to try the "dangerous" drilling move at home without warming up properly (Sari 2003). Reports in the popular press noted that the media storm surrounding Inul was diverting attention away from Indonesia's social problems—corruption among political and religious leaders, civil wars in Aceh and Irian Jaya, abuses against women, and deep-rooted poverty (Asy'arie 2003).[6] One author noted that attacks on Inul's posterior deflected attention away from the "asses" that occupied the political seats in the government.[7]

As suggested by the previous statement, popular cultural practices may reflect a collective desire by disempowered masses to escape the mundane and repressive conditions of their everyday lives. One might also argue that Indonesia's culture industry was at work to manipulate Inul's largely under-class audience of female domestic laborers and factory workers into believing that they too could achieve Inul's transformation from a poor villager (*orang desa*) into a modern urban celebrity (*artis*), a story that was narrated persistently in print tabloids as well as in television dramas of the period.[8]

Yet, the discourse surrounding Inul's dancing body does not suggest a narrative of escape or manipulation. On the contrary, "Inulmania" acted like a lightning rod for igniting popular debates about gender, class, religion, and power.[9] Inul gave rise to a social discourse in which the artistic practice of an individual singer/dancer was used as a forum to express opinions about a wide range of social and cultural issues. It would be difficult to think of a cultural symbol that attracted more passionate and public debate, more pro and contra positions, among such a wide spectrum of Indonesians in early 2003 than Inul's swinging derriere. As cultural critic, poet, and Islamic leader Emha Ainun Nadjib famously pronounced, "Inul's rear end is our collective face" (Emha 2003). In addition to hundreds of reports and commentaries that appeared in Indonesian newspapers, magazines, tabloids, radio programs, and television broadcasts, the story was circulated widely by media outlets in Hong Kong, Australia, Singapore, the United States, and Europe.[10] Inul and her drilling dance had become a "phenomenon," cleverly termed "Fenom-Inul" (Faruk and Aprinus Salam 2003, 27–31).

In this chapter, I describe how and why Inul's dancing body became a central symbol in debates about religion, culture, and politics in the years following the fall of Suharto.[11] In order to understand Inul's performative body as a contested arena of value and valuation during that particular historical moment, I will describe the "distinctive logics of change and forms of valorization characteristic of…musical practices, as these are disseminated through their respective cultural communities and institutional sites" (Straw 1991, 369). Within this context, the Inul phenomenon became a "contact zone of activities and representations" involving "intersubjective clashes" among cultural actors (Feld 2000, 154). A case study of Inul Daratista illuminates contemporary "body politics," the "inherently political nature of symbols and practices surrounding the body politic and the human body" (Ong and Peletz 1995, 6 see also Peletz 1996).

As a field of cultural production, body politics emphasizes human bodies as symbols invested with contested meanings and values. As a theoretical formulation, body politics has important ideological stakes. But like any good theoretical formulation, we need localized case studies that enable us to work out theories, challenge them, and ultimately strengthen our politics around them. This chapter addresses the following questions: What factors enabled Islam, the body politic and a woman's body to be grouped together in the popular imagination at this particular historical juncture? In this case, what was potentially so dangerous about a woman's body that led to its censure? And how was it possible to mount such a public "pro-drilling" stance within a predominantly Muslim country with a long history of strict state control over cultural production and mass media?

Inulmania articulates with the shifting ground of politics, religion, and media that occurred after the fall of Suharto's New Order regime in 1998. I begin by arguing that new technologies for recording music videos and novel ways of distributing them allowed Inul's "product" to circulate. Further, it was the *sound* of a woman's sexuality, expressed openly and powerfully, that caused the ire of certain Islamic fundamentalists. Efforts to ban Inul in 2003 were part of a residual New Order culture of censorship carried out by conservative Islamic organizations. The very public and multifaceted backlash against those New Order–like forces emerged within an expanded mediascape after the fall of Suharto.[12] The fall of Suharto brought about an expansion of private television stations and popular print media, as well as a loosening of the state's control over media content (Widodo 2002). In this context, Inul's body became a stage for a variety of cultural actors—from the most liberal to the most conservative—to try out or "rehearse" an emergent democracy in post-Suharto Indonesia. I map out the social struggles played out over Inul's body and the ideological stakes that these struggles engendered. I provide examples of many different forms of dance on the island of Java to illustrate the fact that women's dancing bodies have been the object of governmental monitoring and Muslim condemnation since the creation of the Indonesian nation-state. These dance forms, along with commentaries by Inul's fans and other female singers, provide a cultural historical context that demonstrates the power of women's bodies in public performance.

Mediating Inul

Under Suharto's New Order regime (1967–1998), information was rigidly controlled and opposing viewpoints squelched. For example, the Suharto regime controlled the press by restricting the number of press licenses, by revoking licenses, and by creating an aura of self-censorship through fear and intimidation. Suharto's resignation in May 1998 initially paved the way for a more liberal and expanded mediascape that allowed the possibility for expressing divergent ideological positions in the public sphere. For example, in 1999, then-president Habibie ratified a new Press Law (40/1999) that removed restrictions on publishing. Deregulating the press and easing the process for creating new publications caused the number of print media publications to mushroom. In the year after the fall of Suharto, 718 new media licenses were granted by the government, as compared to 289 granted during the first 53 years of the country's existence (Tesoro n.d.) The press was still subject to strict state government control. However, deregulation was a sign that the country was moving toward a more liberal public sphere with the potential for broadening the scope of social representation.

How did Inul, a local entertainer in the eastern part of the island of Java, come to the attention of television producers based in Jakarta, the capital city of Indonesia in the western part of Java? In addition to a wildly successful commercial recording industry, dangdut also enjoys regional popularity in live performances at weddings, circumcisions, and other events hosted by individuals or community groups. During the mid- to late 1990s, some of these live events were recorded by people with camcorders. Often these video recordings were commissioned by the hosts of the events for the purpose of selling them after the show. The recordings were then edited and transferred to the new video compact disc (VCD) technology. VCD is a digital movie format introduced by Philips and Sony in 1993 that never became successful in North America. But it became extremely popular in Indonesia and other parts of Asia. The VCD market developed with the introduction of cheap VCD machines, which could be bought for less than US$10 in electronics marketplaces in Indonesia. VCDs circulated widely as non-registered commercial recordings outside the state-regulated commercial economy of recorded music.

VCDs emphasize dangdut's hip-swaying dance—*goyang*—and Inul's dancing body was well-suited to the medium. The sale and distribution of these VCDs boosted Inul's popularity, even though she had not made a single recording with one of the major commercial recording companies in Indonesia. It was reported that several million copies of her VCD had sold before she was offered a recording contract (Walsh 2003). VCDs of Inul's performance circulated widely throughout Indonesia, as well as other countries, including Malaysia, Japan, Hong Kong, and the Netherlands. The Surabaya branch of national television station TransTV broadcast one of her performances for local audiences in 2003. After seeing spectators' positive reaction to Inul's performance on the local television station in Surabaya, producers brought her into the studio to record and broadcast those performances on television stations in Jakarta (Asmarani 2003).

While there may have been many other singers in the past with trademark dance moves that were just as sexually provocative, they were never recorded and their "product" was never circulated, especially on national television. Initially, Inul was seen on programs only broadcast locally in East Java. Producers in Jakarta quickly realized the potential of Inul as a commodity to increase ratings and sell products. In this case, the commercial non-registered VCD industry was used by the mainstream industry to develop talent, a kind of "minor league," to audition and recruit regional acts for national production. This new system of recording, distributing, and marketing brought new kinds of performance to the mainstream. When recordings of Inul's eroticized movements appeared on national television, the effect was thrilling for fans and infuriating for conservative Islamic leaders.

Inul Daratista

Inulmania is the story of Inul Daratista (Ainur or Ainul Rokhimah, b. 1979), a female singer who grew up in the town of Gempol near Pasuruan, East Java, Indonesia. She began her career singing American pop and rock 'n' roll as a teenager before switching to dangdut. Inul's idols include dangdut singer Rita Sugiarto, *pop Indonesia* singer Paramitha Rusady, as well as American/Latina pop superstars Shakira and Jennifer Lopez (Loriel 2003). Inul was considered an interloper among the closed and insular dangdut community of Jakarta. Unlike the coy, purring, and glamorous persona enacted by singers of the 1990s (e.g., Cici Paramida, Ikke Nurjanah, Itje Tresnawati), Inul presented an image of a strong, determined, and sexual woman. She became the single most sought-after singer during 2003–2004.

Inul's image and sound

Local television producers in East Java felt that her performances at private parties were too eroticized for television, and so they persuaded her to develop a new style of performing. Even so, TV producers had to be aware of the camera angles:

> If the camera angle is off by just a little bit, it can give an erotic
> impression. Frontal shots are too suggestive. If we have a naughty
> cameraman who shoots from a low angle, that's even worse. Those
> are the things I have to be aware of. (Lok/Xar 2003)

These two styles of performance—one performed at parties and one for televised broadcast—differed in terms of costume, dance movements, and interaction with the audience, as discussed in the following section.

At parties, Inul appeared outdoors on a stage constructed specifically for
the event. She generally sang solo, accompanied by her six-piece band, whose
members stood in one line across the back of the stage. Her outfits were colorful, tight, and revealing. Males mostly between the ages of 15 and 35 stood in
front of the stage. Some of them danced alone or together in pairs, while others
watched her and the band. It was common for men to come on stage and dance
with her. Women and families in the audience stood farther away from the
stage. The atmosphere was lively and loud.

In televised concerts, Inul appeared on a large stage in a studio, often
accompanied by a group of choreographed dancers. The band stood to one
side and could only be seen when the camera trained its view on them.
TransTV executive Ishadi S. K. described her image and stage performance
as follows:

> TransTV produced several programs starring Inul in 2003. At that
> time, all the stations were competing for her. But TransTV programs
> aimed to be elegant because we targeted the A-B audience [defined by
> income]. Inul was made more elegant with the help of elite choreog-
> raphers and designers like Aji Notonegoro and Robby Tumewu.
> (Ishadi S. K., pers. comm., 30 October 2006)

The audience at these broadcasts was made up of well-dressed middle-class
men and women, and included people in their forties and fifties. Women wearing jilbab (Muslim head scarves) were shown in the audience, which sat during
the performance and appeared orderly. Occasionally, a man who was not one
of the choreogaphed dancers would come on stage and dance with Inul, but
these were planned beforehand.

In both contexts, Inul maintained a strong sexualized presence not only in
terms of her body movements but her vocal presentation and vocal patter to the
audience. These elements became a fixed part of her act. For example, it was
expected that she would perform her signature tune entitled "Goyang Inul"
(Inul's Dance; see figure 7.1), in which she refers to herself in the third person
as she prepares the audience for what they are about to experience.

Para penonton bapak-bapak ibu-ibu semuanya, Jangan heran kalau Inul sedang goyang, Rada panas agak sexy... maafkanlah...	To the audience, respected men and women and everyone present, Don't be surprised when Inul dances, It's a bit hot and sexy... you'll have to excuse me in advance...

FIGURE 7.1 "Goyang Inul" (Inul's Dance).

Despite possible objections by respected elders, male or female, or anyone else in the audience, she asks forgiveness for dancing in her own "hot and sexy" way. But she does not make excuses for "Inul's Dance." The word *maafkanlah* is a command: "Excuse me!" She introduces herself as a strong determined woman who will do what she wants. As she sings in the following verse, "dangdut without dance is like vegetables without salt." Similarly, "Inul's Dance" is a public expression of her natural sexuality. Interestingly, in the televised performance of this song, the choreographed male dancers move across the stage in a crawling position while Inul stands. The public expression of a woman's sexuality, as well as her strong determination, angered her many male critics and excited her many female fans.

The music of Inul

Critics have argued that Inul was nothing special, as mentioned earlier in this chapter, because there were many other performers in small villages throughout Java who performed highly eroticized dance movements in public clubs and at outdoor parties. In relation to the field of female performers, Inul was simply another village dancing girl with a trademark hook (in this case, "the drilling dance"). Comparisons between Inul, who reached a national audience, and performers who would never achieve exposure outside their geographic localities, suggests that only the most talented and innovative performers, however defined, would be singled out for inclusion in national media. This position ignores the process of "mediatization," which frames the subject in new relationships to its audience, introducing the possibility for creating a whole range of new meanings surrounding the subject (Auslander 1999). As discussed earlier, Inul developed different styles of performance, depending on the type of performance. Inul the singer/dancer cannot be separated from Inul the media image. For example, when Inul entered the televisual realm of performance, her recording company commissioned new songs by composer Endang Kurnia (b. 1958), who describes his initial contact with Inul:

> I had seen VCDs of her performing at parties in Surabaya. Everyone said "she's doing this outrageous dance!" Then I got a call from

Blackboard (recording company) who said that they were writing up a contract for someone named Inul in Surabaya and they wanted me to contribute songs for her album. This is before the controversy arose. I supported Inul because she had so much potential and she was so popular with the people. I knew she would become a phenomenon. God gave her the talent to dance, and her voice is not that bad either. Good for her! (Endang Kurnia, pers. comm., 15 November 2006)

It would be more fruitful to compare Inul with other dangdut singers who dominated the genre. Compared to the pouting, coquettish sound of female dangdut singers who had appeared on television in the 1990s, Inul's singing was punctuated by sexualized screams, grimaces, gasps, and yelps. The style of music associated with those singers was closely aligned with *pop Indonesia*, as discussed in the previous chapter.

Inul's singing, on the other hand, was backed by a powerful rock backbeat and screaming guitar parts. The music was composed to match her style of dance and stage presentation: fast tempos, rapidly shifting sections, a proliferation of percussive accents, and instrumental dance sections.

Endang Kurnia composed Inul's two best-known songs—"Goyang Inul" (Inul's Dance) and "Kocok-kocok" (Shake It Up). A fan of Rhoma Irama, Kurnia's style blends dangdut, rock and Sundanese music.[13] In these songs, dangdut elements include instruments (*suling* and *gendang*), long intro, interlude (featuring *suling* and guitar), and a strong emphasis on beats 4 and 1 in the verse. Rock elements include effects-driven electric guitar, slap electric bass, and a rock rhythmic backbeat played on a drum kit. The songs feature fast tempos, alternating sections of rock and dangdut rhythms, power chords, soaring rock guitar solos à la van Halen, and punctuating rhythmic breaks. Sundanese elements include sections that make references to *jaipongan* drumming and Sundanese *suling* (an end-blown flute which is different from the side-blown Indonesian *suling* used in dangdut).

The lyrics of "Kocok-kocok" are delivered from the perspective of a woman who knows what she wants from her lover: honesty, loyalty, stability, love, and attention. She does not want to be one of many lovers waiting her turn in an unstable relationship with an insensitive man.

"Kocok-kocok" works on many interpretive levels. It can be a song about shaking a container that holds numbers in a weekly lottery and social gathering attended by women (*arisan*). The number comes out of its container and reveals the winner of the contest. It can also refer to the instability or shakiness that a woman is feeling about her relationship with a man who has many lovers. Another interpretation, offered to me by a friend and suggested by the last line in the song, is the shaking of a man's penis as he ejaculates. I asked composer Endang Kurnia to comment on this and he replied:

Fine, if you want to see it that way. That's the nature of commercial music. It can be interpreted in different ways. It can be the shaking of the lottery container. It can mean my feelings of love that I don't want shaken up. The scream at the end was also my idea, and if you want to associate that with something "porno," then go ahead. There are many intepretations and that makes it appeal to lots of different people. (Endang Kurnia, pers. comm., 15 November 2006)

The climax comes at the end of the song as Inul screams. Another possible reading is that this scream may be the woman's orgasm during sexual intercourse. As illustrated in the quote above and in chapter 4, songs have

Ku tak mau cintaku dikocok-kocok, ah, Ku tak ingin sayangku dikocok-kocok, Seperti arisan nunggu giliran, Aduh aduh aduh aduh aduh... Mana tahan!	I don't want you to play with my heart, I don't want to be played, Like a game, awaiting my turn, Oh, oh, oh, oh, oh... I can't take it!
Yang ku mau cintamu hanya padaku, Yang ku ingin sayangmu satu untukku, Tiada yang lain cinta yang lain. Aduh aduh aduh aduh aduh... tak mau ahh	I just want your love to be for me, I just want your love only for me, There is no other one, no other love. Oh, oh, oh, oh, oh... I don't want it, Ahhhh!
Dikocok-kocok, 3X Bila arisan dikocok-kocok. Sudah pasti menang, Tapi nunggu giliran. Tapi cinta dan sayangku, Ku tak mau tak mau, tak mau tak mau, Dikocok-kocok ah, Dikocok-kocok, Ku tak mau cintaku, Dikocok-kocok.	Shake, shake, shake, Like a game, shaken up. You've won, But wait your turn. But my love and affection, I don't want it, don't want it, I don't want it, don't want it, Shake, shake, shake, Shake, shake, shake, I don't want my love, Shaken up.
[interlude]	[interlude]
Disayang-sayang, Dimanja-manja, Aku mau Jadi pacarmu, jadi kasihmu, ho,	Loved, Spoiled, I want To be your girlfriend, to be your lover.
Tetapi bila dikocok-kocok Cintaku, Ogah ah ogah aku tak mau, ho.	But if you want to play with My love, No, no, I don't want it.
Cinta bukan untuk mainan, Ku tak mau disamakan dengan arisan, Dikocok-kocok baru keluar . . . ah!	Love is not a game, I won't be played like a game, Shake it up, and then it comes out!

FIGURE 7.2 "Kocok-kocok" (Shake It Up) [courtesy of Endang Kurnia].

many possible meanings, and these multiple meanings give dangdut the potential for appealing to a larger audience of consumers.

The song structure of "Kocok-kocok" is as follows:

[intro—A-A´-B-interlude-C-A´-B-interlude-C´-A´´—outro].

section	Intro			
melody	vocal	gtr. + synth	gtr.	suling
# measures	4	5	6	8
lyric	marilah	--	--	--
vocal interjections	ah!			
time	0.00	0.07	0.14	0.21

section	A	
melody	vocal + gtr. fill	vocal + gtr. fill
# measures	8	8
lyric	Ku tak mau	Seperti arisan
vocal interjections	ah!	ah!
time	0.32	0.43

section	A'	
melody	vocal + gtr. fill	Vocal + gtr .fill
# measures	8	5
lyric	Yang ku mau	Tiada yang lain
vocal interjections	oh!	ah!
time	0.55	1.05

section	B	
melody	vocal	gtr. fill
# measures	20 (8+4+4+4)	3
lyric	Dikocok-kocok	--
vocal interjections	woo! ah!	ah!
time	1.13	1.41

section	interlude	
melody	gtr.	suling
# measures	12	8
lyric	--	--
vocal interjections		
time	1.45	2.00

FIGURE 7.3 *Continued*

section	C						
melody	vocal + synth fill	vocal	suling	vocal + synth fill	vocal	vocal	gtr. fill
# measures	6	4	5	6	5	8	3
lyric	Disayang-sayang	Jadi pacarmu	--	Tetapi bila	Ogah ach ogah	Cinta bukan	
vocal interjections	woo!			ooh!	woo!	ow!	
time	2.12	2.20	2.26	2.32	2.40	2.47	2.58

section	A'	
melody	vocal + gtr.fill	vocal
# measures		
lyric	Yang ku mau	Tiada yang lain
vocal interjections	ah!	ah!
time	3.02	3.13

section	B		gtr. fill
melody	vocal		
# measures	20 (8 + 4 + 4 + 4)		3
lyric	Dikocok-kocok		--
vocal interjections	woo! ah!		ah!
time	3.20		3.48

section	interlude	
melody	gtr.	suling
# measures	12	8
lyric	--	-
vocal interjections		
time	3.52	4.08

section	C'						
melody	vocal + synth fill	vocal	suling	vocal + synth fill	vocal	vocal	gtr. fill
# measures	6	4	5	6	5	8	3
lyric	Disayang-sayang	Jadi pacarmu	--	Tetapi bila	Ogah ach ogah	Cinta bukan	
vocal interjections	woo!			ooh!	woo!	ow!	
time	4.19	4.28	4.34	4.40	4.48	4.55	5.06

section	A"	
melody	vocal	gtr.
# measures	5	1 + fadeout
lyric	Ku tak mau	--
vocal interjections	ah	ow!
time	5.09	5.21

FIGURE 7.3 Song guide "Kocok-kocok."

"Kocok-kocok" is characterized by uneven phrase lengths and sections (see figure 7.3). The song structure consists of an introduction followed by the body of the song (A-B-interlude-C) which is essentially repeated, and followed by a short concluding section (A"). The body of the song does not repeat exactly (the A section is missing in the second iteration), which disrupts the listener's expectation. The irregular phrase lengths of each individual section give the piece a sense of urgency and instability. The uneven phrase lengths force the sections to jut up against each other, which suggests lack of control, physicality, and thrusting toward the climax of the song.

Inul, Islam, and the New Order

A full account of Islam, the state, and society in Indonesia is beyond the scope of this book.[14] The following section introduces key religious groups and individuals that participated in the public discourse about Inul.[15] In the majority Islamic nation, with some 88 percent of the total population of 220 million people, there is a tremendous diversity of opinions regarding the place of Islam in Indonesian politics and society. There was no singular Islamic position toward Inul, just as there is no united Islamic position toward a variety of other issues, such as whether to allow a woman to be president, or whether to implement Sharia (Islamic) law. Moderate and liberal Islamic groups tended to support Inul, whereas the hard-line groups tended to take a stance against her. But as we shall see, these ideological positions crystallized over time in response to opposing positions, and within the political context of the period.

The intersection between Islam and state politics has been a point of contention since Indonesian independence in 1945. Sukarno and the founders of the Republic of Indonesia opposed the inclusion of Sharia law as part the Constitution. Islamic parties made a strong showing in the first general election in 1955, gathering 45 percent of the vote, but not strong enough to build a coalition against the nationalist and communist parties. Militant Islamic groups fought for an Islamic state in Java, Sulawesi, and Aceh during 1950–1965 but were put down by the army. In 1960, Sukarno began using the slogan "Nationalism, Religion, and Communism" (NASionalisme, Agama, and KOMunisme, or Nasakom) to characterize the balance represented by the government ideology.

Suharto's policy was to depoliticize Islam and individualize dissent (Woodward 2001, 29; Bruinessen 2002, 6). But he had many critics who wanted Islam more fully incorporated into the state. Since the late 1980s, Islam began to play a more significant role in Indonesian politics. During the late

1980s, Suharto began to court his critics by creating the Indonesian Association of Muslim Intellectuals (Ikatan Cendekiawan Muslim se-Indonesia, ICMI), a state-sponsored religious apparatus made up of Muslim reformers and bureaucrats that was intended to help deliver political support for Suharto (Liddle 1996). The years 1985–1990 were characterized by "the creation of many new links of patronage, linking the *kiai* [religious leaders] (and allied businessmen) with the local government apparatus" (Bruinessen 2002, 8). Public and private observance of Islam increased with support from the Suharto regime. Religious courts were given equal jurisdiction on certain matters; the ban on wearing *jilbab* (head scarves) was lifted in public schools; and banks based on Sharia law were allowed to form.

After the fall of Suharto, due to new electoral laws, nearly one-third of the newly formed political parties claimed close ties to Islamic ideology or Islamic organizations. Political Islam "refers to efforts that promote 'Muslim' aspirations and carry an Islamic agenda into laws and government policy through the electoral process and representative (legislative) institutions" (Baswedan 2004, 670). However, these parties were not united, nor were they particularly effective. Political Islam does not have one political agenda, but is simply characterized by the accommodation of "Muslim" values in politics (ibid.).

The incorporation of Islam into state politics was not supported by all sectors of Islamic leadership. During the 1980s, Muslim intellectuals created a democracy movement based on religious and cultural pluralism that was not directed toward seeking formal state support of Islamic values. Anthropologist Robert Hefner has called this movement "civil Islam" (Hefner 2000). Its base of support was located in civil institutions including community groups and NGOs. Civil Islam (sometimes called "cultural Islam") advocates a more liberal form of Islam in step with contemporary life on issues including democratization, religious pluralism, and gender equality. Proponents of a democratic and pluralistic civil Islam generally supported Inul, including Abdurrahman Wahid [Gus Dur], former president of Indonesia and former leader of Indonesia's largest Muslim political organization, Nahdlatul Ulama, or NU.

A class of "radical Islam" gained ascendance during the 1980s. These groups have attracted much attention in mass media, although their numbers are significantly disproportionate to the attention they have received. The goal of radical Islam is to create a Muslim state based on the implementation of Islamic law. In 1993, Jemaah Islamiyah (JI) was formed to establish an Islamic state through militancy (Fealy and Hooker 2006; Jones 2003). Its leaders had been active in the mujahidin war against the Soviet Union in Afghanistan during the 1980s (ICG 2002). They have launched attacks on churches, bars, brothels, gambling houses, and nightclubs, including the attack on a Bali nightclub in

2002 that killed 202 people.[16] Other groups, including Laskar Jihad (formed in 2000) and Front Pembela Islam (formed in 1998), have identified what they perceive to be an increasingly immoral society as the target of their ire. These groups took a strong position against Inul.

In this shifting sphere of media, politics, and religion, several Muslim organizations and individuals spoke out strongly against Inul. However, the MUI, a by-product of the New Order, was the most vocal Muslim organization. The MUI was formed in 1975 by the New Order government "to translate government policy [regarding Islam] into a language that the *ummah* [community] understands."[17] The purpose of the MUI was to mobilize support among Muslims for the government's development policies (ibid.). Its founders were university-educated, urban, and close to the centers of power. They built links with other New Order political and economic organizations such as ICMI and Muslim banks (Bruinessen 2002, 8). Their main target of influence was the middle class. As dangdut began to spread more pervasively, through television, radio, and the popular press, its new social location began to compete with MUI's authority.

The MUI does not serve military and security interests directly, but it has a political function (ibid.).[18] The MUI operates through fatwa, authoritative opinions, which, in the New Order, legitimized government policies (ibid.). Fatwa have been issued against liberal Islamic thought, religious pluralism, interfaith marriage, and women leading prayers attended by men. The MUI invoked fatwa number U-287 (2001), a fatwa pertaining to pornography, to condemn Inul. In addition to forbidding sexual acts outside marriage, fatwa number U-287 forbids women to publicly show parts of the body other than the face, palms of the hand, and bottom of the foot. It also forbids tight clothes that reveal the curves of a female's body, the use of cosmetics, and vocal sounds or words that increase men's sexual desires (Majelis Ulama Indonesia 2001).

Although Suharto had been forced from power in 1998, the culture of censorship that had existed during his 32-year reign did not suddenly disappear. Censorship of Inul was carried out within a residual atmosphere of New Order authoritarianism and patriarchy. Fundamentalist voices were stimulated by a public discourse about democracy and were amplified through the expanded "mediascape" of the post-Suharto period. Ulil Abshar-Abdalla, a defender of free speech who has been castigated for his own liberal views of Islam, stated that "the desire to eliminate something that is considered 'different' is still deeply rooted," referring to the Suharto regime..." it used to be the government [doing the censoring], and now it's the people themselves" (Cikini 2003). The expression and acceptance of difference would be dramatized in the case of Inul.

News of the MUI's condemnation spread rapidly in the popular print media, and several other groups supported the MUI decision. In May 2003, the Communication Forum Against Pornography and Pornoaction (Forum Komunikasi Masyarakat Antipornografi dan Pornoaksi, FKMAPP) staged a protest against the television stations SCTV and Trans TV. Shouting "Don't poison our youth with pornography," and "Wipe out the exploitation of navels, behinds and breasts on TV," about a thousand people were reported to have demonstrated against the broadcast of two shows starring Inul ("SCTV dan Trans..." 2003).

The third powerful voice of Islam belonged to dangdut superstar Rhoma Irama, who has a rich and complicated history with Islamic politics and Suharto's New Order regime. As president of PAMMI, Rhoma Irama spoke out against Inul. In his speech calling for a ban on Inul's performances, Rhoma Irama reported a case of a man who said that he raped a woman after watching Inul perform on a VCD (Gunawan 2003, 41). His statements echoed the fatwa issued by the MUI: "Inul's drilling dance (*goyang ngebor Inul*), break dance (*goyang patah*), *goyang ngecor* (another type of eroticized dance), body-shaking dance (*goyang nggeter*), are all categorized as inappropriate ways of showing a woman's body in public and cannot be tolerated" (Hamdani et al. 2004). Rhoma

FIGURE 7.4 Photo of women at an anti-Inul rally, Jakarta, 12 June 2003 [courtesy of *Tempo*].

Irama's statements echoed those by Muslim organizations in Indonesia that have been traditionally opposed to the eroticized female cultural forms that are so prevalent throughout Java and Sumatra. These forms have been viewed as dangerous "because their overt sexuality is thought to lead men astray, destroying marriages and resulting in fights or sometimes even murder" (Lysloff 2001/2002, 4; see also Weintraub 2004, 57–58). Inul's drilling dance, like these older forms, would reportedly lead to an increase in promiscuity, sex outside marriage, moral corruption, and eventually, social chaos. It is important to note that the majority of Inul's fans are women (Inul Daratista, pers. comm., 16 November 2006). Further, there were no investigations, no newspaper stories, no fatwas, and no sanctions against the alleged rapists or the men buying and watching the videos. Invoking Latin music superstar Shakira to emphasize her point, Inul explained that the controversy was a matter of interpretation:

> If one uses his brain I think he can differentiate between music, sexuality, and religion. If someone arrives at a show to see, for example, Shakira's tight pants, sexy midriff, and erotic body movements, then his thoughts will automatically be drawn to sex. It's not that women are such a threat to society. It's because of wrong-headed politics and the mis-use of religion that women have been blamed for society's problems (pers comm., Inul Daratista, 16 November 2006)

The patriarchal and authoritarian stance of Rhoma Irama—the "King of Dangdut"—and the threat of a fatwa against Inul did not gain much support outside the fundamentalist or radical Islamic communities. Rather, subsequent press commentaries quickly turned against Rhoma Irama's attempt to blame the victim. In response to the actions and statements of these conservative Muslim groups and individuals, a number of opposing positions emerged.

A poll in the newsmagazine *Tempo* reported that 78 percent of its readers, mostly middle-class, were against banning her performances. Women's rights groups rejected the notion that this was a case of exploitation, commodification, degradation, or victimization of women. On the contrary, the National Commission on Violence Against Women (Komisi Nasional Anti Kekerasan Terhadap Perempuan, Komnas Perempuan) stated that Inul had suffered psychological trauma *in the name of religion* (Abhiseka 2003). Women's rights activist, author, and playwright Ratna Sarumpaet, whose play *Marsinah Menggugat* (Marsinah's Accusation) about the murder of labor activist Marsinah had been banned in 1997, argued that Inul's case was about freedom of expression (Alwie et al. 2003; Cikini 2003). In response to Rhoma Irama's claims about a causal relationship between Inul and rape, Saparinah Sadli of the

National Commission of Women noted that it was not Inul, but rather the inability of the legal system to protect women that led to the increase in rape cases and violence against women (Nmp 2003).[19]

As news about the case spread, other actors added their voices to the unfolding drama. Conflicting interpretations of Inul represent these divergent perspectives on morality in Islam. Abdurrahman Wahid (Gus Dur) defended Inul against the fundamentalist branches of Islam. Gus Dur was affiliated with NU (Nahdlatul Ulama), an organization that advocates a pluralist democratic form of Islam dedicated to human rights, social justice, and minority rights. The former president correctly stated that Inul could not have single-handedly destroyed Indonesia's moral fabric because it had already been torn apart by corrupt politicians during the New Order. Further, "corrupt people are not condemned, so it's inconceivable that Inul would be" (Ant/jy 2003).

During a performance tour in Kalimantan, Inul was invited to meet with Guru Ijai, a charismatic and nationally respected religious teacher. He announced to his followers that he considered Inul his adopted child (*anak angkat*). It was reported that "he instructed and prayed: 'I hope that Inul will enter heaven. Ignore the slanderous gossip and whatever else might happen. Keep pressing ahead because you are pursuing your livelihood.'"[20]

Despite calls by MUI Secretary Ichwan Syam, who stated "Don't allow Inul to participate in the upcoming 2004 election campaign" (Tma/Ant 2003), political parties seized on Inul's popularity to draw potential voters to their rallies. Since the 1970s, dangdut had been used to gather crowds at political rallies, despite the fact that the majority of people did not vote, and the elections were not conducted fairly. Politicians used the condemnation of Inul by conservative Islamic political groups to draw support to their own liberal positions. In a very public and well-photographed display, Taufiq Kiemas, the husband of then-president Megawati and a member of parliament (Fraksi PDI-P), hugged Inul on a concert stage in February, infuriating members of conservative Muslim groups. The expanded role of a popular music singer came about in an environment of political instability represented by shifting national leadership and an upcoming election in 2004 in which Islamic leaders and politicians were struggling for support.

Inulmania attracted the attention of the international press—a *Time Asia* magazine story and a National Public Radio program (U.S.) appeared in March 2003—as well as the world of international finance.[21] In an article titled "Indonesia's Hip-Shaking Diva is a Good Omen," Australian reporter William Pesek Jr. argued that the controversy surrounding Inul represents "the workings of democracy and free expression taking hold"; the backlash against her is a test of Indonesia's maturity as a nation, "an opportunity for investors to gauge the extent to which religious fervor is spreading—or retreating ..." (Pesek 2003). Inulmania was constructed as an instrument to test the security of international business interests, where a pro-Inul stance might stimulate foreign investment and an anti-Inul stance might scare investors away.

What are we to make of the local, national, and international attention to Inul and the vareity of positions that Inulmania generated? Inul captured a historical moment and came to represent a position oppositional to New Order authoritarianism and conservative Muslim leadership, which had been growing steadily under the New Order. However, it was only after the fall of the New Order, within a climate of freedom of expression encouraged by new media, that she came to play a key role. Popular print media crystallized into two oppositional positions, characterized as *Inulfluenza*, a virus from outside Indonesia that threatens to "infect" the moral fabric of society (similar to arguments made in the popular print media about AIDS) and *Inulviton*, a vitamin-like energizing internal force that invigorates the body politic.[22] Conservative Islamic groups and Rhoma Irama advocated prohibition in order to stem the spread of Inulfluenza. Women's rights groups, artists, intellectuals, fans, moderate Islamic groups, and politicians hoping to rally support from an increasingly energized populace called for a continuous stream of Inulviton. However, as we shall see from the following discussion, Inulmania gave rise to an even wider range of interpretations by ordinary people.

Women, Power, and Performance

Inul's performative body did not spring out of thin air, but is grounded in long-held cultural traditions of women's dance in Indonesia. Viewed from a culturalist position, it is possible to situate Inul's body within a long history of women, power, and performing arts. Western studies of women in Southeast Asian societies have frequently shown that women enjoy relatively "high status," particularly in comparison with women in Indian and Chinese societies (Errington 1990, 1). Scholars of Indonesia have pointed to the notion of bilateral kinship, which results in male and female children being equally valued; complementarity of men's and women's work; the downplaying of sexual differentiation; and the fact that women control money. Women's power in Indonesia is also historically connected to women in the performing arts. For example, female singers in the gamelan tradition of central Java are considered to be *ampuh*, spiritually powerful (Sutton 1984, 128; Cooper 2000, 609–644; Cooper 2004, 531–556). Javanese *tayuban* dancers are an integral part of spirit shrine rituals, village purification, and fertility rites (Hefner 1987) and Sundanese *ronggeng* are traditionally linked to harvest rites and the rice goddess *Dewi Sri* (Foley 1989). A woman's traditional dance called *geol* is used as a spiritual offering to a goddess of fertility in Banyuwangi. In performance, women demonstrate their power to attract males (Sutton 1984; Foley 1989).[23]

Following Ong and Peletz, gender identities are not fixed, but belong to "a fluid, contingent process, characterized by contestation, ambivalence, and change...within the interlocking ideological and material contexts of a dynamic, modernizing region" (Ong and Peletz 1995, 1). These performing arts traditions have articulated with the shifting political and economic terrain upon which women's bodies move (and dance) in local contemporary contexts. Inul was not the first dancer to be the object of regional and national censorship. In several cases, government censorship had been used in attempts to control women's powerful dancing bodies. *Ronggeng*—the singer/dancer/entertainer—were allegedly banned in West Java after independence, whereas performance practices of *sinden* (female singers in the gamelan ensemble) were monitored and regulated during the 1950s and 1960s (Foley 1979; Weintraub 2004). Under the influence of Muhammadiyah reformists and the Muslim political party Masyumi, village officials banned *tayuban* in Pasuruan, Probolinggo, and Malang (Hefner 1987, 91). *Jaipongan*, a genre that combined village styles with disco, modern dance, and martial arts, led to debates about it being banned (Miller and Williams 1998, 93). As discussed in chapter 5, "weepy" songs sung by women with lyrics that mentioned abusive husbands, infidelity, and divorce were banned during the 1980s (Yampolsky 1989).

Striking parallels can be drawn between Inul's performance practice and *tayuban*, a cultural practice that has angered Muslim reformists for decades because of its non-Muslim associations; ritual meals and blessings; serving of alcohol; perception of dancers (*tledhek*) as prostitutes; and men dancing with women.[24] Inul comes from Pasuruan, a region of East Java where *tayuban* was widely practiced. Pasuruan also has a reputation as the most powerful stronghold of Nahdlatul Ulama on the island of Java (Hefner 2000, xiii). Like the East Javanese *tledhek*, Inul sings and dances to earn money. The stage demeanor of both *tledhek* and Inul is flirtatious, enticing, teasing, and sexual. Performance settings in both cases are boisterous, loud, hot, and excited. The rapid movement of the hips, a rudimentary form of the drilling move, is common to *tayuban*. The description of movements used in the *ngremo* section of the dance, as described by Robert Hefner, could easily be applied to Inul: bold stance, swinging arms, and strong foot pounding (Hefner 1987).

FIGURE 7.5 Inul striking a typical dance pose [courtesy of *Tempo*].

On stage, female dangdut performers often dance with men, who are often inebriated. Female dangdut performers, like *tledhek,* believe that inserting *susuk* into their skin will enhance their power to attract males (Sutton 1984, 130; Spiller 2001).[25] Further, in both dangdut and *tayuban,* women participate as audience members, evaluating dancers and enjoying the festival atmosphere of dance parties.[26] Female dangdut singers are "owned by the people" (*milik masyarakat*), much like the *tledhek,* who are considered every man's property (Elvy Sukaesih, pers. comm. 20 July 2005).

What is remarkable about Inul's success is that her singing and dancing were unexceptional in relation to other singers. As one fan stated, "She dresses as other artists commonly do" (Wahyudi 2003). Her performances are erotic, but restrained (Heryanto, quoted in Barraud 2003). And contemporary entertainers use their bodies in more sexually provocative ways, including Anisa Bahar, known for her own eroticized trademark move called *patah-patah.*[27] Inul was just as puzzled as anyone: "Why was I singled out? There are lots of singers whose dance movements are more vulgar and sexy than mine!" (pers. comm., 16 November 2006). Commentators have noted that some female dancers in Hindi films wear less, and move in more sexually provocative ways. Music critic Bre Redana stated that "you could find so many Inuls in any small town in East or Central Java.[28] The drilling move was simply her trademark, a distinctive hook, that set her apart from others.

Interpreting Inul

So what did Inul *do* for fans? F. X. Rudy Gunawan writes that responses to Inul included "amazement, laughter, embarrassment, and anger" (Gunawan 2003). Statements gathered in the popular press do not indicate simple homologies between a cultural text and the meaning of that text, but rather signify the (highly diversified) ways in which actors describe and experience aesthetic pleasure (Hennion 2003, 82). However, at least two trends are identifiable. In true Indonesian-language fashion, people created *plesetan* (play on words) that show not only the depth of feeling that Inul had created, but also the playful *and political* response to Inul's fame. People create *plesetan* by altering the meaning of a common acronym, typically those used for naming official Indonesian institutions. The letters of the acronym are made to correspond to new words, and the resultant meaning makes the original meaning sound ridiculous and also produces a humorous commentary on a current situation. For example, BII (Bank Internasional Indonesia, the International Bank of Indonesia) became "Bangsa Inal Inul," "The Country of Inal Inul"; "Inal Inul" refers to the swaying of one's behind from left to right while walking (Faruk and Aprinus Salam 2003, 31–32). RI (Republic of Indonesia) became "Republik Inul," the "Republic of Inul." PesantrenOnline.com, which advertises itself as an Internet site for Indonesian Muslims, mentions the following: FPI (Front Pembela Islam, the Organization to Defend Islam) became "Front Pembela Inul," the "Organization to Defend Inul," whereas JI (Jemaah Islamiah, the Islamic Fundamentalist Group) became "Jemaah Inul," the "Inul Fundamentalist Group" (Yahya 2003). Names of U.S. government agencies were a favorite target as well: FBI (Federal Bureau of Investigation) became "Fantasi Bokong Inul," or "Fantasizing about Inul's Rear," and CIA (Central Intelligence Agency) became "Cintailah Inul apa Adanya," "Love Inul No Matter What" (Yudhono 2003). Quite apart from subverting the original meaning of the phrase, pleasure emerges from the invention of the new phrases themselves as well as the act of voicing them. There is pleasure in the humorous connection between the newly created phrase and the original meaning of the term. And Inul's fans enjoyed fantasizing about a "Republic of Inul" and an "Organization to Defend Inul" against her detractors. *Plesetan*, representing multiple responses by people about what Inul means to them, had political implications. *Plesetan*, in this case, challenge the monolithic and moralistic interpretation of Inul issued by MUI and other conservative Muslim organizations and individuals.

Second, discourse among fans tended not to focus on the drilling move, or even the quality of her stage act or singing, but the sentiments she evoked in fans when they watched her perform. These sentiments tended to revolve around her ability to dance with "energy" (*energi*). For example, Kartoyo, 21, an employee of the City Public Order Office (Dinas Ketenteraman dan Ketertiban) stated that "...she can *lift* our spirits with her energetic and dynamic movements. Watching her perform, the *stress* of a full workday disappears" (Wahyudi 2003). Nurjaya, 30, a motorcycle taxi (*ojek*) driver, insisted that "...I see her as someone who *motivates* me. I feel more *alert* after watching her perform. For the poor, watching or listening to dangdut performances is far more *encouraging* than listening to politicians or thinking about war" (ibid.). Meriem, 45, a manager at a reputable hotel in Central Jakarta, stated that "I don't get the impression that Inul is raunchy. I personally *admire* her potential in dancing and singing" (ibid.). In these descriptions, Inul's stage presence sounds more like an aerobic workout than a pornographic display. These statements point to the context of live performance and energetic dance as the primary mode for understanding Inul's aesthetic practice, rather than the individual drilling move that had been singled out in the press. The interpretation of the drilling dance as aerobic energy does not point to the erotic nature of Inul's performance, but it does not make excuses for it either. Rather, she "lifts their spirits, motivates them, and encourages them." Comments by fans suggest that they are participating *with* her rather than gazing *at* her.

Female dangdut singers whom I inverviewed in July 2005 were generally dismissive of Inul's artistic abilities, supportive of her commercial success (albeit somewhat mystified by it), and outraged at the censure heaped upon her by authoritarian and patriarchal institutions and individuals. Ellya Khadam, who had hit records in the early 1960s and is reportedly the first successful Indonesian female recording artist to dance while singing, argued that "If there is a negative effect on spectators—male spectators—then they should turn off the TV! Look at something else!" (Ellya Khadam, pers. comm, 18 July 2005). Echoing statements by fans, she acknowledged that Inul's drilling dance could be interpreted in a multiplicity of ways, and that it could have a variety of social effects, not all of them negative. Taking a broader view of women's performance, she argued that male spectators, not female singers, should be held accountable for producing "negative effects." Music and film star Elvy Sukaesih, the "Queen of Dangdut," had been subject to similar kinds of censure at various points in her career. She noted that "when I first danced and sang in public in the 1960s, I swayed my hips too! Inul is not that unusual, and there are far more erotic dangdut singers, but, because of television, she has gotten the most attention....It's like an oil lamp. Let the oil burn and it'll burn out quickly. But throw more oil on the fire and the flames will spread like wildfire. Let it die out already!" (Elvy Sukaesih, pers. comm 20 July 2005). Elvy Sukaesih's statements pointed to the expanded role of mass media in producing the Inul "phenomenon." But without the controversy involving Rhoma Irama, disseminated through television and popular print media, Inul would not have been considered unique or interesting. In an article entitled "Terserah Orang" ("According to One's Interpretation"), Cucu Cahyati, the singer of "Mabuk dan Judi" (Drunkenness and Gambling) is quoted as saying that "It's fine if people think that moving one's hips (goyang) has negative connotations. But that's only one opinion/interpretation" ("Terserah Orang" 1996).

By late 2003, Inul had become a major player in the entertainment industry, winning three national awards from television station SCTV for best television artist (August) and one AMI award (Anugerah Musik Indonesia) for best dangdut album (October). Representations of Inul in the popular print media changed from controversial newcomer to established star. A feature article entitled "Just Like Madonna" appeared in the middle-class women's magazine Femina, signaling her acceptance as a seasoned entertainment figure. Biographical entries appeared on Web sites dedicated to Indonesian celebrities, including Apa dan Siapa and TokohIndonesia.com. And a soap opera entitled "Why Inul?" documented the controversies surrounding her performance, as well as her meteoric rise to the top.

Indeed, within a year, Inul began to fade from the public sphere. This was partly due to new broadcasting regulations, which had been introduced in 2002 (UU Penyiaran), but had only begun to come into play in late 2003 (Ishadi S. K., pers. comm., 8 November 2006). These regulations delimited the kinds of outfits and movements that were allowed on television. According to Inul, new regulations about performing on television had made it impossible for her to express herself maximally:

> Musicians need to be able to express themselves on television. They must be able to perform dance moves that are beautiful, and that do not transgress religious norms. If they are able to do that, people will say, "wow, that's an exciting program!" (Inul Daratista, pers. comm., 16 November 2006.

Despite these new media regulations that restricted her televised performances, Inul has used her celebrity to promote greater freedom of expression for women. She took a public stance against Islamic fundamentalist groups that introduced the so-called "anti-pornography" bill (Rancangan Undang-Undang Antipornografi dan Pornoaksi, RUU-APP) to the Indonesian Legislative Assembly (Dewan Perwakilan Rakyat, DPR) in 2006. Under this bill, people would be banned from "disseminating, listening to, staging, or posting writings, sounds or recorded sounds, film or equivalent, song lyrics, poetry, pictures, photographs and/or paintings that exploit the attraction of the body or body parts of a person dancing or moving in an erotic fashion."[29] Legislation regarding the production and distribution of pornographic materials was already included in Indonesia's Criminal Code, although it was not effectively enforced or implemented (Allen 2007). The RUU-APP, enacted on October 30, 2008, increased the state's authority to regulate women's (and men's) bodies. It is important to note that feminist groups were not involved in drafting the RUU-APP bill, which is less about pornography than it is about censorship of various kinds (Garcia 2007, 67).

Feminist activists were against the "anti-pornography bill" because it (a) criminalizes victims of pornography; (b) fails to distinguish children from adults; and (c) allows people to take the law into their own hands (Khalik 2008). Protests were mounted against the bill for representing the "Talibanization" of society and a movement toward Sharia law (Allen 2007). Inul spoke out against the bill in a number of public forums, appearing with activists Rieke Diah Pitaloka and Ratna Sarumpaet as well as former president Gus Dur. This legislation has potentially severe implications for the masses of people captivated by Inul and others, as well as the commercial, government, and critical institutions that represent them. Despite counterprotests by the Betawi Brotherhood Forum (Forum Betawi Rembug, FBR), which demonstrated in front of her home and disrupted business in front of her karaoke club in 2006, Inul has continued to perform and to advocate publicly for freedom of expression and women's rights.[30]

Summary

Writing about Inul generated an extraordinary variety of perspectives on contemporary Indonesian society.[31] In this chapter, I have focused on the social and material conditions that ground the construction of meaning within specific mediated contexts of cultural production. New methods of recording, distributing, and promoting music videos resulted in wider representation of regional popular styles, including "live" recordings that were produced, distributed, and sold outside the mainstream music economy. VCD production and distribution created an alternative economy of music that was not regulated by the state, opening up the possibility for wider exposure and greater freedom of expression.

Inul's detractors argued that the drilling dance had crossed the lines of respectable moral behavior. Using the top-down rhetoric of the New Order, they argued that it was bad for youth and detrimental to the moral fabric of the nation-state. Under the Suharto regime, information was rigidly controlled and opposing viewpoints quashed. The New Order simply did not allow conditions that would make it possible for such intense and widespread debate to develop. It was a residual culture of censorship, within the hands of the MUI and Rhoma Irama, that set into motion efforts to ban a woman's dancing body. But it was the fall of Suharto and subsequent changes in the sphere of politics and religion that amplified these highly charged ideological positions.

The topic of Islamization in Indonesia—including the creation of new Islamic political parties, the rise of radical Islam, calls for an Islamic state, and the expression of religious identities in public—was too broad to deal with here. In this chapter, I have addressed the central ideological factors surrounding music, censorship, and women in the post–New Order period. The MUI issued a very New Order–like decree, but it was not supported by the central government. The drilling dance found hearty supporters among those groups frequently silenced by the Suharto regime: ordinary people, oppositional political groups, the press, and intellectuals. Due to a more liberal press, politicians, women's rights groups, moderate religious leaders, and intellectuals siezed on Inul to voice their own ideological positions. In the highly mediated sphere of popular culture, Inulmania contributed to a new dialogic space where conflicting ideological positions could be expressed and debated. As Indonesia moved out from under the shadow of the Suharto era, Inul's body became a stage to act out rehearsals for democracy.

Inulmania came and went, but it performed serious cultural work, and its effects on dangdut will be shown in the next chapter. In this chapter, I have emphasized the important ideological stakes of body politics. Bodies invested with diverse meanings and values have powerful implications for, among other things, thinking about changing social relations of power. Inul's body articulates the forms of power relations that emerged in the post-Suharto era and the implications they have for discourses about Islam, pornography, women's bodies, state-civil relations in Indonesia, and changing forms of media. As I have described in this chapter, the fall of Suharto set the stage for the transition to a more democratic Indonesia. But what form would democracy take in a country that had been dominated by the 32-year authoritarian regime of the New Order? Inul's body participated in a discourse about a whole range of issues that are crucial for a democratic polity: women's rights, freedom of expression, and freedom of speech. Within a very concentrated amount of time, hundreds of articles were written about the "drilling dance" and what it could possibly mean within the shifting terrain of politics, religion, and culture in Indonesia. She captured the imagination of millions of people at the local, national, and international levels. As an icon of popular culture, Inul enabled people from a variety of subject positions to grapple with some of these issues and to form their own opinions about them. Inul's body acts as a potent site for analyzing these rehearsals for democracy, as well as debates within Islam over censorship, pornography, and violence against women. A simple drilling dance, perhaps, but one that signifies the desires, aspirations, and will of people in shaping the body politic in post-Suharto Indonesia.

NOTES

1. Inul has been dubbed "Ratu Ngebor" ("Queen of the Drill") and has even been pictured in a publicity shot holding an electric drill.

2. Amidhan is also a member of the People's Consultative Assembly (Majelis Permusyawaratan Rakyat, MPR) and a member of the National Commission for Human Rights (Komisi Nasional Hak Asasi Manusia, or Komnas HAM).

3. Majelis Mujahidin is based on the older Darul Islam and Laskar Jihad, from the most fundamentalist wing of the Islamic students' movement. Both are affiliated with transnational radical Islamic networks (Bruinessen 2002). Majelis Mujahidin advocates enactment of Sharia law at the regional level: suppression of "vice," a ban on the sale of alcohol, forced veiling of women, and restrictions on the movement of women unaccompanied by a male protector (ibid.). Their organization is called the Front for the Defence of Islam (Front Pembela Islam, FPI). FPI's targets include "the Miss Indonesia and Miss Transvestite competitions, the rock band Dewa, Mexican soap operas, the Ahmadiyah and Wahidiyah sects, JIL [The Liberal Islam Network, Jaringan Liberal Islam], and the so-called illegal churches (gereja liar)" (Wilson 2008, 203). Wilson notes that the activities of the FPI are motivated by profit more than morality (2008, 205–06).

4. In a public statement, Rhoma Irama also forbade her from singing any of his songs.

5. "Dance drills, faith spills" is a translation of "Goyang Ngebor, Iman Bocor." I am grateful to Ben Zimmer for helping me with the translation.

6. One example, cited in an article about Inul, reports on vice president Hamzah Haz's extravagant pilgrimage to Mecca in 2003. Haz, the leader of the Muslim-based United Development Party (Partai Persatuan Perkembangan, PPP), had already made the pilgrimage several times. Further, he brought along an entourage of over 100 people.

7. "Inul, Goyang Sejuta Umat" 2003, 24. I would like to thank Ariel Heryanto for bringing this article to my attention.

8. See, for example, the television soap opera Why Does It Have to be Inul? (Kenapa Harus Inul?) (2004).

9. Terms associated with Inul proliferated in the popular print media including "Inulitas," "Inulisme," "Inulogi," "Inulist," "Inulisasi," and "Inuliyah," among others. In this chapter, I will use "Inulmania."

10. For example, Hong Kong: Time Asia (24 March 2003), South China Morning Post (26 February 2003), Asia Times Online (10 May 2003); Australia: Australian Financial Review (28 May 2003), Sydney Morning Herald (1 April 2003), The Australian (6 May 2003), Radio Australia (21 April 2003); Singapore: Straits Times (9 March

2003); the United States: *Christian Science Monitor* (csmonitor.com, World>Asia Pacific, 9 May 2003), National Public Radio (All Things Considered, 16 May 2003), *The Economist* (24 May 2003); England: *BBC News* (1 May 2003); and France: *International Herald Tribune* (14 May 2003).

11. My method consists of reading and interpreting popular print media; formal interviews and informal discussions with dangdut artists, critics, and fans. Data for this chapter are based on a review of over 200 popular press articles published from January 2003 to August 2004 in Indonesia, Australia, and the United States. Articles on Inul can be grouped into the following four categories: newspapers and newsmagazines; magazines; tabloids (music, film, and television); and media promotional publications. Inulmania has generated book publications, including Faruk and Aprinus Salam 2003; Gunawan 2003; and Darmeanan 2004; and scholarly articles, including Wichelen 2005; Heryanto 2008; and Weintraub 2008.

12. The fall of Suharto pointed toward a new era of media freedom characterized by a new press law (1999), granting of four new television licenses (2001–2002), and expansion of radio and the Internet. However, media expansion does not necessarily translate into a democractic society. For example, ownership of television stations was largely in the hands of the state, the Suharto family, and their associates (Sen 2002).

13. Endang Kurnia was trained in the traditional Sundanese art of *wayang golek* as a young boy. Many of his songs can be described as "ethnic dangdut" because he incorporates ethnic Sundanese elements. For example, he has composed songs with Sundanese themes entitled "Antara Karawang-Jakarta" (Between Karawang and Jakarta), "Neng Odah" (Miss Odah), "Sinden Jaipong" (Jaipongan Singer/Dancer) and "Embah Dukun" (The Old Healer), among others.

14. For recent accounts of Islam, the state, and democracy in Indonesia see Hefner 2000; Woodward 2001; Effendy 2004; Fealy and Hooker 2006.

15. I have borrowed the framework for this section from Fealy and Hooker 2006, 44–50. See also Doorn-Harder, N.v. and R. M. Feener 2006.

16. FPI leader Habib Muhammad Riziek Syihab was arrested in June 2008 following an FPI attack on an interfaith rally in Jakarta.

17. The following data about the MUI are based on Bruinessen 1990.

18. According to Bruinessen 1990, all major currents of mainstream Islam were represented in MUI in 1990. But this appears not to be the case twenty years later.

19. I am only reporting on women's rights groups that took a position on Inul and were represented in popular print media. For more about the women's movement in Indonesia, see Blackburn 2001.

20. http://www.tokohindonesia.com/selebriti/artis/inul-daratista/index.shtml

21. Internet sources must be read carefully for accuracy. Often, authors replicate inaccurate information without carefully checking the facts beforehand. For example, "Daratista" is often mistranslated as "the girl with the breasts" (Walsh 2003).

22. The terms "Inulfluenza" and "Inulviton" are from Asikin 2003.

23. Of course, power to attract males sexually is not the same thing as power to shape the legal system, run a company, or administer media institutions, jobs held primarily by men.

24. For example, Muslim reformists in the 1970s called for bans on *tayuban*.

25. *Susuk* refers to a small piece of gold, silver, or precious metal inserted into one's body to make one attractive, to protect oneself against harm, or for treating minor ailments. The practice pre-dates the coming of Islam to Java and is considered forbidden in Islam.

26. Significant elements present in many of these female singing and dancing traditions, which are not present in dangdut are: (1) the presentation of the dance scarf to selected male partners; and (2) the male comic role (although this role is sometimes enacted by the emcee in dangdut).

27. The term *patah-patah*, literally "breaks," is probably derived from the Indonesian version of break dancing, in which the quick and abrupt movements of the hips are timed with the rhythmic breaks of the music.

28. One article states that "there are thousands of other aspiring dangdut singers who may never go beyond the seedy bars and wedding parties, although their stage acts may just be as risqué as hers" (Walsh 2003).

29. Translation of RUU-APP by Aviva Kariningsih Cohen and Dr. Matthew Isaac Cohen.

30. Ariel Heryanto argues that in a period spanning less than six months (early 2003 to June 2003), Inul had changed from a local performer who maintained total control over her performance to a polite, subdued, and ordered member of the privileged social class (2008, 15–31). This shift from local hero to co-opted media celebrity represented an erasure of her power and "subversive subaltern attributes" (29). In a class-based struggle over power, authority, and representation, cultural order had been restored and elites had triumphed over subalterns (ibid.). My view is that elements of her performance retained some of their symbolic power, even in the highly negotiated space of national television. During my fieldwork for this book, 2005–2008, people were still invoking Inul to stake out various positions on freedom of expression, morality, and the representation of women's sexualized bodies in the public sphere. As Heryanto correctly observes, Inulmania was widely acknowledged to be a central impetus in creating the anti-pornography bill (15; Allen 2007, 103). I attribute some of the potency of these symbolic practices to Inul's own agency, both onstage and in her numerous appearances on talk shows and in magazine interviews. Clearly, she made certain changes in her performance style in order to reach more people through the medium of television. But even though it was impossible to "express herself maximally" on national television, the symbolic power of her body resonated well beyond the trajectory of her career.

31. For example, Faruk and Aprinus Salam (2003, 6) identify ten perspectives: (a) sociology of art; (b) cultural studies; (c) morality; (d) gender studies; (e) political economy; (f) rational communication; (g) postmodernist; (h) physical; (i) psychological; and (j) aesthetic.

Chapter 8

"Dangdut Daerah":
Going Local in
Post-Suharto Indonesia

When I asked the prolific composer/arranger Ukat S. (b. 1947) about recent market trends in dangdut in 2006, he used the term "ethnic dangdut" (*dangdut etnik*) to refer to dangdut with an Indonesian ethnic nuance (*nuansa etnik*). He mentioned several of his hit songs that used scales, melodies, rhythms, and instruments derived from music associated with one of the many ethnic groups in Indonesia.[1] He contrasted "ethnic" dangdut with "pure" dangdut (*dangdut piur, dangdut murni*) and "regular dangdut" (*dangdut biasa*) which were, ironically, based on Indian film music and contained nuances of India (*nuansa India*). According to Ukat S., the emphasis on regional Indonesian musical characteristics, rather than Indian ones, had solidified dangdut's status as "Indonesia's national music" (*musik nusantara*).[2]

After the fall of Suharto, another kind of "ethnic dangdut" (which I will call "regional dangdut" or *dangdut daerah*) saturated local music scenes in many parts of the country. Sung in regional languages and marketed to specific ethnic communities, dangdut spin-offs developed in West Sumatra (Minang *saluang dangdut*), West Java (Sundanese *pong-dut*), Cirebon (Cirebonese *tarling*), East Java (Javanese *koplo*), and Banjarmasin (Banjarese *dangdut Banjar*), among others (see figure 8.1). In 2007, "regional-language dangdut" (*dangdut berbahasa daerah*) even obtained its own award category at the annual Indonesian Music Awards (Anugerah Musik Indonesia, AMI) (Ant/Ly 2007). Dangdut, originally associated with Melayu and India in the 1970s, and then resignified as national in the 1980s and 1990s, had evolved into something "ethnic" and "regional" in the 2000s.

"Ethnic dangdut" and "regional dangdut" contrasted with the New Order discourse about dangdut as Indonesia's national popular music par excellence.

FIGURE 8.1 Cassette and VCD covers of "dangdut *daerah*" recordings.

Dangdut was perceived, by some, as the genre with the greatest potential to "go international" during the 1990s (see chapter 6). In the 2000s, what did it mean for a national popular music to "go local"? How were these new forms created, marketed, distributed, and used? How did the specter of the economic crisis and the fall of the Suharto regime in 1998 affect the production of dangdut?

Culture in the New Order was used for political purposes to promote the idea of "Bhinekka Tunggal Ika," or "Unity [expressed] in Diversity." Symbolic representations of atomized cultures were constructed and displayed on national television, in national political discourse, and at national festivals. Yet, in this multicultural representation of difference, everyone ended up looking pretty much the same. Social inequalities based on ethnic, racial, class, and gender differences were edged aside for the sake of national homogeneity. In these spaces, epitomized by the Taman Mini theme park in Jakarta, spectators were encouraged to recognize themselves as equivalent to all others, as a way of sublimating social differences. In this New Order vision, social differences and inequalities were contained in the service of symbolic unity. Emanating from the central government in Jakarta, the idea of political unity based on ethno-linguistic and cultural differences aimed to amalgamate people living in the westernmost part of Sumatra to the easternmost town in the province of Papua ("from Sabang to Merauke," to use another slogan of the era).

A similar kind of center-periphery model describes the relationship between forms of national and regional music of Indonesia (Hatch 1985; Yampolsky 1991; Sutton 2003). In the New Order, national popular music genres were defined as those sung in the national language (not regional languages); whose musical elements (instruments, timbres, melodic, rhythmic and formal organization) were based on Western models, or at the very least, were not identified with one ethnic group or another; and whose recordings were produced in Jakarta by a centralized group of producers and disseminated via national media (radio and television) for a national market of consumers. Local (also called regional or ethnic) popular musics, on the other hand, were sung in local languages; had indigenous musical ingredients; and were produced in local recording studios and circulated via localized media for local markets. Local tended to be coterminous with small communities, linguistically and culturally specific. The hegemonic force of the national radio and television apparatus threatened and displaced local musics for the purpose of promoting national unity (Yampolsky 1991, 1).

In this chapter, I focus on emergent forms of "ethnic dangdut" and "regional dangdut" in the post-Suharto period. These examples problematize notions of "local" (also called "regional" or "ethnic"), "national," and "global." My aim is to show how these localized articulations of ethnicity take on broader meanings outside the national-ethnic model of culture. Ethnicity gets defined and used in all sorts of ways to tell all sorts of stories. Connecting musical content with processes of ethnic and national identification has a tendency to ignore the multiple meanings of a cultural text, and the ways in which these meanings change over time. However, it is important to situate specific dangdut repertoire, musical practices, and modes of circulation within discourses about ethnicity and nation in the post-Suharto period. The localization of dangdut across the archipelago is one of the richest areas of research in Indonesia today, and I will only be able to touch on a few stories in this chapter.

It is crucial to specify how electronic mediation (radio, television, recordings, and the Internet) shaped the kinds of meanings that were possible. For example, where and when did ethnicity get expressed in national media? In the first section of this chapter, I use the term "nationalized regionality" to describe examples of regionality in nationally mediated music ("ethnic dangdut"). In the second section of this chapter, I analyze regional forms of dangdut to exemplify what I will call "regionalized nationality" ("regional dangdut"). These forms of regional dangdut are sung in regional languages and are marketed to people of specific ethnic groups, some of whom (including migrant populations) live in different geographical locations. These forms utilize a dangdut musical framework, but they signify ethnicity in different ways from previous forms of dangdut, and in different ways from each other. First, I will describe local performance and recording within the political economy of dangdut during the late 1990s, as this was important for the development of localized scenes.

The Effects of *Krismon* on Local Performance and Recording

The economic crisis (*krisis moneter,* or *krismon*) that shook Southeast Asia in 1997 had important effects on dangdut performance, recording, and distribution. The lack of capital available for music led to a decrease in live performances and recording opportunities. Dangdut musicians responded by downsizing the resources needed for a performance. Live music remained a viable way for performers to earn a living, but musicians had to shape the accompanying ensemble into different formats, as shown in figure 8.2.

Hiring one musician to play a synthesizer (*electone* or *organ tunggal*) was the least expensive option for sponsors with less savings to spend on parties. By programming the instrumental parts, a musician could create a traveling orchestra. An *electone* keyboard instrument was often used for karaoke, and the keyboard player served as a musical guide or teacher for people who came up to sing a song or two at a club or party. Dangdut musicians were arguably more likely than other musicians to benefit from these performance opportunities because they had a reputation for being versatile. For example, electone groups played dangdut, but they also played Indonesian and regional popular forms, Western pop songs, Indian film songs, Mandarin songs, and anything else to satisfy their audiences.

The economic crisis severely curtailed the production of new music recordings made in the larger recording studios of Jakarta and other large cities. Sales figures of cassettes decreased dramatically, although exact figures are unavailable (Barendregt and van Zanten 2002, 85). Those recordings that were released were quickly copied and sold cheaply and easily through the burgeoning pirate

ensemble type	number of musicians	instruments
combo	8	keyboard I (string); keyboard II (blok), guitar I (bass), guitar II (melody/lead), guitar III (rhythm), tambourine, *gendang*, and *suling*
semi	4	keyboard (programmed), guitar (melody/lead), *suling*, *gendang*
electone or *organ tunggal*	1	keyboard (programmed)

FIGURE 8.2 Performance formats after the economic crisis of 1997 (*krismon*).

industry (*industri bajakan*). This system curtailed sales of legal recordings, but it allowed people on the margins of the recording industry to produce and circulate their wares more easily, especially for the purpose of advertising for live performances. Lack of enforcement on producing and selling recordings of untaxed products led to "do-it-yourself" (DIY) production and distribution practices among local producers, as shown in the previous chapter. Some of them gained national exposure, like Inul, while others built local reputations.[3] Local bands used the opportunity to advertise to local markets, with the possibility of reaching broader audiences as well. Following Inul's success, groups adopted new forms of promotion and publicity. For example, they produced and distributed VCDs of their performances, but the covers did not list the name or address of the producer. A product would be distributed, like the Inul VCDs, but not taxed, and it could not easily be traced back to the group. On the video itself, performances of the group showed banners (*spanduk*) that advertised the group's contact information. But it was not clear who had made the video. If groups were questioned, which was unlikely, they would simply deny that they had produced it. Under these conditions, bands built strong local followings, as illustrated in the following edited passage from my field notes:

> Just north of Bandung, West Java, lies the area of Ciumbuleuit, home to wealthy Indonesians and ex-pats. Off the main road, just past the bus terminal, is a valley that houses a kampung (hamlet) of ordinary Sundanese. Concrete steps lead to stone houses with tin roofs. In the afternoon, children are everywhere, flying kites, eating snacks, playing soccer. I weave my way through corridors and past wood huts and small foodstalls to the home of Massprie Sejati, leader of the band Primadonna (figure 8.3). The band gathers here and practices for upcoming gigs. As the market for dangdut increased after the fall of Suharto, the group changed its focus from Sundanese music and dance to exclusively dangdut with a strong rock flavor (dangdut rock). In 2004 they changed their name from the Sundanese "Mekar Wangi" (Spreading Fragrance) to "Primadonna." Primadonna performs at weddings, circumcisions, and other events hosted by individuals or community groups. They have established links with event organizers and radio stations. Their main revenue comes from shows featuring what they call "sexy dancers," a trend that began in 2004, after the Inul phenomenon. Vonny Safura Dwiputri (Puput), Massprie's 11-year-old daughter, is one of the main dancers [⊙].

In addition to performing dangdut with a heavy rock edge, they play *pong-dut* (also called *dangdut jaipongan, b[l]ang-plak, blak-pong,* or *dangdut Sunda*), a

FIGURE 8.3 Primadonna band [photo: Andrew Weintraub].

regional Sundanese form of dangdut with Sundanese drumming. The main
feature in this music is a Sundanese drumming style from West Java that
accompanies *jaipongan,* a form of Sundanese dance. The drum sound can be
created electronically, or it can be played on one or more sets of Sundanese
kendang (each set consists of three or more drums). When played using actual
drums, one can hear the variations in patterns. Drum jabs/kicks add emphasis
to movements and create excitement for listeners in often unpredictable ways.
At clubs and parties, these patterns can be improvised, within a whole system
of erotic and playful interaction that occurs among male drummers, female
dancers, and their male counterparts (Spiller 2001). Songs can be sung in
Sundanese or Indonesian.

National Regionality: "Goyang Dombret" and "Embah Dukun"

Dangdut inflected by local languages, instruments, and rhythms had existed at
least as early as the 1980s (Hatch 1985, 216). National hits of the 1980s and
1990s included single words and phrases from the regional languages Minang

("Aduh Buyung"), Makassarese ("Sumpah Benang Emas"), and Sundanese ("Duh Engkang"), among others. In dangdut, local words and instruments added local flavor, but they told stories in Indonesian that everyone could relate to: "Aduh Buyung," is about a Minang migrant man named Buyung who travels far from his place of origin; "Sumpah Benang Emas" takes place on a beach in Sulawesi (*pantai Losari*), but it is essentially about problems in a marriage; "Duh Engkang," discussed in chapter 6, is a nostalgic tale in West Java about returning home to a simpler lifestyle, an issue that affects the lives of people in many parts of Indonesia. In these songs, regional elements circulated nationally through television, radio, and recordings. They commented on notions of regionality, but their audience was not limited to a specific locality. Regionality was not imagined as a specific place, but as regionality itself, as in a "national [sense of] regionality." Despite its regional flavor, dangdut with an ethnic nuance acted as a sign that "this is for everyone."

In this section, I will discuss two songs in this vein: "Goyang Dombret," composed by Ukat S., and "Embah Dukun," composed by Endang Kurnia. Both songs circulated nationally in 2000–2001, and both have strong Sundanese regional elements. Ethnic markers include Sundanese instruments (*calung* xylophone and *kacapi* zither), drumming style, dance movements (*ketuk tilu* and *jaipongan*), and melodies that approximate Sundanese scales. Both songs are in Indonesian, but have a smattering of Sundanese words and references, as well as some Betawi and Javanese words.

"Goyang Dombret" is about a female singer/dancer (*ronggeng dombret*) who dances with men at parties held every night during the dry season in fishing villages in the northern parts of West Java including Cilamaya (Karawang), Mayangan (Subang), and Indramayu (see figure 8.4). The dance is accompanied by an ensemble featuring loud drumming. *Ronggeng dombret* dance in a free-style manner that emphasizes their hip movements (*goyang pinggul*). *Ronggeng dombret* dance together, as a group, and invite men to dance with them, especially those who have just returned from fishing all day. After the dance, the men give the *ronggeng* money as part of a cultural practice called *sawer*. Although specific to West Java in theme, the song was circulated nationally in 2000 and was recorded by national recording stars Uut Permatasari and Inul Daratista.

"Goyang Dombret" preserves the ethnic tradition of *ronggeng* who are an active part of village life in Java and Sumatra. But what kind of story does it tell? How is ethnicity being used here? "Goyang Dombret" adheres to Ukat S.'s notion that "ethnicity sells" even if the song is laden with elements of rock, pop, disco, house, and dangdut. The song sells an image of a woman who has many dance partners. She will sing and accompany a man all night, as long as she is paid. Her performance will be better if he pays her more. The man can forget about her

Refrain: Goyang dombret, goyang dombret Goyang dombret, goyang dombret.	Refrain: Goyang dombret, goyang dombret Goyang dombret, goyang dombret.
Kang Dadang paling kasep, Saya suka akang suka sekali, Bang Mandor paling ganteng, Saya demen abang demen sekali,	Dadang is the best-looking, I like him, I like him a lot, And Mandor is the most handsome, I like him a lot too.
Ayo dong Kang bergoyang biar saya temenin, Jangan lupa sawernya buat tambahan saya, Makin banyak sawerannya, Makin asyik goyangannya.	C'mon honey let's dance, keep me company, Don't forget to give me money as a tip, The more money I get, The better I'll dance for you.
[Refrain]	[Refrain]
Saya sinden cuma nyanyi, Silahkan abang bergoyang, Walau harus pulang pagi, Asal saja akang senang.	I'm a singer, and I will only sing, You go ahead and dance, Although you have to go home in the morning, What matters is that you have a good time.
Saya sinden cuma nyanyi, Tapi banyak yang menggoda, Harus bisa jaga diri, Supaya jangan ternoda.	I'm a singer, and I will only sing, But many try to tempt me, One has to hold back, So as not to be disgraced/deflowered.
Nang ning nang ning nung	La la la la la
[Refrain]	[Refrain]

FIGURE 8.4 "Goyang Dombret" (The Dombret Dance) [courtesy of Ukat S.].

after the dance is over, but he cannot forget about paying her. The most important element of this financial exchange is for the man to be satisfied. She expects him to leave, and even encourages him to go home in the morning.

Toward the end of the song, the dialogue ends between the woman (*saya*/I) and the man (*abang*/male). The narrative tone shifts from a personal situated encounter to a more general abstract moral lesson. At the end of the song, presumably after she has been paid, the woman explains that her job is to sing, and nothing else. She narrates a common story about female singers (*sinden*): many try to tempt her, but she must not give in to temptation. She may be telling the man why she is refusing his advances, or she may be offering a piece of advice to women, or she may simply be reiterating a moral lesson she was told long ago. What is striking is the shift in tone, which may have been added in order to evade censorship. This practice of self-censorship toward the conclusion of a song is similar to practices in filmmaking:

> A film can contain (in the sense of both carrying and limiting) contentious images and ideas, as long as it achieves the "correct" conclusion. And audiences, aware of such conventions, can read the film without or against its narrative closure. (Sen 1991)

In order to deter censors who may think that a *ronggeng* does something besides merely singing, the last verse offers a disclaimer and a moral lesson designed to placate any objections by censors. The *ronggeng dombret* only desires one thing, and she is there simply to satisfy her dance partners. Despite its sexualized theme and "porno" lyrics, this song was never banned. It acheives the "correct" conclusion: whether the *ronggeng dombret* merely sings, or does something else, she does not pose a threat to men. However, there are many ways that audiences can read against this type of narrative closure. For example, the song carries an image of an independent sexualized women who expresses her desire for more than one man. She makes it clear that she only needs them for tips. These contrasting meanings leave the text open to interpretation, and speak to women's issues across ethnicities.

Another example of "nationalized regionality" is the national hit "Embah Dukun" (The Old Healer) composed by Endang Kurnia.[4] In 2000, the singer Alam asked Endang Kurnia to compose a song that would pick up on the popularity of ghost stories during this period (*filem hantu*), as well as the antiwitchcraft campaigns during the late 1990s (see Sidel 2007, 142–153). Endang Kurnia (who appears in the video as the old healer) based the song on practices of *dukun*, traditional healers that recite mantras and spells for healing and excorcism rites. To further capitalize on this image, the song makes reference to different linguistic forms of the word "satan" on the island of Java (Javanese, Betawi, Sundanese) (see figure 8.5).

The singer Alam creates a narrative of four different characters, each with a different vocal quality: (1) observer (speaks); (2) storyteller (sings using a soft smooth vocal timbre; laughs; and sings in a higher-pitched growl); (3) *dukun* (spits, shouts, and delivers rapid-fire lyrics that mimic the reciting style of a traditional healer who uses mantras to call spirits); and (4) patient (sings). "Embah Dukun" juxtaposes sections of hard rock and dangdut to emphasize these shifts in narrative tone (see figure 8.6). [◉]

The video for "Embah Dukun" builds conflicting interpretations into the text as a way to attract as wide an audience as possible.[5] The serious tone that sets the mood of the song about a traditional healer is immediately disrupted by the singer Alam, who laughs hysterically when he says "there is a healer working on a patient." Alam is a young rock singer whose dance movements are modeled after Michael Jackson. Alam begins the video wearing a simple t-shirt and white pants, but changes into a yellow warm-up jacket and black pants during his dance numbers. In a seated position, Alam holds up one finger, moves his head from side to side, and thrusts his body back and forth. Alam's scratchy and irreverant vocal quality breaks with the sweet and smooth crooning style usually used by male dangdut singers. The rough tone of his voice contrasts with Alam's "cute boy" appearance.

Waduh, mbah dukun sibuk nich?!]	Wow, healer, so busy, huh?!
A: Ada mbah dukun sedang ngobatin pasiennya, Konon katanya, sakitnya karena diguna-guna [deudeu teuing], Sambil komat-kamit mulut mbah dukun baca mantra, Dengan segelas air putih lalu pasien disembur.	A: There is a healer treating a patient, They say the patient is sick because of a black magic spell [it's too much!], While moving his lips the healer recites a mantra, And with a glass of clear water the patient will be spat on.
Setan gendeng, setan bandel, setan gombal, Setan setan semua yang namanya setan, Jangan ganggu yeuh, jangan suka mengganggu, Pergilah kau setan, jangan ganggu, Mbreuh, bayawak belegug ngaganggu siah ku aing di batako.	Satan, naughty satan, cheating satan, Satan, all the names of satan, Stay away, don't bother this person, Get away, Satan, don't bother her, You stupid jerk, annoying, I'll beat you with a stone.
B: Mbah dukun tolong juga saya, Yang sedang mabuk cinta, Nama si Lela anak kepala desa, Yang membuat aku tergila-gila, serrr!	B: Healer help me too, I'm drunk with love, Her name is Lela and she's the village head's daughter, She makes me crazy with love!
[interlude]	[interlude]
C: Mbah dukun tolong lihat jodohku, Apa mungkin si Lela menjadi milikku, serrr?	C: Healer, help me see my future wife, Is it possible that Lela could be mine?
Mbah dukun jampi-jampi kan aku Agar si Lela semakin cinta padaku Dan tak lupa doaku paling utama Kepada Tuhan Yang Maha Kuasa Semoga cinta kami abadi selamanya, yess!	Healer give me a spell, So Lela will fall in love with me, And don't forget my prayer, the most important one, To God, the all-powerful, So that pure love will come to us forever. Yes!
Mbah dukun, jangan takabur yah, Tuhan yang menentukan mah.	Healer don't be arrogant, God controls everything.
[repeat previous with variations]	[repeat previoius with variations]

FIGURE 8.5 "Embah Dukun" (The Healer) [courtesy of Endang Kurnia].

In 2000, "Embah Dukun" was criticized for promoting *dukun,* ancient healers associated with magic, who were thought to steer people away from Allah. *Dukun* are not a laughing matter for everyone, especially fundamentalist or conservative Muslims. However, the words *konon katanya* ("reportedly") indicate doubt that magic can be responsible for a patient's illness. Through humor, the song pokes fun at traditional healers, and yet people continue to seek them out for advice about relationships, business opportunities, and other matters. Further, the patient seeking help urges the *dukun* not to forget to include the most important prayer to the one and only God (Allah). This song mirrors the syncretic belief system of many Indonesian Muslims who

section	Intro
lyrics	Waduh, embah dukun
# Measures (metrical structure)	4
accompaniment	guitar, piano, synth
gendang	--
vocal quality	speaks
character	observer
time	0.00

section	A		
lyrics	Ada embah dukun sedang ngobatin	Setan gendeng	Janggan ganggu
# measures (metrical structure)	12 (4 + 4 + 4)	1 1/2	7 (4 + 3)
accompaniment	piano, synth	guitar, bass, drums	band
gendang	--	-	Ch1
vocal quality	sings; laughs	spits, speaks rapidly	shouts; recites mantra
character	storyteller	dukun	dukun
time	0.09	0.38	0.43

section	B
lyrics	Mbah Dukun tolong juga saya
# measures (metrical structure)	8 (1/2 + 4 + 1/2 + 3)
accompaniment	band
gendang	Ch1
vocal quality	sings
character	patient
time	0.59

section	interlude	
lyrics	-	--
# measures (metrical structure)	8	4
accompaniment	keyboard, guitar, bass, drums	band w/suling solo
gendang	-	jaipongan
vocal	-	--
character	-	--
time	1.18	1.36

section	C			
lyrics	Mbah dukun tolong lihat jodohku bah	--	Mbah dukun jampi jampi kan aku	Mbah dukun jangan takabur
# measures (metrical structure)	4	2	12 (4 + 4 + 4)	1
accompaniment	band	band w/ suling solo	band	band
gendang	Ch1	jaipongan	Ch1	--
vocal quality	sings	--	sings	talks
character	patient	--	patient	observer
time	1.46	1.55	2.00	2.30

FIGURE 8.6 Song guide "Embah Dukun" (The Healer): intro—A-B-interlude-C.

simultaneously believe in the power of *dukun* as well as Allah. The ending achieves the "correct" conclusion, as in "Goyang Dombret," but it contains conflicting images and ideas about tradition (*adat*) and Islam. Its images and sounds, as well as the polyvocal nature of its text, encourage people to read against the grain and to question its ideological position.

"Goyang Dombret" and "Embah Dukun" were nationally marketed songs with ethnic nuances. They invoked a melange of languages (Indonesian, Sundanese, Javanese, and Betawi), making it hard to locate ethnicity in any one location. They had a hint of regionality, but were intended to cross ethno-linguistic boundaries. They symbolized "[the essence of] regional" for a national audience.

"Regional Nationality": *Saluang Dangdut, Koplo,* and Dangdut Melayu

In the following section, I will analyze three regionalized forms of dangdut: *saluang dangdut* (West Sumatra); *koplo* (East Java), and dangdut Melayu (Riau).

Saluang dangdut

"Saluang Dangdut" (Tanama Record) is a karaoke VCD of ten Minang songs and accompanying dance (see figure 8.7). *Saluang* is a long rim-blown bamboo flute, tuned to a pentatonic system. The male *saluang* player (unnamed in the video) sits immobile during all of the pieces, using circular breathing to produce a continuous flow of sound. He is dressed in a traditional Minang headdress, shirt, and pants. There are two female singers (Irma Junita and Ety Chan), in their thirties, who wear different clothes for different songs. Their outfits include long elegant evening gowns, business outfits, informal sporty attire, as well as traditional Minang headress and costume. Their demeanor ranges from pensive to fun, but not flirtatious or seductive. They either sit together with the *saluang* player, or stand in one position and move to the music using small steps. A group of teenage female dancers in the background performs more active dance movements, including gyrating hips, side-to-side head movements, and choreographies based on traditional dance movements (e.g., planting rice and fishing). They are dressed in jeans, t-shirts, and sportswear. At times, they pose seductively and look directly at the camera.

"Saluang Dangdut" is *saluang* with a national tinge. This production is marketed to and consumed by Minang. It is a karaoke production designed for people to sing along. All songs are in the Minang language, and several are based on a

FIGURE 8.7 *Saluang dangdut* CD cover.

genre of sung poetry called *saluang jo dendang*. The arrangment emphasizes the heterophonic relationship between voice and *saluang*. Programmed keyboard accompaniment in a diatonic scale establishes the harmony of the song.

The unmetered *saluang jo dendang* songs have been adapted to a regular fixed beat. The main dangdut characteristic is the bass line, with accents on beats 1, 4, 6 and 7 of an 8-beat measure. The *gendang* part is not played on an actual *gendang*, but it is suggested by a heavy rhythmic emphasis on beats 7 and 1 (of an 8-beat measure). Essentially, *saluang dangdut* refers to modernized Minang songs accompanied by a keyboard, with a dangdut tinge.

Visual and sonic signs link modernity to a specific locality. The first song features a van as one of the main "characters" in the story; the band's name, "Junita" (named after the main singer), announces itself as an advertisement painted on the side of the van. Minang land (*alam* Minang) is one of the main framing devices. The *salaung* player sits either in a grassy knoll or against a spindly tree trunk. The dancers appear in a forest clearing. Tree branches sway in front of the singers. Cutaway shots of rivers, mountains, rice fields, and flower bushes bring viewers back to the physical location. These images index a nostalgic attachment to a Minang homeland.

The term "dangdut" in the title signals that this localized product has commodity value within the contemporary national music market dominated by dangdut. "Saluang Dangdut" uses dangdut to circumscribe a place (*tanah* or *alam* Minang), a language (Minang), elements of music (instruments, vocal style), performers (Irma Junita and Ety Chan), and references to material culture (architecture, clothing). "Local," in this case, does not refer to one specific geographical location, but rather many geographic communities in which Minangkabau have dispersed in the Minangkabau diaspora (*merantau*), especially in bigger towns and cities of Indonesia (Barendregt 2002, 417). By picking up on some of the nuances of dangdut (dance styles and dangdut bass lines), *saluang dangdut* is *saluang* with a national nuance.

"Saluang Dangdut" contrasts with another Minang video recording of the well-known dangdut song "Jatuh Bangun," composed by Eko Saky and made famous by Kristina, one of several female celebrities who rose to stardom on national television in the 1990s. In this version, entitled "Jatuah Bangun," the title and some of the text have been translated from Indonesian into Minang. The first verse of the Minang "Jatuah bangun" and the Indonesian "Jatuh Bangun" are shown in figure 8.8 (with English translation).

In contrast to "Saluang Dangdut," this production by Minang Record takes place mostly at night.[6] The main dancer, who also lipsyncs the words, is shown against a series of fantastic backdrops: Stonehenge, flowing rivers, an English garden, the Eiffel Tower, European castles, expansive mountain ranges, urban

Minang	Indonesian	English
Jatuah bangun denai mangaja uda	Jatuh bangun aku mengejarmu	Up and down I chase you
Namunnyo uda ndak mau tau	Namun dirimu tak mau mengerti	But you don't want to undertand
Den boakkan saganggam cinto	Kubawakan segenggam cinta	I bring you love
Namun uda mamintak denai	Namun kau meminta diriku	Yet you ask me
Mambaok rambulan ka pangkuan uda	Membawakan bulan ke pangkuanmu	To bring you the moon

FIGURE 8.8 Minang and Indonesian lyrics (with English translation) of "Jatuh Bangun" (Rising and Falling).

nightlife, crowd scenes, fireworks. Instead of local references, the visual imagery has a global orientation.

This is an example of *dangdut trendy* and fits the description by Jeremy Wallach (2004):

> The techno-hybrid grooves of ethnic house music and dangdut trendy are assembled from a bewildering array of musical genres: sampled snippets of African American slang, bits of Hollywood movie dialogue, rhythmic patterned shouts (*senggak*) reminiscent of West Javanese traditional music, and hip hop drum loops. Also added to the mix are sampled xylophones, barrel drums, kettle gongs, bamboo flutes, and other indigenous musical instruments representing various Indonesian ethnicities.

"Jatuah Bangun" assembles its musical sources into a form for local Minang communities, either in West Sumatra or in other places where migrants have relocated. The video, which I viewed on the Internet, is part of a virtual Minang space consisting of online newspapers, discussion groups, and business networks (Barendregt 2002, 417). Like the rapidly shifting visual style, exemplified in the video by background images that move too quickly to identify, the music never stops moving. It is a localized version of a national song filtered through globalized visual images. In this case, going local is identified as going global.

Koplo

The popularity of Inul Daratista naturally gave rise to groups that aimed to capitalize on her success. In the post-Inul period, videos of bands performing "sensational dangdut" (*dangdut heboh*) and "sexy dangdut" (*dangdut sexy*) flooded local markets, especially in Central and East Java. As discussed in chapter 6, eroticized styles of dance had long been a part of rural performance practices, but they did not circulate widely via recordings until the advent of the camcorder and the VCD music industry.

At these "live" events, female singers perform eroticized movements on stage. In videos of these performances, female singer/dancers are filmed frontally and from low camera angles to emphasize their dancing bodies. Males in the audience are packed tightly toward the stage, and they dance in place, wave their arms, and pass money to the singers or to an emcee. Occasionally, men will come onstage to dance.

The performance style originated in Central and East Java by bands including Trio Macan (Lamongan), Palapa (Sidoarjo), Monata (Mojokerto), Sera (Gresik), Evita (Gresik), Sanjaya (Blora), Sakatto (Probolinggo), and Putra Dewa (Tuban).

The repertoire includes dangdut songs in Indonesian, Javanese, and a mixture of the two languages. Song texts in Javanese play well across the archipelago in cities, towns, and villages with Javanese populations. Bands have also achieved success across regions, as evidenced by dangdut *heboh* styles on VCDs marketed as far east as Maluku. Backing bands have individual styles, ranging from lounge bands with matching jackets to rock bands with long hair, t-shirts, piercings, and tattoos.

Trio Macan (Trio of Tigers) is the name of a group (from Lamongan) as well as a genre. The three female dancers in the group wear matching tight-fitting costumes and shiny belts with beaded tassles. They do not wear shoes. Each of the "tigers" has long hair pulled back by a headband. In addition to standard *goyang pinggul* (gyrating hips) and chest shaking, their act consists of various trademark moves. Imitating tigers, they crawl on the stage toward the audience. They swing their heads around (headbanging). From a standing position, they lean back at a 45-degree angle and perform pelvic thrusts in the air. Sitting on their knees and leaning back, they extend their arms all the way back as they thrust or gyrate their hips.

Koplo refers to the performance style, the drum rhythm, and the fast-tempo, metal-inflected music that accompanies Trio Macan. "Koplo pills" (*pil koplo*) are hallucinagenic drugs. *Koplo* music was a way to express a drug-induced sentiment about a style of dance that people considered "unbelievable" or "out of this world." *Koplo* was created in the early to mid-1990s and exploded during the "crazy times" of the post-Suharto era, full of instability and chaos but also energy and hope. On recordings, *koplo* also refers to the electronic remix style, which is usually fast and characterized by active percussion parts.

Koplo was created in East Java, but its origins are unclear. Malik B. Z., the composer of "Keagungan Tuhan" (The Greatness of God), claims credit for inserting a *koplo*-like rhythm from a local East Javanese genre *reog ponorogo* into one of his popular music compositions in the 1970s. Yadi, a keyboard player in Bandung, West Java, theorized that the main *koplo* drum rhythm derives from the drum motif that accompanies the stepping pattern (*mincid*) in Sundanese *jaipongan* (Yadi, pers. comm., 19 December 2006), and this view was confirmed by musicians in the East Javanese cities of Surabaya and Banyuwangi. In the 1980s, *jaipongan* drumming traveled to East Java via cassettes, where it was incorporated into various forms of music. However, *jaipongan* drumming also incorporates dangdut rhythms. Therefore, *koplo* may have originated as a reinterpretion of a dangdut rhythmic pattern that had been translated through *jaipongan*. These rhythms were subsequently reinterpreted by Sundanese drummers playing *koplo* music in localized Sundanese dangdut ensembles. These creative appropriations illustrate intercultural processes among ethnic groups, rather than the dominance of national forms over local ones (see figure 8.9)

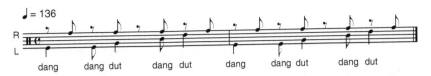

FIGURE 8.9 *Koplo* rhythmic pattern.

Koplo instructs us to think about circulation in a different way from the one-way New Order model of center-periphery (national-regional). A *koplo* performance ethos is rooted in *ronggeng* dance of rural Java. Its music is heavily inflected by a variety of musical styles, including metal, house, dangdut, and *jaipongan*. Intercultural relationships among ethnic groups have contributed to the development of new styles. *Koplo*'s rise in popularity occurred after Inul (originally a rock singer from East Java), merged her trademark "drilling" dance with dangdut. The televisual mediation of Inul occurred at the national level, and these broadcasts traveled back to East and Central Java. In this case, the national mediatization of dangdut brought a regional style back to the region, where it was fused with other regional styles within a local industry. These circuits challenge the older center-periphery model of national-regional music.

Dangdut Melayu

In 2002, singer Iyeth Bustami produced an album entitled "Laksmana Raja di Laut" (Laksmana, the Hero of the Sea).[7] The album was made in Jakarta, marketed nationally, and achieved critical and popular success. In 2003, Iyeth Bustami received an award as the best female dangdut singer of the year ("Kembali ke Akar Melayu" 2003). The album signaled recognition for dangdut Melayu, a type of ethnic dangdut in Riau. Arranger Mara Karma, also from the island of Riau, received the award for best arranger. And singer Hamdan ATT, originally from Ambon, won the best male singer award for a Melayu song "Patah Kemudi" (Broken Steering Wheel) (ibid.).

The text for "Laksmana Raja di Laut" urges listeners to remember Melayu arts and culture (see figure 8.10). The song refers to ethnocultural signifiers, including musical instruments and rhythms, styles of dance, folklore, hair ornaments, and Melayu culture itself. Unlike the visually oriented singer/dancers of her era, whose careers were launched on television (e.g., Inul Daratista, Uut Permatasari, Anisa Bahar), Iyeth's performances featured very little dance.

Verses for "Laksmana Raja di Laut" are constructed in the four-line *pantun* form in which the first two lines form the *sampiran* (place to hang clothes) and

Zapin, Aku dendangkan, Lagu Melayu, Pelipur hati, Pelipur lara.	The zapin rhythm, I sing, A Melayu song, To console my heart, To ease my sadness.
A: Cahaya manis kilau gemilau, Digantung tabir indah mengawan, Ku bernyanyi berzapin ria, Moga hadirin, aduhai sayang, jadi terkesan.	A: A sweet light shining magnificently, Hidden behind a curtain of clouds, I sing and dance with joy, Hoping that all present, my love, will be impressed.
Kembanglah goyang atas kepala, Lipatlah pandan sanggul dipadu, Kita berdendang bersuka ria, Lagulah zapin, aduhai sayang, rentak Melayu.	The flowers dancatop one's head, The ornaments and hair perfectly in place, We sing together and enjoy, A Melayu song, my love, the rhythms of Melayu.
[Interlude]	[Interlude]
B: Laksmana Raja di Laut, Bersemayam di Bukit Batu, [aa haay] Hati siapa [aa haay] tak terpaut, Mendengar lagu zapin Melayu. 2x	B: Laksmana the hero of the sea, Enthroned in the mountain of stone, [hey] Whose heart [hey] will not fall in love, Listening to a Melayu dance-song. 2x
A': Membawa tepak hantaran belanja, Bertahta perak, indah berseri, Kami bertandak menghidup budaya, Tidak Melayu, aduhai sayang, gilang di bumi.	A': Bring a purse to the market, Crowned in silver, beaming with beauty, We dance to keep alive the culture, Melayu culture, my love, spreading its glory on earth.
Petiklah gambus sayang langgam berbunyi, Disambut dengan tingkah meruas, Saya bernyanyi sampai di sini, Mudah-mudahan hadirin semua menjadi puas.	Pluck the gambus, love, a melody, Accompanied by the drum, My song ends here, Hopeful that all who have listened are satisfied.
[repeat B] 2x	[repeat B] 2x

FIGURE 8.10 "Laksmana Raja di Laut" (Laksmana, the Hero of the Sea) [public domain].

the last two lines form the *isi* (contents). They are structured into the rhyme scheme abab, indicated with bold and italics as follows:

Laksmana Raja di **Laut**
Bersemayam di Bukit Bat*u*
Hati siapa tak ter**paut**
Mendengar lagu zapin Melay*u*

"Laksmana Raja di Laut" combines the rhythms of dangdut and *zapin;* the term *zapin Melayu* refers to an archaic form of Malay folk dance and music "performed mostly by the Malays and mixed-blood Malays of Arab descent" (Nor 1993, 1). The term *zapin* refers to the modernized form that has become emblematic of national Malay culture and identity (ibid., ix). Ethnomusicologist Rizaldi Siagian notes that the *gendang* dangdut drum replaced the small hand drum (*marwas*) used in *zapin* ("Kembali ke Akar Melayu" 2003). *Zapin* instrumental parts include *biola* (violin), accordion (played on a synthesizer), *gambus* (played on guitar), and *marwas* (pl. *marawis,* also played on a synthesizer). Dangdut instruments include electric guitar, *suling,* piano, and *gendang.* [⬤]

The song begins with two introductions: (1) intro I, an unmetered highly ornamented vocal section accompanied by rolling piano arpeggios and violin fills;[8] and (2) intro II, a metered section. The form of the song is as follows: [intro I-intro II—A-interlude-B-A´-B] (see figure 8.11).

section	Intro I	
lyric	--	Zapina
measures (metrical structure)	3	Unmetered (accomp. violin, piano, and synth)
percussion	gendang, marawis	--
time	0.00	0.08

section	Intro II	
lyric	--	--
measures (metrical structure)	3	10 (4 + 4 + 2)
percussion	gendang, marawis	gendang, marawis
time	1.02	1.10

section	A	
lyric	Cahaya manis	Kembanglah goyang
# measures (metrical structure)	10 (4 + 4 + 2)	10 (4 + 4 + 2)
percussion	gendang, marawis	gendang, marawis
time	1.34	1.58

section	Interlude	
lyric	--	
# measures (metrical structure)	4	5 (2 + 2 + 1)
percussion	gendang	gendang
time	2.22	2.31

section	B	
lyric	Laksmana	Laksmana
# measures (metrical structure)	8	9 (8 + 1)
percussion	gendang	gendang
time	2.44	3.03

section	A'	
lyric	Membawa tepak	Petiklah gambus
# measures (metrical structure)	10 (4 + 4 + 2)	9 (4 + 4 + 1)
percussion	gendang, marawis	gendang, marawis
time	3.25	3.50

section	B	
lyric	Laksmana	Laksmana
# measures (metrical structure)	8	8
percussion	gendang	gendang
time	4.11	4.30

FIGURE 8.11 Song guide "Laksmana Raja di Laut" (Laksmana, the King of the Sea).

In 2004, "Laksmana Raja di Laut" became embroiled in a controversy over ownership of the song because the composer for "Laksmana Raja di Laut" was listed as anonymous (n.n.). Iyeth Bustami had assumed the lyrics were part of the oral tradition and that gave her the right to record it. It is likely that she heard this tune on one of the Malaysian television shows featuring Malaysian singers that she had watched as a child growing up in Riau, just across the Straits of Malacca from Malaysia. In 2004, after hearing Iyeth's version of "Laksmana Raja di Laut," singer Nurham Yahya, also from Riau claimed that the song was his. On July 22, 2004, he registered the song with the director general of the Intellectual Property Rights Organization (Hak Kekayaan Intelektual, HAKI) (Siagian 2006). If she had indeed copied the song, Iyeth Bustami was therefore liable for copyright infringement, subject to a penalty of $US1000 and a maximum of seven years in prison (ibid.). However, after hearing about HAKI's acknowledgment of this claim, cultural stewards of six traditional communities in Riau initiated a case against Nurham as well as HAKI. They stated that the song lyrics were part of the oral tradition, and their ownership could not be claimed by individuals or institutions (ibid.).

After hearing that the lyrics were allegedly owned by Nurham, Iyeth conducted her own investigation and discovered that Malaysian composer Suhaimi Bin Mohd Zian, also known as Pak Ngah, had composed the melody using the title "Nostalgia Idul Fitri," a song about the Muslim holiday that marks the end of Ramadhan, the Islamic holy month of fasting. Pak Ngah composed the song melody in 1993 for a theatrical production (Tresnawati 2005). The song had been recorded by Malaysian singer Sarifah Aini in 1996. "Nostalgia Idul Fitri" had received substantial radio play throughout Malaysia and parts of Indonesia, including the island of Bengkalis, Iyeth Bustami's home.

Iyeth claims she first heard the song melody for "Nostalgia Idul Fitri" in 1999 (Tresnawati 2005). But it was not Sarifah Aini's version: the lyrics to the "Nostalgia" melody had been changed to "Laksmana Raja di Laut," a common practice in Melayu *pantun* of the Bengkalis region (Rizaldi, pers. comm., 30 December 2006). As is common in the oral tradition, someone had invented lyrics and had set them to an existing melody. People often did this spontaneously, without regard for the composer of the text or the melody, and so it was not widely known that Nurham had composed the lyrics. Rather, the composed lyrics, in the traditional form of *pantun*, had become part of the everyday life and folklore of the people.

Iyeth met with Pak Ngah, who owns the rights to his melodic creation (*hak cipta*) and he subsequently granted permission to Iyeth to use the melody.

In late 2005, a trial was held in the District Court (Pengadilan Negeri/Niaga) located in the city of Medan in North Sumatra.[9] The trial addressed the composition of the melody and the lyrics. Ethnomusicologist Rizaldi Siagian testified that the two melodies were indeed the same. Ownership of the lyrics was more problematic. Representatives of the six communities argued that the lyrics came directly from Melayu folklore, were used in ritual ceremonies, and had no owner. However, authority for stewardship of these traditions was vested collectively in these ancestral communities. The stewards of the tradition had something similar to moral rights over traditional forms of expression. For example, the representatives of these communities were the descendants of Datuk Ibrahim, the founder of Bandar Bengkalis, who was given the title "Datuk Laksmana Raja Dilaut" by Sultan Sri Indrapura of Siak in Riau (ibid.). Some of those individuals testified that Nurham had spoiled the reputation of one of their ancestors by bringing the case to a public hearing in court. They argued that Nurham Yahya's name should be removed as the owner of the lyrics. They also urged Nurham to reimburse Iyeth for the funds she had spent to defend herself in court (Rizaldi, pers. comm., 30 December 2006). In early 2006, Nurham brought the case to a higher court and as of 2009 the case was still pending.

This case demonstrates yet another way that ethnicity has been used in Indonesia. Not only did the district court rule against Nurham's individual claims of ownership to these particular lyrics (registered with HAKI), but the judge ruled that lyrics composed in *pantun* forms, with its symbolic references to Melayu ethnicity, are collectively owned by the Melayu people (Rizaldi 2006). By ruling against a decision passed down by HAKI, the national intellectual property rights organization of Indonesia, the court did not comply with Indonesia's 2002 Copyright Act which states:

> The State shall hold the copyright for folklore and works of popular culture that are commonly owned, such as stories, legends, folk tales, epics, songs, handicrafts, choreography, dances, calligraphies and other artistic works.

Retracing the circulation of the song shows yet another way of thinking about music and ethnicity outside the national-ethnic or center-periphery model. The melody was composed by Malaysian composer Pak Ngah and recorded by Malaysian singer Sarifah Aini. The recording traveled across the very porous border separating Malaysia and Indonesia to Riau where it was combined with a text by an unkown author. Iyeth Bustami brought the song to Jakarta where it was fused with elements of Indonesian dangdut. Circulated nationally, the song made its way back to Riau and at that point it was claimed by composer Nurham Yahya. A court in Medan determined that the song was owned collectively by ethnic Melayu and could not be registered with the State. Even though it was a work of unknown authorship it did not belong to the State.

The debate over "Laksmana Raja di Laut" brings us back to the discourse about Melayu in chapter 2. Pointing to Indonesia (Deli or Padang, for example) as a place of origin, as opposed to Malaysia (Melaca, for example), has become important in recent years because of the specific historical, economic, and political relationship between Indonesia and Malaysia. Political tensions have been simmering for almost 50 years, dating back to 1963, when the Indonesian government opposed Malaysia's claim to certain British colonies on the island of Kalimantan (formerly Borneo). These political tensions between Indonesia and Malaysia continue in the present day over competing claims to Ambalat Island and its seabed off the coast of northern Kalimantan, which is believed to possess oil and gas reserves (Heryanto 2008, 2). Locating the origins of Melayu cultural forms on the Indonesian or the Malaysian side of the Straits of Malacca has become important in competing claims to cultural artifacts, food, and expressive practices as representative of national heritage (Aragon and Leach 2008, 616).

In 2005, music was again at the center of debates about rights claims to Melayu culture. Composer Munif Bahasuan states:

> Currently, there is a misunderstanding between Indonesia and
> Malaysia. Many classic popular Melayu songs from Medan were taken to
> Singapore. Malaysia claims that they are Malay songs. But Indonesians
> claim them, stating that they were composed by Indonesians. Even
> though we're one culture. One of the songs is "Kuala Deli." Musicians
> from Malaysia, and Melayu musicians from Medan, are arguing about
> whether it was composed by a Medan musician. Another example is the
> song "Bunga Tanjung": I know that's a Padang song. But Malaysia is
> claiming it as its own. (Munif Bahasuan, pers. comm., 16 July 2005)

Claims made in Singapore about dangdut originating from Singapore flamed these fires. In an article entitled "Too Much! Dangdut Claimed by Singapore," Rhoma Irama argued for patenting dangdut because he had heard that Singapore was holding an international dangdut contest, and he used the opportunity to voice concerns about Malaysia's claims to the genre (HDS and MW 2005). But as shown in the case of "Laksmana Raja di Laut," identifying the origins of a song was complex and highly contested due to the substantial economic stakes involved.

Ethnic Tinge?

Writing about local versions of *pop Indonesia*, Sutton contends that "some instances of what is touted as 'local' might best be interpreted as tokenistic—

mere ethnic tinge, reinforcing the hegemonic cultural order in which global, Western-based forms dominate" (2003, 3). Dangdut, of course, is not a Western-based form. But more importantly, the "local" examples discussed in this chapter do not reinforce the hegemonic cultural order of Indonesian national forms. Rather, the examples in this chapter show us multiple ways in which meanings about ethnicity and nation have been re-articulated in music after the fall of Suharto in 1998.

New modes of performance, promotion, and distribution gave rise to a new chapter in dangdut history. Based on these widespread practices of localization in many parts of Indonesia, dangdut had become "Indonesia's de facto national music" (Sutton 2003, 13; Wallach 2008). Yet the "nationalized regionality" and the "regionalized nationality" of dangdut, and the processes of identification that emerged, are different from what I have described in previous chapters. *Saluang dangdut,* marketed to Minang who live in towns and cities across the archipelago, was a form of *saluang* with a "national tinge." *Koplo* was based on an intercultural process in which jaipongan rhythms (infused by dangdut rhythmic features) were appropriated by Javanese musicians and worked into a new form. Dangdut Melayu, another nationally marketed form, created stories that looked back to ancestors, homeland, and "tradition."

These examples are important for the history of dangdut. Rhoma Irama's claim that dangdut was rooted in music of North Sumatra, with added elements from India and the West, privileged an ethnocultural wellspring from which dangdut subsequently sprang. According to this way of thinking, its center could never be challenged or moved. For Elvy Sukaesih, dangdut's roots were unquestionably in India. But more importantly, its forms, practices, and meanings were created by Indonesians. Further, "ethnic dangdut" had created a space that enabled Indian associations in dangdut to emerge as something ordinary (*dangdut biasa*) or pure (*dangdut piur*). "Regional dangdut" did not harmonize with Secretary of State Moerdiono's pronouncement in the 1990s that dangdut was "very Indonesian" based on a shared language or repertoire ("one nation, one language, one homeland"). Rather, in the 2000s, dangdut was redefined in terms of "one nation, many languages, and a transnational homeland." Further, if the New Order model for becoming national was to "go international," the post–New Order model of national music was to "go local." Rather than naturally springing from one cultural source (Melayu), or imposing a discourse of sameness promoted by the central government, dangdut, via an increasing number of regional ethnocultural varieties, had become Indonesia's de facto national music, each one signifying different socioeconomic realities and cultural interests.

NOTES

1. For example, "Mabuk Janda" (Crazy about Janda), "Goyang Dombret" (Gombret Dance) and "Putri Panggung" (Princess of the Dance Floor), which all use Sundanese musical elements.

2. In the larger sphere of Indonesian popular music in the 1990s, *etnik* designated a style of *pop Indonesia* that used "instruments, scales, or styles of traditional musics, primarily but not exclusively Indonesian" (Sutton 2003, 5).

3. Recording artists complained that their work was being stolen, but this did not make a difference in remuneration for their labor; they usually received a flat fee, as opposed to royalties.

4. The tune is also known as "Mbah Dukun" (without "E").

5. I viewed the video at the following URL: http://www.youtube.com/watch?v=1_Lva2Mpgqk.

6. I viewed the video at the following URL: http://www.youtube.com/watch?v=vee3Ug447tk.

7. After 10 albums for other producers, this was Iyeth's first self-funded production.

8. Examples of other songs with unmetered introductions include "Khana" (Mansyur S.), "Bimbang" (Anxiety; Elvy Sukaesih), and "Nalangsa" (Loneliness; Anita Kemang), among others.

9. A district court handles cases for the city (*kota*) and county or regency (*kabupaten*) and is the first step toward resolving conflicts.

Chapter 9

Conclusion: Why Dangdut?

In the award-winning film *Suddenly Dangdut* (*Mendadak Dangdut*, 2006), Petris, a spoiled and arrogant pop music singer, and Yulia, her kind and protective older sister and manager, are arrested with a satchel of drugs in the back seat of their car.[1] (The drugs belong to Yulia's boyfriend, who has already fled the scene). Not knowing what else to do, and facing imprisonment, the sisters decide to run. Chased by the police, they flee to a village on the outskirts of the city and arrive at a lively outdoor celebration, where a dangdut band is providing the entertainment. To avoid detection by the police, Petris quickly disguises herself as a dangdut singer (renamed Iis Maduma) and joins the band (hence the title *Suddenly Dangdut*). Initially stiff, she gradually adjusts to the tempo and swing of the music. Aided by band leader Rizal, a charismatic yet deceptive man who resembles a young Rhoma Irama, the two women settle into their new village lifestyle. Petris performs frequently with the traveling troupe, and Yulia looks after her.

Petris has everything in life, but lacks the heart to appreciate it. Yulia is jealous of Petris's beauty and fame, but does not have the courage to speak up to her domineering sister. The stress of being on the run, along with Petris's unceasing frustration and demanding personality, exacerbates the tensions that already exist between them. But through a series of emotional trials and tribulations, the two sisters learn to see each other's point of view, and they grow closer by the end of the film.

In the film, dangdut is confined to the village, a place that exists in a different temporal register and geographical location from the sisters' urban lives. Throughout the film, the sisters can never leave the village, even though the city is nearby. Through this geographical separation, the film produces a sharp class distinction between the urban progressive (*gedongan*) and village backward (*kampungan*) lifestyles. However, by venturing outside their clean urban lifestyle to the gritty life of rural Java, the characters discover important lessons about themselves and each other. On one hand, dangdut is the key tool to their journey of self-discovery. By the film's conclusion, Petris has become a more sensitive and compassionate person. She has discovered her "dangdut soul" (see chapter 4). And Yulia learns how to stand up to her domineering sister. They have not only escaped from their comfortable lifestyle, but they have escaped from themselves. On the other hand, they keep dangdut's material reality at a comfortable distance. They eventually return to their lives, transformed and ready to move "forward."

The movie is interlaced with musical interludes and scenes about the music. The lyrics of the main song "Jablai" (Rarely Caressed) does not relate directly to the story told in the film, but it serves an important symbolic function. Rizal, the band leader, initially attempts to teach the song to Petris, whose musical orientation is the smooth sound of *pop Indonesia*. Petris sings all the notes correctly, but without any ornaments (*cengkok*) or rhythmic accents. He scolds her for singing the melody in such a straightforward and superficial manner, reminiscent of pop singing: "If it doesn't have the ornaments, it's not dangdut!"[2]

The vocal styles that differentiate the musical worlds of *pop Indonesia* and dangdut also symbolically mark the class affiliations of their audiences, as illustrated in the following scene. Rizal invites Yati Asgar, a professional singer whose dangdut credentials are marked by heavy makeup, a sexy leopard-skin print top, a strong religious orientation (her first spoken lines are "*Alhamdullilah, rejeki dari Allah*" or "Praise to God, [my success is] a blessing from God"), and a nickname that indexes "tradition."[3] When Yati advises Petris about singing, she is actually giving her a lesson about living in communal poverty: "When you sing, you sing only for yourself. But to sing dangdut correctly you have to think of everyone in the audience. How can you entertain them so that they will forget their hunger, their poverty, and their everyday troubles in life? That's the most important job of a dangdut singer." This brief segment points to the discourse of authenticity and communality in the genre, described in chapter 4 as "dangdut soul."

The text of "Jablai" has several formulaic elements of dangdut songs, as described in this book. First, it has a narrative structure, beginning with the word "when" and marking time with each verse: one night (verse 1); one year (verse 2); and several years (verse 3). Second, the upbeat danceability of the music contrasts with the downbeat mood of the lyrics (see chapter 5). Third, the text tells a common dangdut story: a woman has sex with a man in a neighboring village and returns home pregnant "with two bodies" (*berbadan dua*). Her parents disapprove of the union, but she refuses to listen to them. After a year, the man has fallen in love with someone else, leaving the woman without any financial or emotional support (see

Waktu tamasya ke binaria, Pulang-pulang ku berbadan dua, Meski tanpa restu orang tua, sayang, Aku rela abang bawa pulang.	When I went out that night, And came home with another body (inside), Although my parents don't agree, my love, I'm ready to make a home with you.
Nggak kerasa udah setahun, Si abang mulai berlagak pikun, Udah nggak pernah pulang ke rumah, sayang, Kepincut janda di Pulo Gebang.	After one year, You started pretending to forget us, You didn't come home at night, my love, And fell for a woman in Pulo Gebang.
Lai lai lai lai lai lai, Panggil aku si Jablai, Abang jarang pulang, Aku jarang dibelai.	Lai lai lai lai lai lai, Just call me si Jablai, He rarely comes home, And I'm rarely given love,
Anak kita skarang udah besar, Mulai bingung kok bapaknya nyasar, Kenapa bapak ngga pulang-pulang, emak, Kata tetangge "emangnya enak."	Our child is now grown, And confused that his father's not around, Why doesn't he come home, mom? And the neighbors say "that's the way it goes."

FIGURE 9.1 "Jablai."

chapter 6). As the years go by, the child grows up without a father. But the blame falls on the woman, as the neighbors shake their heads (see figure 9.1).

The title of the film (as well as the hit song that emerged from it) prompts me to ask, "What is dangdut about this story?" What kinds of representations and meanings about dangdut emerge from this critically acclaimed film? In the promotional literature for the film, the production team (director, writer, producer, and actors) made it clear that they knew very little about dangdut before the production started. Unfamiliar with the genre, they prepared for the film by doing fieldwork in neighborhood dangdut clubs. But this is not a documentary; the movie does not attempt to address the contemporary social function and meanings of dangdut among dangdut fans themselves. If that were the case, the film would have presented examples of dangdut house, dangdut sexy, or dangdut *heboh*, discussed in chapters 7 and 8, as opposed to the retro style of dangdut shown in the film. Rather, dangdut is a colorful backdrop to the story that unfolds between two sisters. The story does not stray from their own individual personal issues.

And yet, the second media release states a common trope about dangdut and "the people" (italics mine): "*As we know*, dangdut music possesses a philosophy about how to entertain "the people" and make them forget their everyday problems."[4]

The media release assumes that dangdut is something that acts *on* people, specifically, by making them forget. Unfortunately, the film does not show how that process of forgetting actually works. In fact, the movie does the opposite: it uses a dangdut story to bring the everyday problems of Petris and Yulia to light. This example leads me back to one of the questions in the introduction to this book: Why dangdut?

Clearly, dangdut was crucial for making the plot work. But it was not the congruence of the story, the music, the images, or the characters with a social community of dangdut fans that made the film successful. Rather, it was the political economy of dangdut—its tremendous commercial popularity and national political meaning that coincided with the film's conception, production, and release. Further, it was the incongruence of national pop singer and movie star Titi Kamal starring as a dangdut singer that was designed to attract her fans (who wondered what *she* was doing starring in a film about dangdut) that helped to make the film a huge commercial and critical success.

I would argue that the movie works because dangdut is a particularly good way to narrate a story about social class relations in Indonesia. For example, at the beginning of the film, and the first time we hear the word "dangdut," a young man spots the attractive Petris and invites her to come along to dance dangdut with him at the show (*neng, ikut abang dangdutan yuch!?*). "You're disgusting," she snarls at him (*najismu!*). In this brief moment, even the mention of dangdut yields a strong negative reaction from the privileged Petris. Further, the egotistical Petris wonders why the man didn't recognize her, to which her sister replies "Don't be so arrogant. Not everyone in Indonesia watches MTV!" This brief interaction situates dangdut in a bygone pre-modern past. Although the sisters' individual lives are transformed by dangdut, the lives of people living in the *kampung* remain basically the same.

Told from a middle-class perspective, this dangdut story resonates with themes I have discussed in this book. A discourse of social distinction characterized dangdut among 1970s middle-class rockers and pop stars, who saw the music as lacking and superficial within the burgeoning commercial music industry of the period. In the 1980s, psychologists and critics recognized dangdut's powerful connection to the people, but found it raw, excessive, and undisciplined. Dangdut was blamed for causing immorality, licentiousness, and a rise in birthrates, among other social problems.

The New Order regime, however, recognized the power of dangdut in the 1970s by hiring groups to sing at political campaign rallies. Government officials of the 1980s and 1990s saw the potential for using dangdut as part of the development narrative of the New Order. And in the 2000s, dangdut engaged with politicized forms of Islam and discourses of morality. Whatever dangdut may have been for these commentators, positive or negative, it held great symbolic power.

In this book I have used sound, images, and texts to show how dangdut as an aesthetic practice and a social discourse narrates stories about class, ethnicity, gender, and nation. Throughout this book I have tried to interpret these stories as symbolic mediations that represent ideological, institutional, and commercial interests.

One of the stories I have narrated is the historical development of a cultural media industry around dangdut in the 1970s. Dangdut expanded its reach in the 1980s by blending with changing forms of media and technology; it traveled on buses via cassettes, and it was transported by film, television, and radio across the islands of the vast archipelago. The increasing presence of non-registered VCDs (video compact discs) in the 1990s and 2000s enabled consumers to visualize a broad range of dangdut styles and introduced a do-it-yourself attitude to the production of regional forms. The localization of media production after the late-twentieth-century economic crisis and the fall of Suharto challenged the center-periphery model of culture and represents a new way of thinking about music and local cultures (see chapter 8).

I have stressed contradictory ways of reading these cultural texts, which emerge in reading practices of any kind. As a commercial form, contradictory interpretations were built into dangdut to attract consumers. In chapter 5, I discussed strategies of polysemy, ambiguity, and camp that encouraged creative and playful interpretations of song lyrics, images, and sound. These narrative strategies affected ways of telling stories and the forms they take. I found it useful to address these tensions and contradictions by analyzing social contexts within which these songs, language, and performance practices were embedded. I introduced this approach to show how new meanings emerged, gained currency, and often conflicted with older meanings.

Dangdut helped to reproduce both hegemonic as well as counter-hegemonic positions in the realm of culture. In chapter 6, I showed how a form of glamorous, soft, dreamy dangdut became a priviledged site for narrating the nation on commercial television throughout the 1990s, when dangdut was being courted within the government official discourse about culture. As a national form, it was imagined as the music for all Indonesians. Women as symbolic representations of the nation were crucial in this narrative project. At the same time, songs could be critical of the national formation through representations of women that challenged the state's image of the ideal woman.

In chapter 7, Inul's "drilling dance" was embraced by liberal groups suppressed during the New Order, while calls for the banning of Inul represented some of the most conservative Islamic groups, whose voices were similarly muffled during the same period. The relationship between dangdut and Islam became one of antagonism by political Islamic organizations, including the MUI and the FPI, which argued that "porno" lyrics, movements, and clothing encouraged social chaos: sex outside marriage; a rise in drunkenness and gambling, violence against women; and the breakdown of morals in society. Yet, there was no clear evidence that proved the negative effects of dangdut lyrics and dance movements on actual people. This case revealed the increasingly important way that dangdut mediates politics and religion. These debates were productive as power in defining the contours of what counts as Islamic, and what does not, in Indonesian national politics.

Labeling a singer or a song "porno" had palpable effects, including restrictions on television and radio broadcasts or in live performances in certain regions. Inul's "drilling dance" of 2003 seemed tame compared to body movements subsequently presented on national television programs in 2007. In a move taken from Janet Jackson, dangdut singer Dewi Persik's breast became unhinged from her top in a live broadcast on TPI.[5] Under pressure from local religious groups, she was subsequently banned from performing in several cities including Bandung, Tangerang, and Depok (Hardi 2008).

On the other hand, "porno" led to greater attention and greater demand. As prohibitions on women's dancing bodies increased, their movements became more eroticized and their outfits more revealing. In post-Inul Indonesia, almost every dangdut band had a group of "sexy" dancers ready to perform at weddings and circumcisions. So, it seems that the "porno wars" stimulated rather than curbed the public appetite for eroticized bodies in both regional performances and national media. These struggles over defining morally acceptable behavior reflected the ideological tensions and contradictions that characterize life in early-twenty-first-century Indonesia.

How could dangdut represent the majority of Indonesians, while also reportedly encouraging sex, decadence, and violence? Rather than defining dangdut as a lack (of "good" taste, morality, musical quality, or "class"), or as something that displaces other genres, I have tried to look at what people were actually doing with dangdut on the ground, as it were. In chapter 5, I described a spectacle of excess in dangdut lyrics, full of soaring highs and depressing lows. These stories showed the range of interpretations made available in dangdut.

Which stories are speakable and which ones are forced to be hidden from view? During the New Order, the Department of Information kept close tabs on artists who spoke out for opposing political parties, including Rhoma Irama, whose songs were critical of the Suharto regime. Songs considered "pornographic" or "mournful" were similarly censored. The state solidified its control over culture through a monopoly on television and radio throughout the 1980s. During the media expansion of the 1990s, as the Suharto regime began to lose support, the state stepped up efforts to incorporate dangdut into its development narrative.

Composers and performers struggled to find ways to evade censorship during the New Order regime, but they also responded to what the people wanted. But what do the people want? And who are the people anyway? These questions could not be fully answered by quantifying the interests of a particular group of class subjects. I had to also focus on the ideological interests of the groups that attempted to define "the people." If there are no masses, but only ways of constituting them, dangdut stories had to be analyzed from the positionality of government cultural ministers, commercial music producers, religious leaders, and middle classes and elites as well. From a music industry perspective, "the people" were either consumers or not. For the state, they were political subjects who could be called into being through political rallies where their favorite music was played. From the perspective of Islamic prosyletizers, their personal and moral behavior was at stake. And for middle classes and elites, dangdut was a symbolic marker for creating what Pierre Bourdieu has labeled [class] "distinction" (Bourdieu 1984).

These questions about the sociological category of "the people" remind us to challenge stories about dangdut as Indonesia's national music. Despite claims to representing *all* Indonesians, dangdut has a very western Indonesia and Islamic flavor. For example, despite every imaginable stylistic and regional music spin-off, and despite the brief popularity of Mandarin dangdut in the 1980s, I was not able to locate even one Chinese dangdut recording during 2006–2009. This does not mean that Chinese Indonesians were not active as musicians or fans. Nor do I wish to discount the tremendous influence of the largely Chinese-owned music recording industry, which produces and distributes the majority of dangdut recordings. However, the public discourse about dangdut is largely by, for, and about Muslims.

For this reason it was important to point out the Melayu-ness of the music, due to the genre's stated origins, its geographical dominance in western Indonesia, and its associations with Islam. Influential musicians pointed to the Melayu origins of the music in North Sumatra. Rather than a linear progression culminating in the development of a single genre, I emphasized a transcultural dialogue among Melayu, Indian, Arab, and American cultures in the localized, mass-mediated urban centers of Jakarta, Surabaya, and Medan. I stressed the debates surrounding claims to Melayu roots based on culture, ethnicity, and lineage. Claims made about origins have important stakes for dangdut's identity as an Indonesian national music, as well as Indonesia's national identification with dangdut. Stories about dangdut as Melayu not only reflect what it means to be part of Indonesia, but, as dangdut superstar Elvy Sukaesih pointed out in chapter 2, they point to the Indonesian-ness of dangdut. These stories have exclusionary tendencies for those Indonesians who may love dangdut, but who do not identify with the Melayu-ness of the music.

Much has been left out of this story. The research for this book was conducted in urban areas of Jakarta, Bandung, and Surabaya because I felt that a pioneering study of dangdut's history should begin in the cities where the music was born. Dangdut's popularity reaches widely across the archipelago, and yet some areas are "more dangdut" than others. Limited by time constraints of fieldwork and lack of knowledge about local linguistic and cultural specificities, I was not able to examine how these forms not only represent different regional interests, but also how they challenge the kinds of stories told in national media. New forms are developing every day, and the tremendous output of regional dangdut forms, with their localized conditions of production and consumption, is one of the most exciting areas for future research.

The book provides glimpses into the lives and work of dangdut's stars, and I have written extensively in chapter 4 about the career of the pioneering composer and performer Rhoma Irama. But a more complete history of dangdut would include whole chapters (or books) about influential singers, including Ellya Khadam, Munif Bahasuan, A. Rafiq, Elvy Sukaesih, and Mansyur S., as well as the groups Sinar Kemala, Soneta, and Radesa. I would hope that future scholarship about dangdut will focus more on some of the most influential composers and arrangers, including Asmin Cayder, Leo Waldy, Fazal Dath, and Eddy Lestaluhu, among others. More detailed musical analysis will illuminate points that I did not notice. I can only hope that the weaknesses of this book will stimulate others to fill in the gaps.

Further study will reveal the transnational nature of dangdut in Malaysia, Singapore, Japan, and the Middle East. For example, there are more than one million Indonesians working abroad, comprising mostly women domestic workers living in the Middle East and other parts of Asia. Further, I have only touched on the battles being waged around intellectual property and cultural rights disputes with Malaysia and Singapore.

What good are stories? Why study them? I believe that dangdut stories do have the possibility of building empathy for other points of view. There is truth in former Secretary of State Moerdiono's statement in the mid-1990s that "dangdut makes us more empathetic to each other." Similarly, Elvy Sukaesih's description of a common dangdut song in the epigraph to chapter 5 urges the listener to step into the shoes of a single mother struggling to make ends meet. By listening to those songs and understanding what they are trying to communicate, there is great potential for dialogue. But a further level of interpretation is necessary to reveal the ideological functioning of music, as well as the discourse surrounding it (for example, why would a high government official invoke popular music during this particular historical juncture?). Stories have to be told and interpreted. Placed within a historical narrative about politics and culture in the late New Order regime, Moerdiono's statement was part of a top-down discursive formation about what it means to be a proper national citizen; about the innerparty rivalries of the Suharto regime; and about payola that linked the government with the state-run television network (see chapter 6).

Despite my ethnographic obsession with "getting it right" and my journalistic impulse to "get the story," the tales that I have spun in this book are necessarily incomplete and selective. This does not mean that they are somehow less valuable for understanding the musical genre of dangdut. But we must learn to pay attention to the silences and gaps in our stories. It is often the counternarratives, the stories not told, and the ones we have chosen to ignore that have the potential to build the most lasting and powerful meanings.

NOTES

1. Titi Kamal won the 2006 MTV Indonesia movie award for best actress. The film won four 2007 Indonesian Movie Awards, including best supporting actress (Kinaryosih), best duo (Titi Kamal and Kinaryoshi), best singing actor/actress (Titi Kamal), and favorite duo (Titi Kamal and Kinaryoshi).

2. "Mendadak Dangdut" (http://www.sinemart.com/mendadakdangdut/rilis.php) (accessed 7 June 2008).

3. Her last name stands for "asli Garut," or "authentically Garut"; Garut is a town in West Java historically known for its strong cultural and artistic traditions.

4. "Mendadak Dangdut" (http://www.sinemart.com/mendadakdangdut/rilis.php) (accessed 7 June 2008).

5. I viewed the video of the TPI broadcast at the following Web site: http://www.youtube.com/watch?v=b7ocXKKsnao [accessed 26 June 2008].

Glossary

The following definitions are my own, unless otherwise noted.

Betawi	Indonesian name for the Dutch "Batavia" (the former name for Jakarta).
blok	rolling arpeggio patterns played on a keyboard. Also called *bloking*.
cengeng	sentimental, tearful, or mournful.
cengkok	melodic pattern, embellishment, or ornament.
chalte	four-beat rhythmic pattern with accents on beats 4 and 1. Also spelled *calte*.
Deli	1. region in North Sumatra; 2. the site of a sixteenth-century Islamic sultanate.
electone	trademark used for electronic keyboard instruments produced by Yamaha; cf. *organ tunggal*.
gambus	name for a plucked lute presumably brought by immigrants from the Hadramaut region (Yemen). Can refer to a long-necked fretless lute (called *gambus*) or a pear-shaped lute (also called *'ud*).
gedongan	"progressive," modern; rich; from the word *gedung* (building).
gendang	in dangdut, a set of two single-headed drums that combines the physical qualities of Indian tabla and bongo. Also called *gendang tamtam*.

gendang kapsul	small cylindrical drum with two heads, named after its "capsule" shape.
Golkar	*Golongan Karya*; functionary work group.
goyang	shake; movement; dance.
joget	style of dance.
kaherva	rhythmic pattern often used in Indian film music that is similar to *chalte* in dangdut. Also spelled *kaherawa* and *kaherwa*.
kampungan	"backward"; implies inferiority, lack of refinement, lack of formal education, and a low position in a hierarchical ordering of social classes. From the word *kampung*, a hamlet or village.
koplo	1. performance style developed in the 1990s in East Java; 2. drum rhythm; 3. fast tempo, heavy metal-inflected music.
krismon	*krisis moneter*; the economic crisis that hit many parts of Southeast Asia in 1997.
kroncong	string-band music. Also the name of a guitar-like instrument as well as a distinctive type of accompaniment (Kornhauser 1978, 124).
lagu dakwah	song with Islamic religious message. Also spelled *da'wah*.
langgam	1. "the Indonesian name for any diatonic song consisting of four 8-bar phrases, each phrase being a melodic setting of 2 lines of the text" (Kornhauser 1978, 159); 2. a direct borrowing from 32-bar song form AA′BA′ (ibid.).
Melayu	Malay. In terms of ethnic identity, a flexible and evolving notion based on language, geography, religion, customs, and ceremonies.
Minang	Minangkabau; ethnic group in West Sumatra.
New Order	(Orde Baru) the political regime that came to power under President Suharto in 1966–1967 after the bloody tragedy that ended President Sukarno's Old Order government (Orde Lama).

organ tunggal	electronic keyboard synthesizer used to accompany singing and dancing. Also called *electone.*
orkes gambus	music ensemble and type of music featuring the *gambus.*
orkes harmonium	music ensemble and type of music featuring the harmonium, a small reed organ from Europe via India.
orkes Melayu	"Malay orchestra," an ensemble and type of music popular during the 1950s to the 1970s. Abbreviated O.M.
PAMMI	Persatuan Artis Musik Melayu Indonesia, the Union of Melayu Musical Entertainers of Indonesia.
pantun	four-line verses in which the first two lines form the *sampiran* (hook or hanger) and the last two form the *isi* (contents).
pongdut	Jai*pong*an dang*dut.* genre of regional Sundanese dangdut.
pop Indonesia	genre of Indonesian popular music.
pop Melayu	genre of Malay music popular in Indonesia during the 1960s and 1970s.
porno	pornographic, smutty, vulgar.
qasidah	genre of Indonesian vocal music, often sung in Arabic, that expresses Islamic themes.
radio amatir	ham radio; amateur radio operator.
rakyat	ordinary people, masses, the public.
rebana	frame drum.
ronggeng	1. professional female singer/dancer/entertainer in rural performing arts of Java and Sumatra; 2. dance events featuring a female singer/dancer/entertainer.
RRI	Radio Republik Indonesia, the national radio station network.
saluang	long rim-blown bamboo flute used in Minang music of West Sumatra. It has four holes and is tuned to a pentatonic system.
sandiwara	popular theater form of the twentieth century.

seriosa	European-influenced semi-classical vocal genre accompanied by Western instruments.
Sharia	Islamic law. Also spelled *syariah* and *syariat*.
sinden	female singer.
sinetron	*Sinema Elektronik*; television drama.
Suharto	Indonesia's second president who served from 1967 to 1998. Cf. New Order.
Sukarno	Indonesia's first president, who served from 1945 to 1967.
suling	bamboo flute. In dangdut, a set of side-blown six-hole flutes, each tuned to a different key.
Tempo	newsmagazine similar in scope to *Time* magazine.
tilawah	reciting the Qur'an.
TPI	Televisi Pendidikan Indonesia, the Indonesian Educational Television station.
TVRI	Televisi Republik Indonesia, the Indonesian National Television station network.
VCD	video compact disc; a digital movie format introduced by Philips and Sony in 1993.

References

A. Karim Nun. 1955. *Aneka*, November 10, 15.

Abadzi, Helen. 2007. "When India Conquered Greece: Hindi Films of the 50s in Greece." http://www.soundofindia.com/showarticle.asp?in_article_id=1096044732. (7 August 2007).

Abhiseka, A. 2003. "'Ngebor' Dance Divides the People." *The Jakarta Post*, http://www.thejakartapost.com/Archives/ArchivesDet2.asp?FileID=20030504.@01. (4 May 2003).

Acciaioli, Greg. 1985. "Culture as Art: From Practice to Spectacle in Indonesia." *Canberra Anthropology* 8 (1/2): 148–172.

Advertisement, PT Virgo Ramayana Record. 1980. "Camelia Malik dan Reynold." *Aktuil*, April 7, 32.

Agus. 2000. "Planet Senen: Di Sini Dangdut Pertama Kali Bersemi." *Arda*, August, 6.

Allen, Pam. 2007. "Challenging Diversity?: Indonesia's Anti-Pornography Bill." *Asian Studies Review* 31:101–115.

Alwie, T., I. Farida, and A. Muhajir. 2003. "Biarkan Publik Menilai." *Gatra.com*, http://www.gatra.com/2003–05–16/artikel.php?id=27823. (17 December 2005).

Amir, Sam. 1958. "S. Effendi." *Minggu Merdeka*, 13 July, 2.

Andaya, Leonard. 2001. "The Search for the 'Origins' of Melayu." *Journal of Southeast Asian Studies* 32 (3): 315–330

Anderson, Benedict. 1990. *Language and Power: Exploring Political Culture in Indonesia.* Ithaca, NY: Cornell University Press.

Ant/Ati. 2003. "'Duet Maut' Inul Daratista-Anisa Bahar Diprotes." *Kompas Cyber Media*, http://www.kompas.com/gayahidup/news/0303/15/021032.htm. (15 March 2003).

Ant/jy. 2003. "Taufik Kiemas: Goyangan Inul Masih Dalam Batas Kewajaran!" *Kompas Cyber Media*, http://www.kompas.com/gayahidup/news/0305/03/210422.htm. (17 December 2005).

Ant/Ly. 2007. "AMI Dangdut Awards Siap Digelar." *Rileks.com*, http://www.rileks.com/music/?act=detail&artid=31102006116271. (24 February 2008).

Aragon, Lorraine and James Leach. 2008. "Arts and Owners: Intellectual Property Law and the Politics of Scale in Indonesian Arts." *American Ethnologist* 35 (4): 607–31.

Aribowo. 1983. "Proklamasi Identitas." *Fokus*, December 8, 16–17.

Aripurnami, Sita. 1996. "A Feminist Comment on the Sinetron Presentation of Indonesian Women." In *Fantasizing the Feminine in Indonesia*, edited by L. J. Sears. Durham, NC: Duke University Press.

Armbrust, Walter. 2008. "The Ubiquitous Non-Presence of India: Peripheral Visions from Egyptian Popular Culture." In *Global Bollywood: Travels of Hindi Song and Dance*, edited by S. Gopal and S. Moorti. Minneapolis: University of Minnesota Press.

Arps, Bernard. 1996. "To Propagate Morals through Popular Music: The Indonesian Qasidah Moderen." In *Qasida Poetry in Islamic Asia and Africa;* Volume 1: *Classical Traditions and Modern Meanings*, edited by S. Sperl and C. Shackle. Leiden: E. J. Brill.

"Artists from the Kampung." 1977. *Kompas*, 7 April, 1.

Asikin, S. 2003. "Virus Goyang Bernama Inulfluenza." *Suara Merdeka*, http://www.suaramerdeka.com/harian/0303/02/nas7.htm. (2 March 2003).

Asmarani, D. 2003. "A Village Girl Shakes It Up." *Straits Times*, 9 March.

"Asmin Cayder, Lagu Ciptaanya Sering Timbulkan Heboh." 1992. *Pos Film*, 29 March.

Asy'arie, M. 2003. "Goyang Inul dan Goyang Pejabat." *KOMPAS Cyber Media*, http://www.kompas.com/kompas%2Dcetak/0302/22/opini/141845.htm. (3 June 2003).

"Asyiknya Digoyang Dangdut." 2001. *Kompas*, 9 September.

Atmodarminto, Wiyogo. 1989. Keputusan Gubernur Kepala Daerah Khusus Ibukota Jakarta Nomor: 1072 Tahun 1989.

———. 1990. Letter from Jakarta Governor Atmodarminto.

Auslander, Philip. 1999. *Liveness: Performance in a Mediatized Culture*. London: Routledge.

"Balada Dangdut, Berpangkal dari Lagu." 1997. *Kompas*, 10 September.

Barakuan, Magdalena. 1964. "O.M. Chandraleka." *Purnama*, 21.

Barendregt, Bart. 2002. "The Sound of Longing for Home: Redefining a Sense of Community through Minang Popular Music." *Bijdragen tot de Taal-, Land- en Volkenkunde* 158 (3): 411–450.

Barendregt, Bart, and Wim van Zanten. 2002. "Popular Music in Indonesia since 1998, in Particular Fusion, Indie, and Islamic Music on Video Compact Discs and the Internet." *Yearbook for Traditional Music* 34: 67–113.

Barnard, Timothy P., and Hendrik M.J. Maier. 2004. "Melayu, Malay, Maleis: Journeys through the Identity of a Collection." In *Contesting Malayness: Malay Identity Across Boundaries*, edited by T. P. Barnard. Singapore: Singapore University Press.

Barnard, Timothy P. ed. 2004. *Contesting Malayness: Malay Identity Across Boundaries*. Singapore: Singapore University Press.

Barraud, A. 2003. "Indonesia: Pornography or Performance?" *ABC News Radio (Asia Pacific)*, http://www.abc.net.au/ra/asiapac/programs/s836743.htm. (9 August 2004).

Barthes, Roland. 1972 (1957). "The World of Wrestling." In *Mythologies*. Translated by Annette Lavers. New York: Hill and Wang.

"Basofi Sudirman: Dengan Dangdut Kita Sukseskan Pembangunan." 1994. *Citra* 218: 2.

Baswedan, Anies Rasyid. 2004. "Political Islam in Indonesia: Present and Future Trajectory." *Asian Survey* 44 (5): 669–690.

Batubara, A. Halim. 1954. "Lagu2 Melaju." *Aneka*, 1 May, 16.

———. 1955. "Emma Gangga." *Aneka*, 20 January, 13.

Becker, Judith. 1975. "Kroncong, Indonesian Popular Music." *Asian Music* 7 (1): 14–19.

Behrend, Heike. 1998. "Love à la Hollywood and Bombay in Kenyan Studio Photography." *Paideuma* 44: 139–153.

Berg, Birgit. 2007. "The Music of Arabs, the Sound of Islam: Hadrami Ethnic and Religious Presence in Indonesia." PhD dissertation, Music, Brown University, Providence, RI.

"Berjuang dalam Goyang." 1989. *Matra*, 13–22.

"Bintang 'Serodja.'" 1959. *Bintang Minggu*.

Biran, H. Misbach Yusa. 2001. "The History of Indonesian Cinema at a Glance." In *Film in Southeast Asia: Views from the Region*, edited by D. Hanan. Hanoi: SEAPAVAA.

Blackburn, Susan. 2001. "Women and the Nation." *Inside Indonesia* (April-June), http://www.insideindonesia.org/edit66/susan1.htm. (11 September 2007).

Bourdieu, Pierre. 1984 (1979). *Distinction: A Social Critique of the Judgement of Taste*. Cambridge, MA: Harvard University Press.

Brackett, David. 2000. *Interpreting Popular Music*. Berkeley: University of California Press.

Broughton, Simon, and Mark Ellingham. 2000. *Rough Guide to World Music; Volume 2: Latin and North America, the Caribbean, Asia and the Pacific*. London: Rough Guide.

Browne, Susan. 2000. *The Gender Implications of Dangdut Kampungan: Indonesian 'Low-Class' Popular Music*. Working paper no. 109. Victoria, Australia: Centre of Southeast Asian Studies, Monash University.

Bruinessen, Martin van. 1990. "Indonesia's Ulama and Politics." *Prisma: Indonesian Journal of Social and Economic Affairs* 49: 52–69.

———. 2002. "Geneaologies of Islamic Radicalism in Post-Suharto Indonesia." *South East Asia Research* 10 (2): 117–154.

Capwell, Charles. 1995. "Contemporary Manifestations of Yemeni-Derived Song and Dance in Indonesia." *Yearbook for Traditional Music* 27: 76–89.

———. 2004. "The Music of Indonesia." In *Excursions in World Music*, edited by B. Nettl. Upper Saddle River, NJ: Pearson Prentice Hall.

Chopyak, James D. 1986. "Music in Modern Malaysia: A Survey of the Musics Affecting the Development of Malaysian Popular Music." *Asian Music* 18 (1): 111–138.

Cikini. 2003. "Inul 'Ngebor' Dukungan Gus Dur Siapkan Banser." *Kompas Cyber Media*, http://www.kompas.com/metro/news/0305/01/093710.htm. (1 May 2003).

Cohen, Matthew. 2006. *The Komedie Stamboel: Popular Theater in Colonial Indonesia, 1891–1903*. Athens: Ohio University Press.

Collins, James T. 2001. "Contesting Straits-Malayness: The Fact of Borneo." *Journal of Southeast Asian Studies* 32 (3): 385–395.

Coombe, Rosemary. 1992. "Publicity Rights and Political Aspiration: Mass Culture, Gender Identity, and Democracy." *New England Law Review* 26: 1221–1280.

Cooper, Nancy. 2000. "Singing and Silences: Transformations of Power through Javanese Seduction Scenarios." *American Ethnologist* 27 (3): 609–644.

———. 2004. "Tohari's Trilogy: Passages of Power and Time in Java." *Journal of Southeast Asian Studies* 35 (3): 531–556.

"Dan Oma Serta Upit Ikut Kampanye." 1977. *Tempo*, 9 April, 54–58.

"Dangdut Siang Bolong TPI Kupas Tuntas Persoalan." 1995. *Pos Film*.

"Dangdut, Sebuah 'Flashback.'" 1983. *Fokus*, 8 December, 13–18.

"Dangdut, Setelah Halal di TV-RI." 1979. *Tempo*, 5 May, 50–54.

Darmeanan, M. 2004. *Inul: Goyang Ngebor Goyang Pemilu 2004*. Tangerang: Penerbit Buku Populer 'Totalitas.'

David, Bettina. 2008. "Intimate Neighbours: Bollywood, Dangdut Music, and Globalising Modernities in Indonesia." In *Global Bollywood: Travels of Hindi Song and Dance*, edited by S. Gopal and S. Moorti. Minneapolis: University of Minnesota Press.

———. In press, Von verführerischen Frauen und verantwortungslosen Männern: Dangdut-Popmusik in Indonesien-Hamburg: Asien-Afrika-Institut, Universität Hamburg.

———. Forthcoming. "The Erotics of Loss: Some Remarks on the Pleasure of Dancing to Sad Dangdut Songs." In *Sonic Modernities: Popular Music and New Social Formation in the Malay World*, edited by B. Barendregt and W. van Zanten.

Des. 1977. "Wawancara Mini dengan Oma 'Superstar' Irama." *Aktuil*, 7 March.

Dhondy, Farukh. 1985. "Keeping Faith: Indian Film and Its World." *Daedalus* 114 (4): 125–140.

Dick, Howard W. 1985. "The Rise of a Middle Class and the Changing Concept of Equity in Indonesia: An Interpretation." *Indonesia* 39: 71–92.

"Diwaktu soeboeh" [Di waktu subuh]. Moekty, vocal, with Madjelis Gamboes Modern [from] Laboean Deli. 78-rpm. Columbia TP 6. Recorded late 1930s or early 1940s.

Doorn-Harder, Nelly van, and R. Michael Feener. 2006. "Indonesia." In *Muslim Cultures Today: A Reference Guide*, edited by K. M. Coughlin. Westport, CT, and London: Greenwood Press.

"Dua Orang Raja." 1978. *Tempo*, 14 January, 41–43.

"Dunia Ellya Khadam." 1972. *Tempo*, 27 May, 36.

Effendi, S. 2003. "Fenomena Inul dan Pendidikan Tinggi (Tanggapan untuk Winarso Dradjat Widodo)." *Kompas Cyber Media*, http://www.kompas.com/kompas%2 Dcetak/0305/05/opini/291898.htm. (5 May 2003).

Effendy, Bahtiar. 2004. *Islam and the State in Indonesia*. Athens: Ohio University Press.

"Elvi Sukaesih di Ujung Pandang." 1979. *Aktuil*, 7 June, 35.

"Elvy Sukaesih Tolak Anggapan Dangdut Adalah Melayu." 1994. *Pos Film*, 6 November.

Ema. 1999. "Dangdut Menggoyang Dunia." *Pos Kota*, 31 January, 5.

Emha, Ainun Nadjib. 1979. "Jiwa Dangdut Kita pada Dasarnya Sangat Besar." *Aktuil*, 7 June.

———. 2003. "Pantat Inul Adalah Wajah Kita Semua." *Kompas Cyber Media*, http://www.kompas.com/kompas-cetak/0305/04/utama/293700.htm. (4 May 2003).

Ensiklopedi, Tokoh Indonesia. "Elvy Sukaesih: Si Ratu Dangdut." http://www.tokohindonesia.com/ensiklopedi/e/elvy-sukaesih/index.shtml (accessed 20 January 2005).

———. "Iis Dahlia: Sang Primadona Dangdut." http://www.tokohindonesia.com/selebriti/artis/iis-dahlia/index.shtml (accessed 20 January 2005).

Errington, Shelly. 1990. "Recasting Sex, Gender, and Power: A Theoretical and Regional Overview." In *Power and Difference: Gender in Island Southeast Asia*, edited by J. M. Atkinson and S. Errington. Stanford, CA: Stanford University Press.

Faruk and Aprinus Salam. 2003. *Hanya Inul*. Yogyakarta: Pustaka Marwa.

Fealy, Greg, and Virginia Hooker, eds. 2006. *Voices of Islam in Southeast Asia: A Contemporary Sourcebook*. Singapore: Institute of Southeast Asian Studies.

Feld, Steven. 2000. "A Sweet Lullaby for World Music." *Public Culture* 12 (1): 145–171.

Feld, Steven, Aaron A. Fox, Thomas Porcello, and David Samuels. 2008. "Working-class Country." In *Music, Words and Voice: A Reader*, edited by M. Clayton. Manchester and New York: Manchester University Press.

Fokus Kita. 1975. *Tempo*, 22 March, 3.

Foley, Kathy. 1979. "The Sundanese Wayang Golek: The Rod Puppet Theatre of West Java." PhD dissertation, University of Hawaii, Honolulu.

———. 1989. "Of Gender and Dance in Southeast Asia: From Goddess to Go-Go Girl." In *Proceedings of the 20th Anniversary CORD Conference*. New York: Congress on Research in Dance.

Foucault, Michel. 1972. *The Archaeology of Knowledge*. New York: Tavistock.

Frederick, William. 1982. "Rhoma Irama and the Dangdut Style: Aspects of Contemporary Indonesian Popular Culture." *Indonesia* 34: 102–130.

Garcia, Michael Nieto. 2007. "Indonesian Publishing: New Freedoms, Old Worries, and Unfinished Democratic Reforms." In *Identifying with Freedom: Indonesia after Suharto*, edited by T. Day. New York: Berghahn Books.

"Gebyar Dangdut di Layar Kaca: Terikat Hukum Bisnis Selera." 1994. *Citra*, 28 March–3 April, 3.

"Generasi Baru, Dangdut Dut...." 1997. *Tabloid Berita Mingguan Adil*, 16–22 July.

Gerke, Solvay. 2000. "Global Lifestyles under Local Conditions: The New Indonesian Middle Class." In *Consumption in Asia: Lifestyles and Identities*, edited by C. Beng-huat. London: Routledge.

Goldsworthy, David. 1979. "Melayu Music of North Sumatra." PhD dissertation, Music, Monash University, Monash.

Gopal, Sangita, and Sujata Moorti, eds. 2008. *Global Bollywood*. Minneapolis: University of Minnesota Press.

Gumelar, Sandy. 2000. "Karena Nekad Ngamen, Langusung Ditangkap Tentara." *Arda*, August, 9.

Gunawan, R. F. X. 2003. *Mengebor Kemunafikan: INUL, Seks dan Kekuasaan.* Jakarta: Galang Press.

"Gunong Deli." Miss Delia and Leiman S. S., vocal. 78-rpm. His Master's Voice P 22811. Recorded 1940.

"Hak Asasi Dilarang." 1977. *Tempo,* 17 December, 17–18.

Hamdani, D., Sulistiyo, B., and Haryadi, R. 2004. "Menyibak Kelambu Pornografi." *Gatra. com,* http://www.gatra.com/2003-05-26/artikel.php?id=28674. (10 February 2004).

Hansen, Thomas B. 2005. "In Search of the Diasporic Self: Bollywood in South Africa." In *Bollyworld: Popular Indian Cinema through a Transnational Lens,* edited by R. Kaur and A. Sinha, New Delhi: Sage.

Harahap, Riza. 1994. "Pesta Demokrasi Praktisi Dangdut Mencari Figure Pemimpin." *Jayakarta,* 5.

Hardi, Erick P. 2008. "Walikota Bandung Tolak Dewi Persik." *Tempointeraktif,* http://www.tempointeraktif.com/hg/nusa/jawamadura/2008/04/10/ brk,20080410-120947,id.html. (10 April 2008).

Harnish, David, and Anne Rasmussen, eds. Forthcoming. *Divine Inspiration: Music and Islam in Indonesia.* New York: Oxford University Press.

Harsono, Andreas. 1988. "Membela Musik Dangdut." *Suara Merdeka,* 15 December, 2.

Hatch, Martin. 1985. "Popular Music in Indonesia." In *Popular Music Perspectives 2: Papers from the Second International Conference on Popular Music Studies, Reggio Emilia, September 19–24, 1983,* edited by D. Horn. Goteborg, Exeter: IASPM.

HDS, and MW. 2005. "Gawat! Musik Dangdut Mau Diambil Singapura." *100% Dangdut,* 27 April.

Hefner, Robert. 1987. "The Politics of Popular Art: Tayuban Dance and Culture Change in East Java." *Indonesia* 43: 75–94.

———. 2000. *Civil Islam: Muslims and Democratization in Indonesia.* Princeton, NJ: Princeton University Press.

Heins, Ernst. 1975. "Kroncong and Tanjidor: Two Cases of Urban Folk Music." *Asian Music* 7 (1): 20–32.

Hendrowinoto, Nirwanto, Ki S., et al. *Seni Budaya Betawi Menggiring Zaman.* Jakarta: Dinas Kebudayaan DKI Jakarta, 1998.

Hennion, Antoine. 2003. "Music and Mediation: Toward a New Sociology of Music." In *The Cultural Study of Music: A Critical Introduction,* edited by M. Clayton, T. Herbert and R. Middleton. London: Routledge.

Heryanto, Ariel. 1999. "The Years of Living Luxoriously: Identity Politics of Indonesia's New Rich." In *Culture and Privilege in Capitalist Asia,* edited by M. Pinches. London: Routledge.

———. 2003. "Public Intellectuals, Media and Democratization: Cultural Politics of the Middle Classes in Indonesia." In *Challenging Authoritarianism in Southeast Asia,* edited by A. Heryanto and S. Mandal. New York: Routledge Curzon.

———. 2008. "Pop Culture and Competing Identities." In *Popular Culture in Indonesia,* edited by A. Heryanto. London and New York: Routledge.

Hoetabarat, Jack. 1980. "Elvy Sukaesih: Itu Paha Stand In." *Aktuil* 7 (12): 50–51.

Holt, Fabian. 2007. *Genre in Popular Music.* Chicago: University of Chicago Press.

ICG (International Crisis Group). 2002. "Indonesia Backgrounder: How the Jemaah Islamiyah Terrorist Network Operates." In *Asia Report* no. 43. Jakarta/Brussels.

"Inul, Goyang Sejuta Umat." 2003. *Tempointeraktif* 49 (16 May 2009).

Irkham, Agus M. 2005. "Televisi, Kaya Laba Miskin Wacana." www.suaramerdeka. com/harian/0507/18/opi4.html. (12 June 2006).

Jafisham and Irawan Soemardi. 1979. "Elvy Sukaesih: Menemukan Ibu Kangungnya." *Aktuil*, 10 September, 20, 26–27.

"Janasib I & II" [Ya Nasib]. S. Sech Albar, vocal, with the S. Albar Orchestra. 78-rpm. Canary HS 258. Recorded ca. 1939.

Jones, Sidney. 2003. "Jemaah Islamiyah: A Short History." *Kultur* 3 (1): 105–114.

Jubing, Yustina, and Asianto. 1991. "Lagi Ngetrend, Lagu Asing 'Diterjemahkan.'" *Nova*, 7 July, 10.

"Kalamil Foead" [Kalamil Fuad]. Orkes Gambus directed by B. Ihsan. 78-rpm. Tjap Angsa AM 36. Recorded late 1930s.

"Kembali ke Akar Melayu dengan Zapin-Dut." 2003. *Kompas*, http://www.kompas. com/kompas-cetak/0310/19/utama/634316.htm. (26 November, 2006).

Khalik, Abdul. 2008. "PKS Seeks Porn Bill as 'Ramadan Present.'" *Jakarta Post*, http://www.thejakartapost.com/news/2008/09/12/pks-seeks-porn-bill-039ramadan-presento39.html. (1 October 2008).

Kitley, Philip. 2000. *Television, Nation, and Culture in Indonesia*. Athens: Ohio University Press.

Kornhauser, Bronia. 1978. "In Defense of Kroncong." In *Studies in Indonesian Music*, edited by M. Kartomi. Clayton, Victoria: Monash University.

Kristanto, J. B. 2005. *Katalog Film Indonesia, 1926–2005*. Jakarta: Nalar.

"Kudaku Lari." Hasnah Tahar, vocal, with Orkes Melayu Bukit Siguntang directed by A. Chalik. 78-rpm. Irama M 313-11. Recorded ca. 1957.

Kusumah, Budi. 1991. "Bunuh Aku dengan Cintamu." *Tempo*, 25 May, 62–64.

Larkin, Brian. 1997. "Indian Films and Nigerian Lovers: Love Stories, Electronic Media and the Creation of Parallel Modernities." *Africa* 67 (3): 406–440.

———. 2003. "Itineraries of Indian Cinema: African Videos, Bollywood, and Global Media." In *Multiculturalism, Postcoloniality, and Transnational Media*, edited by E. Shohat and R. Stam. New Brunswick, NJ: Rutgers University Press.

"Lebih Jauh Dengan Rhoma Irama." 1988. *Kompas*, 29 May.

Lev, Daniel. 1990. "Notes on the Middle Class and Change in Indonesia." In *The Politics of Middle Class Indonesia*, edited by R. Tanter and K. Young. Clayton, Victoria: Centre of Southeast Asian Studies, Monash University.

Liddle, R. William. 1996. "The Islamic Turn in Indonesia: A Political Explanation." *The Journal of Asian Studies* 55 (2): 613–634.

Lindsay, Jennifer. 1995. "Cultural Policy and the Performing Arts in Southeast Asia." *Bijdragen: Tot de taal-, land-, en volkenkunde* 151: 656–671.

———. 1997. "Making Waves: Private Radio and Local Identities in Indonesia." *Indonesia* 64: 105–123.

"Lingkaran Berhadiah Penonton Semarak Dangdut." 1995. *Dang Dut*. August, 29.

Lockard, Craig. 1998. *Dance of Life: Popular Music and Politics in Southeast Asia.* Honolulu: University of Hawaii Press.

Lok/Xar. 2003. "Menggoyang Rezeki, Menghibur Rakyat." *Kompas Cyber Media,* http://www.kompas.com/kompas-cetak/0302/09/latar/121685.htm. (9 February 2003).

Loriel, A. 2003. "Ratu Goyang 'Ngebor.'" *TokohIndonesia.com,* http://www.tokohIndonesia.com/selebriti/artis/inul-daratista/index.shtml. (10 May 2009).

Loven, Klarijn. 2008. *Watching Si Doel: Television, Language, and Cultural Identity in Contemporary Indonesia.* Leiden: KITLV Press.

Lysloff, R.T.A. 2001/2002. "Rural Javanese 'Tradition' and Erotic Subversion: Female Dance Performance in Banyumas." *Asian Music* 33 (1): 1–24.

Mahmood, K. 2003. "Erotic Dance Challenges the Norms of Liberal Indonesia." *IslamOnline.Net,* http://www.Islam-online.net/English/artculture/2003/03/article12.shtml. (25 February 2003).

"Majelis Ulama Indonesia." 2001. NOMOR: U-287 TAHUN 2001, edited by MUI.

"Malam Amal Komponis Lily Suheiri." 1960. *Fikiran Rakyat,* 10 November, 3.

Mandayun, Rustam F. 1991. "Gemerincing Dunia Dangdut." *Tempo,* 60–66.

Mankekar, Purnima. 2004. "Dangerous Desires: Television and Erotics in Late Twentieth-Century India." *The Journal of Asian Studies* 63 (2): 403–431.

Manuel, Peter. 1988. *Popular Musics of the Non-Western World.* New York: Oxford.

Manuel, Peter, and Randall Baier. 1986. "Jaipongan: Indigenous Popular Music of West Java." *Asian Music* 18 (1): 91–110.

Matusky, Patricia, and Sooi Beng Tan. 1997. *Musik Malaysia: Tradisi Klasik, Rakyat, dan Sinkretik.* Pinang: The Asian Centre.

Melzian. 1994. "Pedoman Dangdut Berasal dari Melayu." *Pos Film,* 20 November, 4.

"Mendadak Dangdut: Media Release." 2006. http://www.sinemart.com/mendadakdangdut/rilis.php. (7 June 2008).

Miller, Terry, and Sean Williams, eds. 1998. *The Garland Encyclopedia of World Music: Southeast Asia.* New York: Garland Publishing.

Milner, Anthony. 2008. *The Malays.* West Sussex, UK: Wiley-Blackwell.

Miloer, M. 1978. "Serangkaian Show Pretty Sisters & Surya Group di Malang: SAS Group di Semarang." *Aktuil* 251: 52–53.

"Moerdiono Bergoyang Dangdut Bersama Camelia Malik." 1994. *Suara Pembaruan,* 4 September.

"Moerdiono dan Habibie Berjoget Ria." 1992. *Pos Kota,* 24 May.

Mohamad, Goenawan. 1984. "Catatan Pinggir: Goyang." *Tempo,* 30 June, 15.

Mousli, S. L. 1980a. "Achmad Rafiq." *Aktuil,* 5 May, 36–7.

———. 1980b. "Rhoma Irama: Dangdut Bukan Musik Musiman." *Aktuil,* 5 May, 34–35.

———. 1980c. "Tentang Filem Dangdut: Sutradara Yopie & Danu Umbara." *Aktuil,* 21 April 1980, 58–59.

Murray, Alison J. 1991. *No Money, No Honey: A Study of Street Traders and Prostitutes in Jakarta.* Singapore: Oxford University Press.

Navis, B. 1976. "Rhoma Irama: Dibaptis Aktuil Sebagai Superstar." *Aktuil,* 19 July, 16–17.

Negus, Keith. 1996. *Popular Music in Theory*. Middletown, CT: Wesleyan University Press.

Newbury, Michael. 2000. "Celebrity Watching." *American Literary History* 12 (1/2): 272–283.

Nizar, M. 1994. "Dangdut Sebuah Perjalanan." *Citra*, 20–26 June, 7.

Nizar, M., and Maman Suherman. 1994. "Sejarah Perjalanan Dangdut: Pohon Dangdut Bertangkai Money." *Citra*, 28 March–3 April, 2.

Nmp. 2003. "Inul Korban Kekerasan Fisik dan Psikologis." *KOMPAS Cyber Media*, http://www.kompas.com/kompas-cetak/0305/04/utama/291812.htm. (4 May 2003).

Nor, Mohd Anis Md. 1993. *Zapin: Folk Dance of the Malay World*. Singapore: Oxford University Press.

Nurbianto, B. 2003. "'Dangdut' Singer Inul Is Too Hot for Many [sic] Indonesia?" *The Jakarta Post*, http://www.infid.be/inul.html. (22 February 2003).

"O.M. Chandralela: Dengan Alatanja Jang Modern." 1964. *Purnama*, 21–22.

Ong, Aiwa, and W. Peletz, eds. 1995. *Bewitching Women, Pious Men: Gender and Body Politics in Southeast Asia*. Berkeley: University of California Press.

"Panen Dangdut, Dangdut, Dangdut." 1975. *Tempo*, 22 March, 44–49.

Paramida, Cici. 2005. "Menyongsong Generasi Baru Dangdut." In *Dangdut Music Rakyat: Catatan Seni Bagi Calon Diva Dangdut*, edited by D. B. Suseno. Yogyakarta: Kreasi Wacana.

Parciack, Ronie. 2008. "Appropriating the Uncodable: Hindi Song and Dance Sequences in Israeli State Promotional Commercials." In *Global Bollywood: Travels of Hindi Song and Dance*, edited by S. Gopal and S. Moorti. Minneapolis: University of Minnesota Press.

Peletz, Michael. 1996. *Reason and Passion: Representations of Gender in a Malay Society*. Berkeley: University of California Press.

Pelpie. 1954. "Hasnah Tahar." *Aneka*, 10 June, 17.

"Perjalanan Musik Dangdut." 1992. *Suara Pembaruan*, 17 January.

Perlman, Marc. 2001. "Indonesia," VI, 1. In *New Grove Dictionary of Music and Musicians*, edited by S. Sadie: Oxford University Press.

Persda. 1992. "Penayangan Dangdut di TVRI Diperketat." *Kompas*, 4 February.

Pesek, William, Jr. 2003. "Indonesia's Hip-Shaking Diva Is a Good Omen for Indonesia." *The Manila Times*.

"Pesta Bumi Musik Ind. Th 1972." 1973. *Vista*, 27 January, 16–17.

Pioquinto, Ceres. 1995. "Dangdut at Sekaten: Female Representations in Live Performance." *Review of Indonesian and Malaysian Affairs* 29: 59–90.

———. 1998. "A Musical Hierarchy Reordered: Dangdut and the Rise of a Popular Music." *Asian Cultural Studies* 24: 73–125.

Piper, Suzan. 1995. "Performances for Fifty Years of Indonesian Independence: Articles from the Indonesian Press, translated by Tony Day and Suzan Piper." *Review of Indonesian and Malaysian Affairs* 1/2: 37–58.

"Pokok & Tokoh." 1979a. *Tempo*, 3 March, 38.

"Pokok & Tokoh." 1979b. *Tempo*, 2 June, 19.

"Pokok & Tokoh." 1984. *Tempo*, 21 January, 23.

Pudyastuti, Sri. 1992. "Dangdut Goyang Terus Pop Kok Loyo." *Tempo*, 16 May, 108.

Purwanto, G. S., and Budaya Purwadi. 2000. "Camelia Malik: Sudah Saatnya Dangdut Go International." *Pro-TV*, July, 2, 6.

"Rajuan Bina" [Rayuan Bina]. O. M. Irama Agung. 78-rpm. Irama M 386–32. Recorded ca. 1957.

Ramedhan, Erwin. 1977. "The Disco Way of Life in Jakarta: From Subculture to Cultural Void." *Prisma* 6: 16–19.

Rasmussen, Anne. 2001. "The Qur'an in Indonesian Daily Life: The Public Project of Musical Oratory." *Ethnomusicology* 45 (1): 30–57.

Ray, Manas. 2000. "Bollywood Down Under: Fiji Indian Cultural History and Popular Assertion." In *Floating Lives: The Media and Asian Diasporas*, edited by S. Cunningham and J. Sinclair. Queensland: University of Queensland Press.

Reid, Anthony. 2001. "Understanding Melayu (Malay) as a Source of Diverse Modern Identities." *Journal of Southeast Asian Studies* 32 (3): 295–313.

———. 2005. *An Indonesian Frontier: Acehnese and Other Histories of Sumatra*. Singapore: National University of Singapore Press.

"Rhoma Irama … Sampai Titik Darah yang Penghabisan." 1987. *Mutiara*, 20 October, 19–25.

Robison, Richard. 1996. "The Middle Class and the Bourgeoisie in Indonesia." In *The New Rich in Asia*, edited by R. Robison and D. Goodman. London: Routledge.

Rosyid, I. 2003. "Majelis Ulama Solo Minta Polisi Larang Pentas Inul." *Tempo Interaktif*, http://www.tempointeraktif.com/hg/nusa/jawamadura/2003/02/20/ brk,20030220–04,id.html. (20 February 2003).

Ruchiat, Rachmat, et al. 2000. *Ikhtisar Kesenian Betawi*. Jakarta: Dinas Kebudayaan DKI Jakarta.

Said, Salim. 1991. *Shadows on the Silver Screen: A Social History of Indonesian Film*. Translated by T. P. Siagian. Edited by J. H. McGlynn and J. P. Boileau. Jakarta: Lontar Foundation.

Sari, D. Y. 2003. "Fenomena Goyang 'Ngebor'!" *Kompas Cyber Media*, http://www. kompas.com/kesehatan/news/0302/14/183816.htm. (14 February 2003).

"Sakee Thoo Deevai Jamai." Ebrahim Masrie, vocal. 78-rpm. Beka B 15560. Recorded 1928.

Sarsidi, G. B. 1995a. "Era Ken Dedes Dan Soneta Girls." *Dang Dut*, July, 7.

Sarsidi, G. B. 1995b. "Fenomena Rhoma Irama Bersama Soneta." *Dang Dut*, June, 7.

Sastromuljono, Adityo. 2005. "Pengantar Minum Racun." *Musiklopedia Zine*, http:// www.musiklopedia.com/zine/index.php?option=com_content&task=view&id=21 &Itemid=1. (22 February 2008).

"Satria Berdakwah, Raja dari Bawah." 1984. *Tempo*, 30 June, 27–33.

"Sayang Manis." Dorah, vocal, with Special Singapore Malay Orchestra directed by Mr. Jahri (Jaar). 78-rpm. Odeon A 206109.

"SCTV dan Trans Didatangi Demo Penentang Pornografi." 2003. *Suara Merdeka*, http://www.suaramerdeka.com/harian/0305/14/nas13.htm. (14 May 2003).

Sen, Krishna. 1991. "Si Boy Looked at Johnny: Indonesian Screen at the Turn of the Decade." *Continuum: The Australian Journal of Media & Culture* 4 (2): 136–151.

————. 2002. "Indonesia: Media and the End of Authoritarian Rule." In *Media Reform: Democratizing the Media, Democratizing the State*, edited by M. E. Price et al. London and New York: Routledge.

————. 2003. "Radio Days: Media-Politics in Indonesia." *The Pacific Review* 16 (4): 573–589.

Sen, Krishna, and David Hill. 2000. *Media, Culture and Politics in Indonesia*. South Melbourne: Oxford University Press.

"Serodja." 1959. *Aneka*, 10 April, 19.

Setiawan, B. 1989. "Dangdut." In *Ensiklopedi Nasional Indonesia*. Jakarta: P. T. Cipta Adi Pustaka.

Setiyono, Budi. 2001. "Ngak Ngik Ngok." http://budisetiyono.blogspot.com/2005/08/ngak-ngik-ngok-perjalanan-sebuah.html. (26 February 2008).

Shamsul, A. B. 2001. "A History of an Identity, an Identity of a History: The Idea and Practice of 'Malayness' in Malaysia Reconsidered." *Journal of Southeast Asian Studies* 32 (3): 355–366.

Siagian, Rizaldi. 2006. "Hikmah Kasus HAKI: 'Laksmana Raja Dilaut.'" *Kompas Cybermedia*, http://www.kompas.com/kompas-cetak/0602/05/seni/2409553.htm. (5 February).

Sidel, John Thayer. 2006. *Riots, Pogroms, Jihad: Religious Violence in Indonesia*. Ithaca, NY: Cornell University Press.

Siegel, James. 1998. *A New Criminal Type in Jakarta: Counter-Revolution Today*. Durham, NC: Duke University Press.

Simatupang, G. R. L. L. 1996. "The Development of Dangdut and Its Meanings: A Study of Popular Music in Indonesia." PhD dissertation. Department of Anthropology and Sociology, Monash University.

"Sinar Malacca." Rubiah, vocal, with Special Singapore Malay Orchestra directed by Mr. Jahri (Jaar). 78-rpm. Odeon A 206109.

Sjamsulridwan. 1952. "Film Malaya Hendak Kemana?" *Sunday Courier*, 3 August, 11.

Soemardi, Irawan. 1979. "Estimasi Pasaran Kaset di Indonesia." *Aktuil*, 7 June, 40.

Soepandi, Atik, et al. 1992. *Musik Samrah*. Jakarta: Proyek Pelestarian dan Pengembangan Tradisional Betawi.

Soeprapto. 1985. "Sambutan Gubernur Kepala Dearah Khusus Ibukota Jakarta." Government Document.

Spiller, Henry. 2001. "Erotic Triangles: Sundanese Men's Improvisational Dance in West Java, Indonesia." PhD dissertation, Music, University of California, Berkeley.

————. 2007. "Negotiating Masculinity in an Indonesian Pop Song: Doel Sumbang's 'Ronggeng.'" In *Oh Boy! Masculinities and Popular Music*, edited by F. Jarman-Ivens. New York: Routledge.

Steele, Janet. 2005. *Wars Within: The Story of Tempo, an Independent Magazine in Soeharto's Indonesia*. Jakarta: Equinox Publishing.

Stevens, Alan M., and A. Ed. Schmidgall-Tellings. 2004. *A Comprehensive Indonesian-English Dictionary*. Athens: Ohio University Press.

Straw, Will. 1991. "Systems of Articulation, Logics of Change: Communities and Scenes in Popular Music." *Cultural Studies* 5 (3): 361–375.

Sullivan, Norma. 1991. "Gender and Politics in Indonesia." In *Why Gender Matters in Southeast Asian Politics*, edited by M. Stivens. Clayton: Monash Centre of Southeast Asian Studies.

Surawijaya, Bunga. 1991. "Goyang Dangdut." *Tempo*, 25 May, 49–60.

Suryakusuma, Julia. 1996. "The State and Sexuality in New Order Indonesia." In *Fantasizing the Feminine in Indonesia*, edited by L. J. Sears. Durham, NC: Duke University Press.

Sutton, R. Anderson. 1984. "Who Is the Pasindhèn?: Notes on the Female Singing Tradition in Java." *Indonesia* 37: 119–133.

———. 2002. "Asia/Indonesia." In *Worlds of Music*, edited by J. T. Titon. Belmont, CA: Schirmer, Thomson Learning.

———. 2003. "Local, Global, or National? Popular Music on Indonesian Television." In *Planet TV: A World Television Reader*, edited by S. Kumar and L. Parks. New York: New York University Press.

Suyitno, Ayid. 1991. "Musik Dangdut Dan Kelebihannya." *Pos Film*, 20 January.

Takari, Muhammad. 1997. "Akulturasi Kebudayaan Musikal Dalam Seni Pertunjukan Dangdut." In *Seminar Seni Pertunjukan*. Gadjah Mada and STSI Surakarta, Surakarta.

Takonai, Susumu. 2006. "Soeara Nirom and Musical Culture in Colonial Indonesia." *South East Asian Studies* 44: 145–203.

Tan, Sooi Beng. 1993. *Bangsawan: A Social and Stylistic History of Popular Malay Opera*. Singapore: Oxford University Press.

Tanaka, Katsunori. n.d. Liner Notes for Sound Recording: *Original Road to Dangdut*. Far Side Music, Ltd.

———. 2005. Liner Notes for Sound Recording: *The Dangdut Queen*. London: Rice Records.

Taylor, Timothy. 1997. *Global Pop: World Music, World Markets*. New York: Routledge.

"Terserah Orang." 1996. *D & R*, 21 September 1996.

Tesoro, Jose Manuel. "Indonesia: Learning the Ropes of Press Freedom." *Asiaweek*, http://www.unesco.org/courier/2000_02/uk/connex/txt1.htm. (16 May 2009).

Theo. 1986. "Muchtar B: Pulang Hanya untuk Mandi dan Ganti Baju." *Kompas*, 5 October.

"Thoo Gair Nahee Mai Gair Nahee." Ebrahim Masrie, vocal. 78-rpm. Beka B 15560. Recorded 1928.

Tma/Ant. 2003. "Jangan Tampilkan Inul Dalam Kampanye." *Gatra.com*, http://www.gatra.com/2003-03-13/artikel.php?id=26241. (13 March 2003).

Tobing, Paul L. 1992. "Giliran Musik Dangdut Dikecam." *Suara Pembaruan*, 8 November.

Tresnawati. 2005. "Pak Ngah Pencipta Notasi 'Laksmana Raja di Laut.'" *Suara Merdeka*, http://suaramerdeka.com/harian/0502/17/budo1.htm. (17 February 2005).

Wahyudi, L. S. 2003. "Watching Inul Makes Our Stress Bearable." *The Jakarta Post*, http://www.thejakartapost.com/Archives/ArchivesDet2.asp?FileID=20030506.G05. (6 May 2003).

Wallach, Jeremy. 2004. "Dangdut Trendy." *Inside Indonesia* (April-June), http://www.insideindonesia.org/edit78/p30_wallach.html. (11 December 2007).

————. 2008. *Modern Noise, Fluid Genres: Popular Music in Indonesia, 1997–2001*. Madison: University of Wisconsin Press.

Walsh, Brian. 2003. "Inul's Rules: A New Idol is Putting Some Sex and Sizzle into Indonesia's Pop Music Scene." *Time Asia Magazine* (11), http://www.time.com/time/asia/magazine/article/0,13673,501030324–433338,00.html. (24 March 2003).

Waterman, Christopher. 2002. "Big Man, Black President, Masked One: Models of the Celebrity Self in Yoruba Popular Music in Nigeria." In *Playing with Identities in Contemporary Music in Africa*, edited by M. Palmberg and A. Kirkegaard. Uppsala, Finland: Nordiska Afrikainstitutet, Abo Akademi University.

Wee, Vivienne. 1985. "Melayu: Hierarchies of Being in Riau." PhD dissertation. Australian National University, Melbourne.

Weintraub, Andrew N. 2004. "The 'Crisis of the Sinden': Gender, Politics, and Memory in the Performing Arts of West Java, 1959–1964." *Indonesia* 77: 57–78.

————. 2006. "Dangdut Soul: Who Are 'the People' in Indonesian Popular Music?" *Asian Journal of Communication* 16 (4): 411–431.

————. 2008. "'Dance Drills, Faith Spills': Islam, Body Politics, and Popular Music in Post-Suharto Indonesia." *Popular Music* 27 (3): 367–392.

Wichelen, Sonja van. 2005. "'My Dance Immoral? Alhamdulillah No!' Dangdut Music and Gender Politics in Contemporary Indonesia." In *Resounding International Relations: On Music, Culture, and Politics*, edited by M. I. Franklin. New York: Palgrave Macmillan.

Widodo, Amrih. 2002. "Consuming Passions." *Inside Indonesia*, www.insideindonesia.org/edit72/Theme%20-%20Amrih.html.

Williams, Raymond. 1961. *Culture and Society*. Harmondsworth: Penguin.

————. 1977. *Marxism and Literature*. Oxford: Oxford University Press.

Williams, Sean. 1989. "Current Developments in Sundanese Popular Music." *Asian Music* 21: 105–36.

Wilson, Ian Douglas. 2008. "'As Long as it's Halal': Islamic Preman in Jakarta." In *Expressing Islam: Religious Life and Politics in Indonesia*, edited by G. Fealy and S. White. Singapore: ISEAS.

Woodward, Mark R. 2001. "Indonesia, Islam, and the Prospect for Democracy." *SAIS Review* 21 (2): 29–37.

Yahya, H. 2003. "Mencerna 'Goyang' Rhoma-Inul." *PesantrenOnline.com*, http://www.pesantrenonline.com/artikely/detailartikel.php3?artikel=180. (3 May 2003).

Yampolsky, Philip. 1987. *Lokananta: A Discography of the National Recording Company of Indonesia, 1957–1985*. Madison, Wisconsin: Center for Southeast Asian Studies, University of Wisconsin.

————. 1989. "Hati Yang Luka: An Indonesian Hit." *Indonesia* 47: 1–17.

————. 1991. "Indonesian Popular Music: Kroncong, Dangdut, and Langgam Jawa." Liner Notes to Smithsonian/Folkways SF 40056, v. 2, *Music of Indonesia series*, edited by P. Yampolsky. Washington, DC: Smithsonian Folkways.

———. 1995. "Forces for Change in the Regional Performing Arts of Indonesia." *Bijdragen: Tot de taal-, land-, en volkenkunde* 151: 700–725.

———. 1996. "Melayu Music of Sumatra and the Riau Islands." Liner Notes to Smithsonian/Folkways SF 40427, v. 11, *Music of Indonesia series*, edited by P. Yampolsky. Washington, DC: Smithsonian Folkways.

———. In Progress. Discography of 78-rpm Recordings Issued for the Indonesian, Malaysian, and Singaporean Markets, 1903–1942.

"Yoenadji" [Yunaji]. S. Albar, vocal. 78-rpm. His Master's Voice NS 278. Recorded ca. 1937.

Yudhistira and Pudyastuti. 1987. "Rhoma: Tidak Mengayuh, tapi Mengalir." *Jakarta Jakarta*, January.

Yudhono, J. 2003. "Akhir Pekan: Cintailah Inul Apa Adanya." *Kompas Cyber Media*, http://www.kompas.com/gayahidup/news/0303/08/132940.htm. (8 March 2003).

Yurnaldi and S. Rakaryan. 1997. "Musik Dangdut Mencapai Puncaknya." *Kompas*, 13 July 20.

Yuval-Davis, Nira. 1997. *Gender and Nation, Politics and Culture*. London: Sage Publications.

"Zahrotoel Hoesoen" [Zahrotul Husun]. S. Albar, vocal. 78-rpm. His Master's Voice NS 278. Recorded ca. 1937.

Zar. 1992. "Sejarah Dangdut: Kini Selera Dikuasai Disko Dangdut." *Citra*, 8–14 July, 23.

Zurbuchen, Mary. 1990. "Images of Culture and Development in Indonesia: The Cockroach Opera." *Asian Theatre Journal* 7: 127–149.

Index

Page numbers in italic refer to illustrations.

pop Indonesia (genre)
  and dangdut, 20, 113, 161–62
  and ethnic tinge, 222–23, 224 n.2
  lyrics in, 134
  and social class, 77, 84, 86, 107–9
  and Rhoma Irama, 94–95
  and Tarantula, 117–20
  vocal quality of, 119, 172 n.8, 226
pop Melayu, 75–78
pop Sunda, 134
popular music studies, 12, 30 n.5
porno, 114, 132, 134, 139, 143, 172 n.12,
  173, 186, 195, 209, 229–30
PPP (Partai Persatuan Pembangunan), 6,
  91, 173 n.6, 198 n.6
Presley, Elvis, 51, 57, 74, 93
production teams, 138–39
Purwacaraka, 5

Radesa, 232
radio
  Ceylon, 79 n.2
  and Melayu music of the 1930s, 38
  NIROM (Nederlandsch-Indische Radio
    Omroe Maatschappij), 55 n.13
  and promotion of dangdut, 86
  regulations, 81
  RRI (Radio Republik Indonesia), 41,
    50
Rafiq, A. (Achmad), 19, 27, 72–75, 75,
  113, 232
rakyat, 81–111
  definition of, 17–18, 21, 81–82, 231
  music and, 5–6
Ramlee, P., 42, 44, 50, 51
recording industry
  1930s, 37
  1970s, 147 n.1
  1990s, 160–162
  and pirated recordings (bajakan), 205
  and royalties, 163–64
  See also commodification of music
recording techniques, 117–20
rock music, 102, 180
ronggeng
  representation of, 24
  in North Sumatra, 36–37, 40, 45, 63
  Sundanese, 191
  dombret, 207–09
Rubiah, 41–43, 53

rumba, 39, 40, 45, 58, 64
RUU-APP (Rancangan Undang-Undang
  Antipornografi dan
  Pornoaksi), 195–96

Saky, Eko, 214
saluang, 212–14
samrah, 38
sandiwara, 41, 42, 43, 46, 50, 55 n.16, 87,
  124
Sattar, Juhana, 44, 69
senandung, 36, 41, 47
seriosa, 44
Sharia, 184, 185, 196, 198 n.3
Shaw Brothers, 42
sinetron, 153, 164–65
social classes
  and film, 225–28
  and going international, 159
  middle classes, 30 n.3
  and pop dangdut, 120
  and rakyat, 81–111
  and Rhoma Irama films, 104
  and television audiences, 5
  See also audience; rakyat
Soneta, 5, 87, 89, 95, 96, 99, 101–2, 232.
  See also Rhoma Irama
stambul, 37, 72
Subardja, Benny, 85
Sud, Eddy, 152, 165
Sudirman, Basofi, 152, 154
Suharto, 18, 81, 91, 92, 151, 155
  See also Golkar; nation-state;
  New Order
Suheiry, Lily, 41–42
Sukaesih, Elvy, 27, 113, 123–131, 124, 125,
  168, 194, 232
  and Melayu music, 34
  and Rhoma Irama, 87, 95
  vocal style of, 119, 126–27, 134, 165
Sukarno, 30 n.11, 57, 76–77, 79 n.1, 81,
  184
Sundanese music, 165, 205–6, 216
Sylado, Remy, 109

tabla, 60, 65–66, 120, 167. See also
  India, music of
Tahar, Hasnah, 45–50
Tamala, Evie, 27, 153
tango, 38, 40, 45, 58